Negotiating Economic Development

Identity Formation and Collective Action in Belize

LAURIE KROSHUS MEDINA

The University of Arizona Press
Tucson

The University of Arizona Press
© 2004 The Arizona Board of Regents
First printing
All rights reserved
∞ This book is printed on acid-free, archival-quality paper.
Manufactured in the United States of America

09 08 07 06 05 04   6 5 4 3 2 1

Library of Congress Cataloging-in-Publication Data
Medina, Laurie Kroshus, 1962–
Negotiating economic development : identity formation and collective
action in Belize / Laurie Kroshus Medina.
p. cm.
Includes bibliographical references and index.
ISBN 0-8165-2361-4 (cloth : alk. paper)
1. Citrus fruit industry—Social aspects—Belize. 2. Economic
development—Social aspects—Belize. 3. Group identity—Belize.
4. Cooperation—Belize. I. Title.
HD9259.C53B425 2004
338.1'74304'097282—dc22
2003025377

Publication of this book is made possible in part by the proceeds of a
permanent endowment created with the assistance of a Challenge Grant
from the National Endowment for the Humanities, a federal agency.

Contents

Figures

Tables

Preface

When I began this research in 1986, the Belizean citrus industry was confronting exciting new prospects and dangerous new possibilities. To counter the revolutionary movements that had emerged in Central America and the Caribbean in the late 1970s and early 1980s, the United States was working to impose its own definitions of "development" and "democracy" on the region. The U.S. government punished wayward countries with military interventions, while it rewarded compliant countries with development assistance and new trade opportunities. Among the new trade opportunities, the United States opened its markets to citrus products from Caribbean and Central American countries that conformed to U.S. prescriptions, producing two dramatic results in Belize: first, the earnings of Belizean farmers and citrus processing companies nearly doubled; and second, Coca-Cola Foods purchased 193,600 acres of land in Belize for its Minute Maid subsidiary to begin citrus production. While the higher prices sparked a boom in citrus production in Belize, Coca-Cola's efforts to rewrite the laws that regulated the Belizean citrus industry threatened to undermine the power that Belizean citrus farmers exercised vis-à-vis the two transnationally owned citrus processing companies that already operated in Belize.

Coca-Cola's investment in Belize raised questions about how the agendas of the U.S. government and Coca-Cola would intersect with the aspirations of farmers and workers in Belize. Since the Belizean citrus industry produces for export, its fortune had always been tied to shifting patterns of global trade. During the mid-1980s, as U.S. concern with Central America and the Caribbean intensified, the power exercised by foreign governments and transnational companies over development in the Belizean citrus industry appeared overwhelming. Yet citrus farmers and workers I came to know in Belize believed that their own actions could shape the available options to better suit them. Their actions and their insistence that those actions mattered pushed me to consider more carefully the potential of human agency to remake structures of inequality. To what degree and through what means were farmers and workers able to remake the development options offered them? In posing such questions, I became part of a larger trend among social scientists trying to keep up with their subjects by injecting agency into social theory.

However, wageworkers and farmers in the citrus industry did not necessarily exercise agency in the ways that the marxist analyses I had been reading would expect or approve. Their mobilizations were usually contingent and temporary rather than sustained; often they organized around identities and interests defined in ethnic or national rather than class terms. Further, Belizean farmers and wage laborers were continually bombarded with messages—albeit contradictory ones—about their identities and interests: they were subject to intense efforts by U.S. and Belizean governments, processing company administrators, and one another to shape how they interpreted and responded to the circumstances in which they lived. This recognition led me beyond considerations of the relationship between structures and agency to explore how the exercise of agency is related to processes of subjection and the production of subjectivities. I sought to understand, through further research and theorizing, exactly what motivated the mobilizations of citrus farmers and workers around particular issues, identities, and interests. How did farmers and workers learn to identify themselves with particular categories? What led them to embrace particular sets of interests? How did they use those identities, once they claimed them?

The research evolved into more than a decade of thinking back and forth between social science theories and the actions of both Belizean farmers and workers and the powerful others who seek to control their actions. To me, the excitement of both anthropological field research and anthropological theory is rooted in their always problematic relationship. Initially, I had prepared to undertake the research by reading about the processes that generate enormous inequalities in the global political economy and the ways that economic development addresses or exacerbates such inequalities. I had synthesized a framework that oriented my research and enabled me to make sense of the world. The process of doing research submitted that framework to a reality test that quickly revealed its gaps and shortcomings, as my theoretical model proved unable to account for all that I saw and heard in the field. I thus returned to theory, reading and thinking further, in order to elaborate a more complex framework that could account for my data. In pursuit of a more adequate accounting, I worked back and forth between the abstract and the concrete through discussions with other academics and citrus farmers and through continued research for more than a decade, as global political-economic shifts led Belizeans to make unanticipated choices that just a few years earlier I would have deemed unthinkable.

As I have worked to make sense of unforeseen complexity and shifting circumstances, I have incurred enormous intellectual and personal debts. I owe the greatest debt and the deepest gratitude to those wageworkers and farmers in the Belizean citrus industry who have immeasurably enriched both my life and my understanding of how the world works, as they have given so generously of their time, their insights, their interpretations, and in many cases their friendship. In order to protect their confidentiality and prevent them from being harmed in any way for their contributions to this study, I cannot name them here or in the account that follows. I have attempted to reciprocate in practical ways with small favors and more abstractly by presenting my work in Belize to contribute to contemporary Belizean debates about issues that concern workers and farmers in the industry; however, my debt to these men and women remains unredeemed and irredeemable.

There are a number of people I am able to thank by name for assistance they have given me in their capacities as officials of organizations in the industry. I am grateful to a number of union leaders who have provided help and guidance over the years, especially the late Pablo Lambey, Raymond Mejia, and Simon Arana of the United General Workers Union, and Fidelis Lambey, the union's secretary. I am also grateful to Benjamin Caballeros and Antonio August for helping me to locate workers who belonged to the Belize Workers Union (and to Caballeros for enlivening so many evenings with improbable but hilarious stories). Similarly, a series of administrators at the Citrus Growers Association have provided invaluable assistance over the years, especially Fred Garcia, Clinton Hernandez, and Bridget Cullerton. I owe a special debt to now-retired CGA field man Elliot Antonio for introducing me to the citrus industry. I also appreciate the good humor with which adminis-trators at the Citrus Company of Belize and Belize Food Products allowed me to interview both them and their employees.

In the capital, many government officials made time for interviews and shared archival materials with me. David Gibson and Egbert Grinage were especially helpful during their appointments as permanent secretary in the Ministry of Industry. I am also grateful to the staff at the National Archives for helping me to discover, locate, and duplicate documents and reports rel-evant to the research.

Dr. Joseph Palacio, fellow anthropologist and resident tutor at the Uni-versity of the West Indies School for Continuing Studies in Belize, has pro-vided support and good advice over the years, and I am grateful for both. I would also like to thank the Society for the Promotion of Education and Research for their sponsorship of annual conferences and publications that have permitted me to share my data and interpretations with Belizean audi-ences and learn from their responses.

I thank Simeon Joseph and Mrs. Jo, the families of Kamal and Claudio Hasbun, and Arthur and Bev Usher for assistance with housing in Dangriga, and Roy Pascasio, Leo Liu, and Omar for facilitating the vehicle that enabled me to travel the countryside. I am especially grateful to Sandra Maravilla Hasbun for her enormous hospitality and friendship. Andre Duquesney also deserves thanks for his critical readings of so many manuscripts and his cogent discussions of the intersections of anthropological theory and citrus politics. In Los Angeles, I also want to thank the families of Carmelita Smith, Albert Smith, and Mario and Patricia Alamina for their friendship, shared over many plates of Belizean rice and beans or chirmole.

I gratefully acknowledge the funding that made possible the research for this book. The National Science Foundation (BNS #8904185), Fulbright IIE, and the Department of Anthropology at UCLA funded the longest stays in the field. The Latin American Studies Program at UCLA and the College of Social Science at Michigan State University provided funds for shorter trips to Belize that enabled me to follow the somewhat surprising turns of events in the citrus industry over the last decade. At Michigan State University, the Department of Anthropology provided a course reduction and the Center for Latin American and Caribbean Studies generously provided summer funding that helped move this manuscript toward completion.

I want to express my gratitude as well to my teachers, mentors, and col-leagues for their engagement with this project. Allen Johnson, Karen Brodkin,

Nazif Shahrani, Peter Hammond, and Susanna Hecht provided both the critical questions and the support required for me to launch this research and continue to develop it. More recently, colleagues and students in the Culture, Resources, and Power program in the Department of Anthropology at Michigan State University have helped me to hone my arguments and to sustain that combination of optimism and outrage necessary for engaged scholarship that directs theory toward real-world issues. I am especially grateful to Anne Ferguson and Bill Derman. The work of senior "Belizeanists" Rick Wilk and Nigel Bolland has provided me with admirable examples of committed scholarship. Both their published work and their comments on my work have strengthened my analysis. I have also benefited from the work of fellow Belizeanists Michael Stone, Karen Judd, Mark Moberg, and Melissa Johnson. I am grateful to the reviewers for the University of Arizona Press, whose comments helped to strengthen the manuscript. And I convey an enormous thank you to Mónica Russel y Rodriguez, for encouragement and insightful comments on drafts of this manuscript and for sharing the things other than work that make a life whole.

To all of the people I have been able to name and to those whose names I am not able to call, I am extremely grateful. Though all have contributed to my research and analysis, none of them should be held responsible for the sense I have made of the ideas they raised. Errors or shortcomings in this ethnography are of my own making, evidence perhaps that the data may always exceed my tools for grappling with it.

Finally, I offer thanks to my family. My parents, David and Joan Kroshus, have taken care of cars and bill payments, encouraged collect phone calls, and even visited Belize to experience anthropological research firsthand. My husband, Chema, has been engaged with this project for nearly as long as I have. His help in Belize enriched the research in many ways and made it possible for us to make the research and the people we came to know in Belize a part of our life. For his contributions to the research and his willingness to incorporate the research into our shared life, I am profoundly grateful. The births of our son, Alejandro, as this manuscript neared completion and our daughter, Amalia, as it went to press, have immeasurably multiplied the joy in that shared life.

Abbreviations

ACP	African, Caribbean, and Pacific
BFP	Belize Food Products
BHDU	British Honduran Development Union
BFHL	Belize Food Holdings Limited
BSI	Belize Sugar Industries
BWU	Belize Workers Union
CBERA	Caribbean Basin Economic Recovery Act
CBI	Caribbean Basin Initiative
CCB	Citrus Company of Belize
CDB	Caribbean Development Bank
CDC	Colonial Development Corporation (later the Commonwealth Development Corporation)
CDU	Christian Democratic Union
CGA	Citrus Growers Association
CIA	Central Intelligence Agency
CSO	Central Statistical Office
CWU	Christian Workers Union
DFC	Development Finance Corporation

EIB	European Investment Bank
EU	European Union
FAO	Food and Agriculture Association
GWDU	General Workers Development Union
GWU	General Workers Union
ICFTU	International Confederation of Free Trade Unions
IMF	International Monetary Fund
LUA	Labourers and Unemployed Association
NAFTA	North American Free Trade Agreement
NBCCA	National Bipartisan Commission on Central America
NGO	nongovernmental organization
OPIC	Overseas Private Investment Corporation
PAC	People's Action Committee
PUP	Peoples United Party
SCU	Southern Christian Union
SPEAR	Society for the Promotion of Education and Research
UBAD	United Black Association for Development
UDP	United Democratic Party
UGWU	United General Workers Union
UN	United Nations
USAID	U.S. Agency for International Development
WFTU	World Federation of Trade Unions
WTO	World Trade Organization

Negotiating Economic Development

1 Introduction
Collective Identities, Shared Interests, and the Negotiation of Development

At a meeting of the Citrus Growers Association, the prime minister of Belize delivered a speech that differentiated citrus growers according to the size of their acreages. "We needn't hide ourselves from it," he asserted. "This industry is so structured that the few big growers own more acreage than the many small owners. . . . [T]hat's the reality." His government was primarily concerned "to make sure that the little man is helped," he asserted. Since the majority of CGA members owned fewer than ten acres of citrus, many farmers recognized themselves as the "little man" the prime minister sought to help; they nodded approvingly. However, after the prime minister had left, a citrus farmer who owned several hundred acres expressed concern about the potential divisiveness of the prime minister's speech. This farmer cautioned: "A word to my colleagues: certainly we would not like to conduct the affairs of the association in a scenario of big and small farmers. And I certainly hope that when issues of far-reaching importance arrive around our table, it is not a collusion of . . . the small farmers [against] the large farmers, because that's the beginning of the end. So, my colleagues, let's hope that will not be the trend whereby issues are decided."

An ethnic Garifuna waterfront worker in the Belizean citrus industry asserted during an interview that most of the workers in the citrus orchards were "aliens." Noting that they claimed to be ethnic Mestizos from Cayo District of western Belize, he said, "They say they are from Cayo, but cho! That's not true!" His assertion about the foreign origins of orchard workers resonated with government officials' portrayal of agricultural workers as immigrants from Central America. However, while government officials argued that immigrant labor was necessary to sustain the agricultural industries at the heart of the Belizean development strategy, this worker's assertion reflected the indignation of Garifuna and Creoles—Belizeans of African descent—about the increased competition for work that resulted from the immigration of tens of thousands of Central Americans—classified as Mestizo in Belize—during the 1980s. Such sentiments fueled many small confrontations, including one described with equal indignation by an older Mestizo citrus worker who had been born in Belize. As he was traveling by bus, he recalled, a young Garifuna woman boarded and began to push her way up the aisle, squeezing between those who were already standing. She stopped next to his seat and asserted in a commanding tone, "That's my seat, paisa!" She addressed him with a term applied by Garifuna to people they assume to be immigrants from Guatemala. Angered by this challenge to his Belizeanness, the Mestizo man retorted, "I'm not a paisa! I'm a Belizean! And more Belizean than you, because I'm older [and thus have been Belizean longer]!" The young woman turned and pushed further back through the crowded bus aisle.

In the face of revolutions and the resurgence of revolutionary movements of the Left throughout Central America and the Caribbean in the late 1970s and early 1980s, the U.S. government sent a bipartisan commission to the region to evaluate the dangers to U.S. interests posed by these movements and to recommend ways to counter and contain these dangers. The National Bipartisan Commission on Central America concluded:

> The hemisphere is challenged both economically and politically. . . . First, the commanding economic issue in all of Latin America is the impoverishment of its people. . . . The contraction of the hemisphere's economies, and the impoverishment of its people, must be reversed. Real growth must be restored. . . . Second, the political challenge in the hemisphere centers on the legitimacy of government. . . . Powerful forces are on the march in nearly every country of the hemisphere, testing how nations shall be organized and by what processes authority shall be established and legitimized. Who shall govern and under what forms are the central

issues in the process of change now under way in country after country throughout Latin America and the Caribbean. . . . [W]e must do all we can to nurture democracy in this hemisphere. (NBCCA 1984:11–12)

This ethnography explores the relationship between the production of collective identities and the negotiation of development policies, at the interface of global and local processes. With an ethnographic focus on the citrus industry in Belize, the book examines how citrus farmers and workers, citrus processing company owners, and politicians compete to construct shared identities and interests; how they mobilize collective actors; and how their collective action shapes the goals, policies, and practices associated with development. As they work to mobilize collective actors, people involved in the industry elaborate competing definitions of who "we" are and what interests "we" share. For example, the citrus farmer quoted above worried that the prime minister's assertion of differences among citrus growers might generate conflict between large and small growers, while he preferred to emphasize their shared identity and interests as citrus farmers. The waterfront worker who questioned whether orchard workers really belonged to the Belizean nation believed these suspected immigrants were less deserving of a share of the benefits of Belizean development. Such efforts to persuade one another about who "we" are and what interests "we" share are implicated in struggles over what development will mean in Belize and how it will be implemented. To whom should resources be allocated and why? Who should participate in Belizean development and in what capacity? Who should benefit from Belizean development and how? At the same time, the quotation from the U.S. government's National Bipartisan Commission on Central America indicates that agendas for Belizean development also originate outside of Belize, as foreigners identify the "problems" confronted by countries like Belize and delineate solutions.

Global and Local Forces in the Belizean Citrus Industry

Both development policies and collective identities in the Belizean citrus industry are negotiated at the interface of global and local processes. Locally, the industry comprises some five hundred citrus farmers, two processing companies, and many hundreds of wage laborers. The heart of the citrus industry has been Stann Creek District of southern Belize, though citrus holdings extend west into Cayo District and south into Toledo District as well

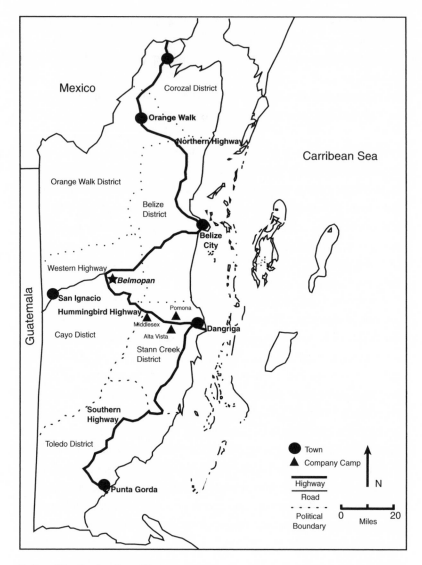

Belize. (Map by Jon Carroll)

(see the map of Belize). A majority of the industry's five hundred citrus farmers live along the Stann Creek Valley Road, which winds its way down from
the Maya Mountains to the coast. The vast majority of farmers own fewer
than fifty acres; most own fewer than twenty. At the other extreme, a few
men owned farms of several hundred acres when I began research in the industry. Each year in the late 1980s and early 1990s they expanded—one hundred,

two hundred, sometimes three hundred acres a year—until some eventually passed the two-thousand-acre mark. Numbering only a couple dozen, these larger-scale farmers produce the bulk of all independently grown citrus. Regardless of such disparities in acreage, all commercial citrus producers are required by law to belong to the Citrus Growers Association (CGA), a producers organization mandated by Belizean law to protect growers' interests.

Two processing companies in the Stann Creek Valley, Belize Food Products (BFP) and the Citrus Company of Belize (CCB), convert the oranges and grapefruits from growers' farms into frozen juice concentrate for export. A consortium of Belizean and Trinidadian investors owned the Citrus Company of Belize; many of the Belizean investors were themselves large citrus farmers. When I began research for this book, Belize Food Products was a subsidiary of Nestlé, the transnational corporation based in Switzerland. Each company owned orchards of several thousand acres. Since this made them citrus growers, the companies also belonged to the Citrus Growers Association.

Hundreds of wage laborers tend the orchards of the processing companies and the large citrus estates, while many smallholders manage their farms using family labor. However, some smaller growers also hire labor, especially those who work for wages and are too pressed for time to do all of the work on their farms themselves. When I began research on the industry, the United General Workers Union (UGWU) represented orchard workers at the two companies and the largest citrus estate, factory workers at the two companies, and waterfront workers who loaded the finished product onto ships for export.[1]

The contexts in which citrus farmers, processing companies, and workers in the Belizean citrus industry operate are powerfully shaped by actors who are not local. Since the industry produces for export, it responds to global markets and the geopolitics of international trade. Its first small boom was the result of the initiation of a British government program to increase the vitamin C intake of British schoolchildren by importing citrus products from the colonies for distribution in schools. Its most recent boom resulted from U.S. efforts in the 1980s to expand Caribbean economies and articulate them more closely with the U.S. economy, in order to prevent Caribbean countries from falling prey to "Communist expansionism." The intensity of Belizean citrus growers' maintenance or expansion of their orchards depends on the prices they receive for their fruit, which reflect both global demand and the costs of Brazilian producers and processors, who produce the bulk of citrus concentrate traded internationally. But prices paid to Belizean farmers also depend on the trade preferences extended to Belize by the United States and Britain, and on the success or failure of Florida citrus farmers' efforts to limit citrus imports to the United States.

The two citrus processing companies have also been under varying degrees of transnational ownership, and international development agencies or foreign investors have funded much of the industry's expansion throughout the recent citrus boom. The provision of funds for citrus expansion reflects the development priorities of foreign development agencies concerned with expanding Belizean exports to enable the country to service the debts incurred in the very process of developing.

The industry's labor force was reshaped by political-economic violence and civil wars in neighboring Central American countries during the 1980s, which fueled migration to Belize. At the same time, global antagonisms and regional alliances have animated citrus workers' union politics in both local and national arenas.

Dominant perspectives and policy priorities from the United States are beamed into Belize via TV and radio as well. Thus, concepts whose content has been defined beyond Belizean borders—here I will focus on the concepts of development, nation, and democracy—have shaped the perspectives of farmers and workers in Belize.

Forces that originate outside Belize powerfully shape the development trajectory of the Belizean citrus industry; indeed, it could be argued that the Belizean citrus industry exists in order to satisfy the needs of people in other countries. However, Smith argues against taking a one-sided view of global-local articulations, "assigning potency and causality only to the external forces" and describing the dynamics within local communities "as if they came about only to meet the needs of actors operating at the higher levels of the system" (Smith 1993:76). She suggests that we examine the ways actors in local arenas shape the structures imposed on them by the expansion of global capitalism by focusing on sites where local and global forces are mediated. The export-oriented Belizean citrus industry provides such a site, where citrus farmers, processing company shareholders and executives, and wage laborers in the industry maneuver within and against international flows of capital, labor, concepts, and priorities, as they compete to define and pursue collective interests in local arenas. Their efforts to mobilize collective actors and negotiate social alliances have pushed the industry's development in directions that conform in some ways—but diverge in others—from the trajectories laid out by foreign agencies.

While the citrus industry constitutes the book's primary site for the exploration of global-local interfaces, the Belizean state is a second site where global and local pressures are mediated in struggles to define development priorities and collective identities. In spite of some contemporary assertions that nation-states are being eclipsed and made irrelevant by the increasingly global organization of economic activity, the Belizean state plays an important role in mediating global and local pressures, as it works to build a Belizean nation and develop its economy. As the state attempts to manage and nurture the national economy, it negotiates and channels development funding, regulates Belizean industries and trade, and articulates rationales for its policies and priorities. These policies and priorities are strongly conditioned by forces originating outside Belize. This study focuses particular attention on Belize's involvement with three transnational discourses, those on development, nation, and democracy. Appadurai has called such discourses "ideoscapes," fluid configurations of "ideas, terms, and images" that circulate globally (Appadurai 1996:33, 36). The meanings associated with these traveling concepts come to vary across time and place, as they are defined and redefined through their articulation into local discourses. International bodies and agencies such as the IMF or the World Bank, dominant nation-states such as the United States or the United Kingdom, and the U.S. media that is beamed into many Belizean homes via cable have all worked to impose particular definitions on these terms. The former have linked these concepts to sets of material incentives and constraints as well. In postcolonial Belize, ideas and forces emanating from the United States in particular—through government contacts, influence over multilateral agencies, and television signals—have been significant in defining development, nation, and democracy.

Belizean political elites, constituting the upper echelons of the Belizean state, respond to the priorities marked out by global ideoscapes and the coercive force that can be brought to bear by Belize's creditors and trade partners, as they elaborate official state discourses. However, the Belizean state also answers to the Belizean electorate. Thus, as the Belizean government has incorporated the concepts of development, nation, and democracy into official explanations of who Belizeans are, what they want, and how best their goals can be achieved, the meanings and practices associated with these concepts have been localized. These official discourses have generated constellations of identities and interests that distribute membership in the Belizean nation, rights to shape the nation's development, and rights to benefit from national development. Such official definitions may be either deployed or sub-

verted by actors in local arenas. This study examines the articulation of local, national, and international processes across these two sites.

Collective Actors and Collective Action

Recognition of the ways development in the Third World has been conditioned by First World policies and interests is not new. Dependency and "development of underdevelopment" theorists from the Third World identified
these relations several decades ago, focusing on relations *between nations*
(Cardoso and Faletto 1979; Frank 1966). Later neo-marxist critiques of both
development orthodoxy and dependency perspectives presented a more complex and nuanced analysis, asserting that the direction development takes in
any particular country is shaped through the formation of social alliances
within that country and their articulation with wider relations of power internationally (deJanvry 1981). Neo-marxist analyses such as deJanvry's focused
on the different impacts that alternative class alliances had produced in Latin
American countries. However, deJanvry's analysis did not account for *how*
particular social alliances had been forged; the model was historically and
sociologically "empty" (Roseberry 1993). If we agree that such alliances determine the direction and shape of development efforts, then social scientists
ought to thoroughly investigate the processes through which particular social alliances have been produced in specific historical circumstances. Beginning with this assumption, the research for this book was undertaken to
explore how such alliances are generated or sustained, how collective actors
are mobilized behind particular agendas. More specifically, how do citrus
farmers, wage laborers, and processing company shareholders and administrators define and pursue shared interests? How do they articulate their interests to the interests of actors beyond the Belizean citrus industry?

My pursuit of these questions in Belize revealed further shortcomings of
neo-marxist analyses of development and underdevelopment: their focus on
class alliances *assumed* the unproblematic existence of classes as collective
actors and largely ignored other significant dimensions of collective identity.
Though I have characterized participants in the industry as farmers, workers, or processing company owners and administrators, they belong to many
other categories as well. The industry incorporates people affiliated with all
of the ethnic categories officially recognized as collective members of the
Belizean nation: Creole, Spanish/Mestizo, Garifuna, Mopan and Kekchi Maya,
East Indian, Lebanese, Chinese, Mennonite, and White. (Although race la-

bels such as "mestizo" and "white" are not capitalized in standard U.S. usage, these terms are capitalized here to reflect their official designation in Belize as *ethnic* labels. The term "black" will also be capitalized, although it is not an official ethnic label in Belize, since U.S. readers will expect the three terms to be treated similarly.) Both men and women participate in the industry as farmers and wage laborers, often in gender-differentiated capacities. Factory owners, farmers, and workers include immigrants from other countries (Guatemala, Honduras, El Salvador, Mexico, Jamaica, Trinidad, the United States) as well as people born in Belize. Those born in Belize include both natives of Stann Creek District and migrants from other districts of Belize. Some workers, farmers, and company shareholders are members and active supporters of one or another political party, either the Peoples United Party (PUP) or the United Democratic Party (UDP), while others take pains to distance themselves from party politics altogether.

Participants in the industry thus locate themselves along multiple axes of identity, claiming class, national, racial-ethnic, gender, political party, and regional or local affiliations. Some individuals occupy more than one position along even a single axis of identity. For example, some of the largest citrus farmers are also processing company shareholders; some wageworkers are also smallholder citrus farmers, who hire wage laborers on their citrus farms. Moreover, as the various dimensions of people's social positioning intersect, they modify one another. For example, immigrant status often modifies a person's status as a worker, such that immigrant workers may earn lower wages or receive less effective union representation than Belizean-born workers. Similarly, women farmers may face challenges their male counterparts do not.

If each participant in the industry is positioned along multiple axes of identity that modify one another in complex ways at their intersections, then we cannot take for granted the existence of solidarity along any single axis of identity. Indeed, although formal organizations such as the Citrus Growers Association and the United General Workers Union had existed for decades prior to my undertaking this research, neither of these organizations represented a single, unified collective actor that was continuous over time: "citrus growers" or "workers." Instead, members of the two organizations embraced multiple, often divergent, identities and interests that shifted situationally. Concerned with the formation of social alliances that shape the development process, I was led to ask: How have participants in the citrus industry been mobilized as collective actors around particular identities? In pursuit of what goals or interests? What impact has their collective action had on the shape development has taken in the citrus industry and in Belize more generally? These questions and their answers must be situated in relation to contemporary perspectives on the construction of personal and collective identities and the mobilization of collective actors.

Identity Formation: The Creation of Categories, Subjects, and Agents

Identity does not derive from within individuals as the manifestation of some internal essence. Rather, identity is a social product: both the available categories and the personal identities people claim (or have imposed on them) are socially constructed. Thus, identity formation involves dual processes: (1) the construction of social categories or "subject positions," and (2) the placement of individuals within particular categories, that is, the creation of "subjects." Individuals are constituted as subjects through social processes that place them in social categories or subject positions and train them to "recognize themselves in particular ways" (Wetherell and Potter 1992:28; Foucault 1979; Laclau and Mouffe 1985). The individual subject thus brought into being is "subjected" in a double sense: "subject to someone else by control or dependence, and tied to his own identity by a conscience or self-knowledge" (Dreyfus and Rabinow 1982:212). In other words, human subjects develop self-identities by accepting or embracing the conceptual categories in which others have positioned them. An individual who possesses an identity is also possessed by the forces that have constituted that identity.

Both social categories and subjectivities are products of discourse: people make sense of the material and social world and their place in it through discourses that "explain" existing circumstances and rationalize certain courses of action. As Foucault used the term, discourse refers to "practices that systematically form the objects of which they speak" (Foucault 1973:49; 1979). In this sense, discourse both reveals and constructs the conceptual frameworks that make possible—but also limit—people's thoughts, words, and actions. Discourse constitutes *objects* (such as identity categories or notions of development and democracy) by ordering our perceptions of the world around us.[2] Discourse constitutes *subjects* by ordering our self-perceptions— our sense of who we are and what import that has. As discourses shape daily practices, interpersonal relations, and social institutions, they are in turn *made material.* Thus, discourse analysis is a means for exploring the sociohistorical production of meanings and practices that blurs distinctions between material and ideational realms, between talking and doing, between words and things, to examine how discourse produces "practical effects" (Abu-Lughod 1991; Ong 1987; Rattansi 1995).

As individuals and institutions put these categories into practice to organize both self-identities and social interactions, they come to "inhabit" them, to make themselves at home in them (Omi and Winant 1994). Positionings or identities that resonate across a wide range of situations may become heavily invested, so that discourses that seek to define identities and interests in specific situations must work on these already-constituted subjectivities (Rattansi 1995). Moreover, as people use these categories to distribute resources and opportunities, the categories become manifested materially.[3] For example, in Belize, as employers at the citrus processing companies hire people they classify as Mestizo for work in the orchards, they establish links between racial-ethnic classification and occupation that both reflect and produce assumptions about which kinds of workers are appropriate for which kinds of jobs. When they pay women less than men to perform the same job, they make gender differences and inequality palpable. As immigrants from Guatemala share scarce resources among themselves, they construct and affirm national solidarities. And as a Belizean challenges a suspected immigrant's right to occupy a seat on a public bus, she positions both herself and the "alien," claiming rights for herself as a Belizean that the immigrant ought not to enjoy.

In this context, it is important to remember that people are not simply the passive recipients of subjectivities. Human beings are *agents,* active subjects engaged in "conscious efforts . . . to understand and work on their situations" (Levine 1993:10). Thus, it follows that while each individual's subjectivity—their sense of self—is shaped through discourse, those individuals are also involved in shaping the discourses that define reality for themselves and others. Discourses do not spontaneously form themselves and then travel at will; rather, human agents formulate discourses and strategically invoke them. They also adjust or rework familiar discourses or abandon them in favor of alternatives. At the same time, it is precisely the "subject"—located in particular social positions associated with particular interests—that can be understood to act strategically as agent.

Where discourses and associated practices of identity intersect, they create different—and unequal—kinds of people along multiple axes of identity simultaneously. For example, Elena Contreras, a Guatemalan immigrant to Belize, was hired to harvest oranges by one of the processing companies. This job was already typed as appropriate for Mestizo immigrants like Elena, but in-appropriate for Belizeans. However, Elena has sometimes been denied work during the industry's off-season, because, as a woman, she is not perceived as an appropriate breadwinner by male employers. Garifuna men who work on the waterfront position themselves simultaneously in class, racial-ethnic, and gender categories, as they move heavy barrels of frozen juice concentrate from trucks to a waiting ship. Using the Garifuna language to coordinate their efforts, they both position themselves as Garifuna and exclude their non-Garifuna company supervisor from their communication. While the physical strength required for waterfront work affirms their masculinity, the relatively high wages they earn reinforce links between masculinity and breadwinner status. Thus, individuals embrace and are socially assigned multiple identities that intersect and shape one another in complex ways. At their intersections, identities may reinforce or contradict one another; they may displace, assimilate, or modify one another. Which identity is relevant in a given context, what that identity entails—given its intersections—and what interests it connotes are matters that social agents negotiate situationally. Collective identities organized along one axis of identity are always vulnerable to disruption by mobilization along other axes of identity. Thus, all forms of collective agency must be investigated as contingent, continually emergent phenomena.

The Production of Collective Agents

The emergent nature of collective identities and collective agency provides the starting point of analysis for some theorists of new social movements. Many social movements defined as "new"—those based on race, ethnicity, gender, or sexuality, for example—are understood to be fundamentally concerned with issues of identity. While some scholars take for granted the collective identities that form the basis for social movements, Melucci (1988) warns against assuming the existence of a collective actor. Instead, he casts collective identity as a process, rather than an a priori fact (Escobar 1992:72). Accordingly, he suggests that the question of how collective actors are constituted or maintained should be the fundamental issue addressed by social movements research. I use that question to frame this study, exploring how collective identities and collective agency have been generated at particular points in time in the Belizean citrus industry and how they have shaped the development process. Further, rather than taking shared interests as an objective feature of the social structure, I explore how collective interests are themselves constituted through the same struggles (Hall 1988:45).[4]

Some social movements researchers have focused on what they define as "new" about contemporary social movements around gender, sexuality, peace, or environmentalism, in contrast to "old" social movements that were understood to be based on class antagonisms. Rather than engaging this particular debate, I argue that, regardless of how different contemporary social movements may be from their predecessors, all social movements are more complex than previous theorizations accounted for. For example, as class-based organizations, neither the Citrus Growers Association—a producers association—nor the United General Workers Union fits the mold of a "new" social movement; but both defy assumptions about class-based "old" social movements. Neither the United General Workers Union nor the Citrus Growers Association represents a continuous, unified collective actor. Since union and CGA members belong to many categories in addition to those of "worker" or "citrus farmer," how they will identify themselves and what interests they will embrace in any particular situation have been determined through struggle. This ethnography explores how aspiring leaders deployed competing discourses to forge collective agents out of the multiple, crosscutting bonds enacted in everyday life. It thus seeks to answer Melucci's key question: how are collective agents formed? In focusing on a producers organization and a union, this book provides a bridge from work on "old" social movements in Latin America, that is, those based on class, to contemporary research on "new" social movements that take collective identities to be more situational and socially constructed.

In order to understand how collective identities are formed and collective agents spurred to action, Melucci (1988) suggests that we must examine the two "faces" of social movements. One face consists of "submerged networks"—interpersonal relations—through which people collaborate to produce interpretations of their material and social circumstances on a routine basis. While Melucci focuses on those interpretations that are subversive of official explanations and prescriptions, I examine how these everyday interpretations, and the actions they authorize, may both subvert and conform to official discourses. The second face comprises moments of public mobilization and collective action. In order to understand how and why people mobilize as collective agents at particular moments, we need to explore the everyday practices that form and nurture the discourses, identities, and interests that may later be invoked to generate collective action (Melucci 1988; see also

Scott 1985). We also need to analyze the discourses elaborated to mobilize collective agents at points of conflict. People pursuing divergent agendas often deploy discourses that provide opposing interpretations of the same set of circumstances. They compete with one another to define what identities are relevant in the situation at hand, to explain why those identities are relevant, and to suggest avenues for collective action. Rather than judging the truth or falsity of competing discourses, I focus on their *efficacy,* on how particular discourses succeed in binding together collective agents in support of particular projects (Hall, Lumley, and McLennan 1977).[5]

Accordingly, this account explores both "faces" of collective action: chapters 4 and 6 explore everyday constructions of identity and interest generated by wage laborers and farmers in the Belizean citrus industry; chapters 5 and 7 examine the ways that would-be leaders defined particular constellations of identity and interest in efforts to mobilize collective agents during two open struggles in the industry. Citrus farmers' routine constructions of affinity and antagonism shaped the possibilities for constructing collective agents during a struggle over the sale of Belize Food Products. Likewise, workers' daily experiences in an ethnically segmented labor force shaped the kinds of solidarities that could be mobilized during the struggle for control of the union.

Organization of the Book

Chapter 2 provides an overview of Belizean history and the historical construction of official discourses on the Belizean nation, economic development, and democracy. Official government discourses on development, nation, and democracy mediate pressures from within and beyond Belizean borders; they weave together concerns about economic development and identity formation to define the Belizean nation and its aspirations. These official discourses construct a somewhat contradictory framework for interpretation and action, whose effects are assessed in subsequent chapters.

Chapter 3 explores the historical development of citrus production and power relations in the industry over the twentieth century, linking events in the Belizean industry to international relations and markets. The first half of the chapter focuses on the political organization and mobilization of citrus farmers in contests with the processing companies over fruit prices and confrontations with the government over access to land and credit for expansion, demonstrating how citrus farmers have appropriated official democracy and development discourses for their own ends. The second half examines the history of labor organizing in the industry and explores its links to wider political processes in Belize and beyond.

Chapters 4 and 5 examine the two faces of collective action among citrus workers. Chapter 4 explores how eight wage laborers in the industry identify themselves in relation to the ways that others position them, and how they measure official discourses against their daily practices in an ethnic- and gender-segmented labor force. The multifaceted identities they fashion for themselves provide the potential for alliances in several directions or schisms along a number of fault lines, including gender, kinship, ethnicity, nationality, work area, job title, place of residence, and political party affiliation. Chapter 5 analyzes a conflict that erupted in the union, which initially involved a broad rank-and-file action against the union leadership. It examines the emergence of two opposing discourses that emphasized ethnic and national explanations for tensions in the union and recommended divergent courses of action to resolve the union's problems. Drawing on the interpretations crafted by the workers introduced in chapter 4, this chapter explores how these opposing discourses were elaborated and how they succeeded in mobilizing workers around particular sets of shared identities and interests to generate two competing collective agents.

Chapters 6 and 7 provide a parallel analysis of the two faces of collective action among citrus farmers. Chapter 6 explores how six citrus growers routinely construct identities and interests through social interactions. It examines the degree to which farmers take up or ignore, accept or rework, official constructions of identity and interests, with attention to the ways in which their perspectives are grounded in their daily work and interactions with kin and neighbors. Like wage laborers, farmers embrace multifaceted identities defined in terms of gender, ethnicity, nationality, political party affiliation, and citrus acreage. Chapter 7 explores competing attempts to define collective identities and interests in the course of negotiations for the sale of Nestlé-owned Belize Food Products. Two coalitions of large citrus estate owners competed to purchase the foreign-owned company. During the negotiations, each coalition invoked official discourses on development, nation, and democracy and articulated them to its own project to construct and channel collective agency. Focusing especially on the views of the farmers introduced in chapter 6, this chapter presents smallholder citrus farmers' responses to the discourses presented by elites and explains how small farmers collectively elaborated an oppositional discourse and forced elites to accommodate it.

Chapter 8 draws conclusions about the social alliances and social schisms produced by the two contests explored here, their impact on development directions in the industry and in Belize more generally, and their articulation with international political and economic forces. The chapter also examines the contradictions and instabilities inherent in these alliances, which necessitate the continual renewal or renegotiation of shared identities, interests, and visions of development. It concludes with consideration of how global realignments of politics and economics may be reshaping the social alignments that will shape future development in the industry and in Belize.

The Ethnographic Process: The Relations of Production of Knowledge

The research that provides the basis for this account was carried out over a number of years. I initiated the project in 1986, when I carried out research in southern Belize for nine months. I conducted archival research; I interviewed farmers, wageworkers, processing company officials, political leaders and regional representatives, the staffs of government ministries involved in the citrus industry, and labor leaders at the national level; and I carried out participant observation at meetings of workers and farmers, as well as in places where they gathered informally. Following this extended period of research, I made short trips back during the summers of 1987 and 1988. During these visits, citrus farmers and workers I had interviewed or interacted with during 1986 updated me on events that had occurred in the industry since my last visit. Recognizing that I was an avid follower of what they called "citrus politics," many were eager to bring me up to date regarding the current state of those politics. In 1989 I returned to Stann Creek District for another year of research. Again, I relied on interviews, archival research, and participant observation, but I also added a formal survey of random samples of members of the Citrus Growers Association and the unions. I had married by then, and my husband, Chema, accompanied me. Though he was not an anthropologist, but rather a furniture and cabinet maker, he played a significant role in the research from this point on. Following this second extended research period, I also spent portions of the summers of 1991, 1992, 1994, 1997, 1998, and 1999 in southern Belize. During each of these visits I mixed formal interviews with citrus officials and informal interviews with farmers and workers to catch up on events in the industry and learn about their perspectives on these events. Over the years, I also relied on the annual reports published by the Citrus Growers Association and correspondence with a small

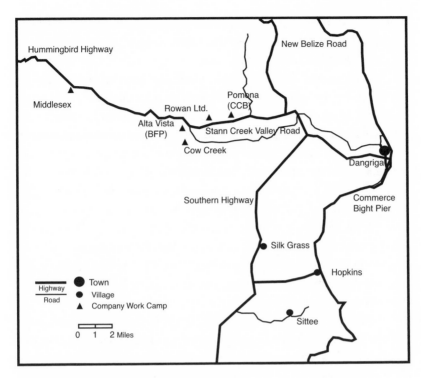

The Stann Creek Valley. (Map by Jon Carroll)

number of farmers and workers to keep up with current events in the industry and their opinions about them.

The farmers and workers I interviewed were spread along more than one hundred miles of roads, from southern Stann Creek District to Cayo District (see figure 1). This was not the typical field site of traditional anthropological research, which many an anthropologist has referred to as "my village." Rather, I lived in the coastal town of Dangriga, the majority of whose residents were neither citrus farmers nor citrus industry workers, and I traveled widely to interact with growers and wage laborers. Citrus farmsteads were scattered along the few roads in the Stann Creek Valley; some workers lived in Dangriga, but the majority of them lived in company camps in the Stann Creek Valley, at Pomona, Rowan Ltd., Alta Vista, Cow Creek, and Middlesex (see the map of the Stann Creek Valley). Most mornings were spent in Dangriga, typing notes, washing clothes, and purchasing food supplies. In the late afternoons, my husband and I visited farmers or workers, who had by that hour finished their daily labor on the farm or the job. Some evenings were filled with visits to workers or farmers who lived in the town of Dangriga, but most involved driving up the Stann Creek Valley to visit those who lived on their farmsteads or in company camps.

In this account, I draw heavily on participant observation in routine interactions among farmers, wage laborers, and processing company owners and administrators, and in the organizational meetings where collective identities and shared interests were publicly debated and farmers and workers were actively recruited into one perspective or another. I focused especially on public meetings in which Belizeans negotiated identities primarily with one another rather than only with me. While interviews with me were shaped by people's perceptions of my identity and interests, in union and CGA meetings people were working to convince *one another* about who they were and what interests they shared, in a context in which these arguments mattered a great deal to participants. I attended as many of these meetings as I could, and after each one I interviewed farmers or workers to learn what sense they had made of the proceedings.

I conducted both formal and informal interviews with growers and workers to elicit their opinions as current events unfolded and to learn their perspectives on past events in the industry. As I interviewed people following a CGA or union meeting, or as I tracked the movement of rumors up and down the valley, I discovered that I was participating in the interactive, collaborative process through which opinions are formed in rural Belize: through conversations with kin and neighbors, industry happenings are analyzed and evaluated, and courses of action are debated.[6] I paid careful attention to the way people positioned themselves in social categories and the interests they claimed, as they presented their interpretations of current and past events in the industry. Many of the informal interviews were not one-on-one encounters; rather, they incorporated other family members or neighbors who were present. In these contexts, I also noted the way farmers' and workers' self-positionings were received by other participants in the conversation.

I also conducted archival research, reading government reports from the ministries of labor, agriculture, or industry; earlier studies of the industry undertaken by private individuals or potential funding organizations; and the minutes of CGA and Citrus Control Board meetings. The latter were especially helpful in generating questions about past events that I could pursue in interviews with farmers and processing company officials.

Finally, I conducted formal surveys of random samples drawn from the CGA and the labor unions in the industry. After gaining through the early phases of the research a good sense of the questions people in the industry found critical or contentious, in 1989–90 I drew random samples of CGA and union members in order to survey a cross section of members of each organization. Initially I had interviewed farmers whose names I was given by CGA leaders as representatives of different categories of growers, based on the size of their citrus acreages, and farmers I met at the CGA office or in travels with the CGA field man. I had interviewed workers I had met in the course of participant observation, or those who began interviewing *me* after seeing me participant observing. I added the survey of random samples of the organizations involved in the industry to discover whatever diverse dimensions of identity were present among citrus growers and workers. Especially given the assertion, made without documentation, that agricultural laborers were almost entirely "foreign," it seemed important to collect data to test this claim. After the formal survey, I later added many of the farmers and workers whose names I had drawn to the list of people whose opinions I solicited regularly about current events in the industry.

I drew a sample of thirty farmers from the CGA, whose membership in 1989 was 398. All thirty farmers agreed to participate in the study; many hoped that my research would benefit them by documenting and publicizing their concerns. By 1989, when I conducted the survey, the UGWU had divided in two. Orchard and factory workers, who numbered approximately three hundred during the off-season and six hundred at the height of the harvest, had seceded to form a branch of the Belize Workers Union (BWU). Though the leader of the BWU was disturbed by my desire to draw a random sample rather than allowing him to select the members I would interview, at the urging of his wife, who enjoyed our visits and was pleased by my ability to speak Spanish, he ultimately allowed me to use the union's membership lists to draw a sample of fifty names. We were able to interview forty-nine of the fifty workers whose names we had drawn; one member of the sample, a young man, avoided us by having his roommates tell us he was not at home. (When another worker explained what was happening, we stopped asking for him.) Another sample member provided answers so clearly untrue that I could not figure how to make sense of them. By 1989 only waterfront workers still belonged to the United General Workers Union (UGWU). At that time the UGWU's membership was under one hundred, and I drew a random sample of ten. Though most waterfront workers who had talked with me during my earlier research indicated that they would be happy to answer my questions, other individuals whose names I had drawn were alarmed by my presence and suspicious of my motives. Most of them visited the union office to seek the opinions of others about whether or not to cooperate with me before agreeing to be interviewed. The secretary, who had known me since 1986, reassured them that I was "okay." Although all members of the sample agreed to be interviewed, one man subsequently indicated his desire not to be interviewed by setting appointments with my husband and me several times and then failing to appear on each occasion. I drew another name to replace him.

If identities—shifting, contextual, contested—are important in the negotiation of Belizean development goals and priorities, the negotiation of identities with the farmers, processing company executives, and wage laborers with whom my husband and I worked significantly shaped the research process. In an important sense, we were all positioned in international fields of power that related us to one another even before we had met, and these positions provided the starting points for our negotiation of relationships during the research process. As Haraway (1988) has argued, knowledge is always produced from a particular vantage point or social location: it is "situated." Accordingly, in what follows I identify some of the positionings from which this research was produced to make explicit the situatedness of my knowledge and the conditions of its production.

Indeed, during the research process, Belizeans continually positioned me in gender, racial, and national categories that they deemed extremely important. Belizeans insistently positioned me as White and American, though different people accorded differential significance to these classifications. Both Whiteness and Americanness facilitated my relations with elites in the citrus industry, suggesting to them that we likely shared attitudes, lifestyles, and to some degree status. Belizean elites often educate their children in the United States, or they travel there for shopping or vacations. As elites, they are expected to interact easily with middle-class professionals from the United States, as they may be called on to do so in the context of developing their business interests. Accordingly, many citrus elites felt comfortable incorporating me into some of their social events as well as into "citrus politics." In fact, seeing themselves as active agents with the potential to shape the industry's development, some elites were actually keen to be interviewed by me, in order to share their priorities for the industry and counter the perspectives they suspected their rivals might have provided to me.

For wage laborers, on the other hand, their positioning of me as White and American had another kind of resonance. Their classification of me into these categories generated social distance at best and a good deal of suspicion at worst. For example, in 1986 the UGWU general secretary agreed to allow me to interview him, but then he narrated stories that were nonsensical. Confused, I asked for a second interview, with the same result. Finally, he explained: when his union had been actively involved in international socialist labor organizations, young women like myself had appeared in Dangriga to "interview" him about his trips to Cuba or other places not approved by the United States. Suspicious of my motives and "mission," he spent two interviews evaluating what I was after before beginning to talk more seriously with me. While I can neither verify nor disprove his assertions about U.S. efforts to gather information about his union, the U.S. embassy official in charge of monitoring labor in Belize offered a succinct appraisal of the Dangriga union leader. "He's a communist," he told me, applying the most dangerous label it was possible to use in the Central America of the mid-1980s.

On my return in 1989, most of the workers who had known me earlier welcomed my renewed research in the industry. However, many other workers were wary of me. For some of them, my positioning as White and American was central to their apprehension about my research. While some workers declined to have any extended interaction with me, a couple of UGWU leaders decided to interview *me* about my intentions, my background, and my motives. The interviews clarified for me some of the issues that concerned them and emphasized the significance of my racial and national identities. "Do you recognize the power you have as a white American? That people respect and fear you?" one union leader asked. Under the circumstances, I did not feel particularly powerful. At the same time, I recalled the worker who had not kept his three appointments with me: apparently he had not felt that he could simply tell me he did not want to be interviewed. "Do you think it's possible for a white person not to be racist? Are you aware that every American that has come down to this union comes down here to tell us what to do?" he continued. White racism and Americans' tendency to tell other people what to do were clearly related issues for him; he perceived the latter to flow from a sense of superiority that derived from the former. He cited an example of U.S. religious workers who had admonished his congregation that they would have to abandon Garifuna cultural traditions if they hoped to become better Christians. They thought their way was the *only* way, he added. His questions placed me squarely within long-standing racial and international relations of unequal power. My interviewers were also concerned about the motives of those who funded my research: "Why does the National Science Foundation want to know about us? What is UCLA's stake in this?" I explained that the intention of my research was not to tell Belizeans what they should do, but rather to learn from them. I wanted to explore how Belizeans struggled to shape the development process in which they were involved, to learn about how Belizeans worked with and against agendas for Belizean development that originated outside Belize in order to generate new knowledge about how development can be negotiated. Though I do not imagine that my reference to producing "new knowledge" provided a very convincing answer, both of my interlocutors shared with me a concern about how Belizeans could and did exercise agency in the face of international structures of power decidedly not stacked in their favor. At any rate, both union leaders who interviewed me subsequently decided to work with me. Their questions emphasized the concerns behind their initial reluctance to do so and probably provided a partial explanation for the refusal of other waterfront leaders to work with me. As I had learned during my earlier research with the union, since its affiliation with Eastern bloc nations and trade union federations in the 1970s, the UGWU's membership has felt itself to be under siege, often rightly so. As one member explained in 1990, "We want to check your credentials to find out if there are things we should not be telling you about."

However, part of the reticence of some union leaders to allow me to conduct research with union members also reflected internal competition over control of the union. With this tension unresolved, I was hesitant to work too closely with either members or leaders who supported my research, in order to avoid exacerbating internal conflicts in the union or creating problems for members who were willing to work with me. Thus, I limited the number of visits I made to waterfront workers after 1989.

Most valley workers also located me in social categories that distanced me as a potentially powerful and dangerous outsider, and many people had predicted that immigrant workers would be unwilling to be interviewed by me. However, many of them were quite open. I attribute this in part to my growing ability to communicate in Spanish (and my lack of shame at committing errors), and in later phases of the research my husband's presence was significant in facilitating relations with Central American immigrants. My husband is himself Guatemalan, and the experience of being Central American in Belize, which he shared with immigrant workers, provided a starting point for solidarity that extended to incorporate me as well. His presence decreased the initial social distance between immigrant workers and me.

Thus, while Spanish speakers initially positioned me in racial and national terms as a *gringa,* a term laden with connotations of difference, distance, and hierarchy, most quickly shifted to the ambivalent diminutive *gringita.* As we got to know one another better, and some of them began to see me in a more complex way as a person as well as a bearer of significant racial and national social positions, many shifted again to a Spanish rendering of my name.

In addition to the farmers, workers, and officials who formed part of my formal research project, my husband and I also interacted with Dangriga's eight thousand inhabitants. Since many of them did not form part of the citrus industry and did not know us, they responded to us largely on the basis of our physical features. My pale skin was read as a sign of class, racial, and national privilege, an interpretation buttressed by our rental of a cement—rather than wood—house and possession of a four-wheel-drive vehicle. I worked to confound and complicate my social positioning by doing my own wash, walking rather than driving around town, and interacting most frequently with non-elites. Though these actions confused people, who inquired about what had happened to my vehicle, they did not alter the nature of the hierarchies that accorded me privilege in the first place. On the other hand, my husband was lumped into the "Spanish" ethnic category, as are most Guatemalan immigrants to Belize, and the derogatory terms Belizeans apply to Spanish persons in general and immigrants in particular were often shouted or grumbled at him. As he questioned others about what these words meant, he learned to be offended by the epithets; at the same time he was impressed with the ability of some of his detractors to repeat their insults in three languages to ensure they got their message across. On the streets of Dangriga, he was called *paisa* many times, a term that Belizeans apply as an insult to Spanish-speaking Central Americans; young Garifuna men spit on him twice. I pleaded with him to interpret such affronts as "data." I deploy some of these encounters in what follows to make such an interpretation plausible.

The gender locations of my husband and myself were also significant in shaping the way the research unfolded and the data we collected. At the outset of the research, as a single woman of twenty-three interviewing primarily men who were twenty to forty years my senior, I worked hard to identify myself as researcher-anthropologist: wielding a notebook in one hand and a tape recorder in the other, I conducted formal interviews. But in spite of my efforts to define myself as a researcher, Belizeans positioned me relentlessly as a "girl." For instance, an employee often announced my arrival at the office of a prominent citrus grower, tape recorder and notebook in hand, with the words, "Your girlfriend is here." Since men derive prestige from being perceived to carry on multiple sexual relationships, the citrus farmer generally responded with a question: "Which one?" Being positioned as a girl provided some advantages. Many men felt less threatened by my research than they might have if I had been older or male. For example, one processing company executive who had resisted my requests for an interview was cajoled by his colleagues: "Talk to the girl. She's only a girl; what harm can she do?" (The holdout had given my gender and presumed heterosexuality a different reading: "She doesn't seem to be interested in finding a man, so she must be CIA.") However, my gender location was sometimes a liability, limiting the kinds of interactions in which I could appropriately participate and curtailing my movements across the social landscape to some degree. Both men and women often cautioned me to limit my movements. Further, since I was especially concerned to make my intentions clear to the wives or girlfriends of the citrus farmers and workers with whom I worked, I interviewed people in their homes with their families present whenever possible.

My husband's participation in later phases of the research made casual, informal relationships with workers and growers and their families easier than they had been when I was single. His assistance also increased my mobility, making it possible for me to do research with male workers living in company barracks where it would have been inappropriate for a woman to go alone. Moreover, Chema had access to gendered experiences not accessible to me, such as the class- and ethnicity-charged interactions he recounted to me after drinking a beer in a club with other men.

The power relations that shaped the research process—and those that shape struggles to constitute collective identities and direct the development process—also require comment in terms of the writing of this account. Tylor (1986) has called for anthropologists to experiment with more mutualistic forms of ethnography, involving increased collaboration between anthropologists and the people with whom we work and more polyphonic texts that permit multiple voices to speak. While this suggestion offers a partial corrective to the way the practice of anthropology is linked to international power relations, it carries with it a dangerously romantic hope that by shifting our writing strategies we will dissolve the power differences that have enabled us to carry out research in the first place. Visweswaran points out that, as anthropologists, "what we come to know is engendered by relations of power" that it is *impossible* to refuse or wish away (Visweswaran 1994:77). Belizeans were much more aware of this fact than I was at the beginning of the research; they taught me this uncomfortable truth by insistently positioning me in racial, national, and class categories that connoted privilege and power. In the pages that follow, I attempt to present the perspectives of differently positioned individuals. For example, in chapters 5 and 7 I present accounts of extended conflicts in the citrus industry, played out in part through public meetings, many of which I was able to attend. These accounts present what other participants told me about the meaning and significance of the events that took place during the meetings. Their interpretations did not necessarily correspond to the understandings I had generated myself. (However, the research process paralleled the way that growers and workers formulated their own accounts: they developed interpretations by eliciting one another's opinions, and I became a participant in that process.) I do not present a single, authoritative account of what "really" happened and what it "really" meant, and, in some sense, "multiple voices" speak in this text. However, it is I who have summoned their words to these pages and orchestrated the voices of citrus farmers and workers as they speak here.

The ideal of cooperative text-making lies beyond the possible for a study such as this one, which involves people who embrace conflicting interests and perspectives, who believe that one another's interpretations of events are at best wrong and at worst lies. Further, participants in this study are widely differentiated in terms of their access to the printed word and their ability to wield power over one another. Thus the project of writing must contend not only with the power I wield but also with the unequal power that characterizes the relationships of workers, farmers, and factory owners to one another. The more involved I became in interviewing workers, the more I limited my contacts with citrus company executives—their employers—in order to avoid being taken as a "company spy." At the same time, I was aware that my movements in the company camps where many workers lived were easy to follow; I could guarantee the people I interviewed that I would protect their confidentiality by not attributing quotes or viewpoints to them by name, but it was not difficult to ascertain who I was visiting in the camps. As a result, rather than attempting to diminish power differences between Belizeans and myself through cooperative text-making, I have felt it necessary to take authoritative measures to disguise the identity of some participants in the study from other participants who wield power over them. Thus,

I use actual names only for those persons who hold public offices, since they are publicly accountable for the speeches and pronouncements they made in their official capacities. I have assigned pseudonyms to all others, and I have altered some details in presenting their accounts in order to protect their anonymity.

2 The Articulate State

Discourses of Development, Nation, and Democracy

This chapter outlines major trends in Belizean history and the historical construction of the collective identities that define sameness and difference in Belize.[1] It also examines how the processes of economic development and identity formation have been woven together in the present through the construction of official discourses on development, nation, and democracy.

The Colonial Period: Peopling a Territory, Extracting Its Resources

Prior to European colonization, Maya had inhabited the territory now known as Belize for centuries (Thompson 1988; Shoman 1994).[2] At the onset of European colonization in the Americas, Spain laid claim to a vast territory that included present-day Belize. Though the Spanish made some efforts to convert the indigenous inhabitants to Christianity, Spain was more concerned with the regions of its new empire that were yielding up precious metals. Spain's relative disinterest and weak control over the territory that would become Belize enabled British pirates and buccaneers to establish a settlement on the Belizean coast during the seventeenth century. That settlement, which would later become Belize Town and then Belize City, served as a base for harvesting logwood trees from Belizean coastal swamps to meet a growing demand for logwood in England, where it was used for dyeing cloth in the expanding textile industry (Bolland 1977:25). The logwood cutters operated along the coast, while the Maya lived inland. Since the woodcutters were unable to recruit or control Mayan labor, when logwood prices rose in the early eighteenth century, they purchased enslaved Africans from Jamaica to increase logwood production. Slaves soon outnumbered Europeans in the coastal settlement. During its first century, Spain complained repeatedly to Britain about the woodcutters' presence and attacked the settlement several times. In 1763 and 1786 treaties, Spain conceded use rights to Britain for the extraction of logwood from Belize but reasserted its sovereignty over the area (Bolland 1977:10, 31). Directly subject neither to British nor Spanish rule, the settlers, who called themselves "Baymen," created their own political and legal system to administer the settlement, comprising the Public Meeting that established laws and elected magistrates who enforced them.

In the 1770s, a synthetic replacement for logwood sent prices plunging, and the settlers redirected their enslaved labor force toward mahogany cutting to meet growing European demand for luxury furniture made of tropical hardwoods. Since mahogany trees were scattered throughout inland forests, an emerging settler elite parceled out among themselves large tracts of land along the rivers that provided the primary avenues of transport.[3] Ensuing competition led to the consolidation of land in the hands of fewer and fewer elites (Bolland 1977:43–45; Grant 1976:37). As the mahogany cutters moved inland, attacks by the indigenous Maya defending their territory became more frequent. Counterattacks by the settlers forced the Maya to withdraw deeper into the interior (Bolland 1977:21–23).

Although logging activities expanded inland during the eighteenth century, Belize Town on the coast remained the social and economic hub of the settlement. The Maya who resided in the interior were not seen as part of the Belize settlement, whose population was distinguished by slave and free status, with "color" distinctions drawn among the latter: white, colored, and free black. Over the eighteenth century, free people of color grew in importance both numerically and in terms of their economic power, as some colored children born to slave women of white slave owner fathers were manumitted and permitted to own property. By 1826, free colored people owned two-thirds of the private land and slaves in Belize, but white elites limited their participation in the settlement's political institutions (Grant 1976:45). Though they were allowed to become members of the Public Meeting, they were required to own two times the amount of property required of whites for membership (Dobson 1973:112–13).[4]

The nineteenth century brought major changes to the settlement: emancipation of slaves, immigration that more than doubled the population, and official status as a British colony. In 1834 the British government imposed emancipation on unwilling slave owners throughout its Caribbean holdings. However, concerned that land ownership "would discourage labour for wages," Britain simultaneously raised the price of land in Belize, to prevent freed slaves from acquiring land and thus ensure a ready labor supply after emancipation (Bolland 1988:119–20). Employers used debt peonage to secure labor, providing their now-free laborers with advances—to sustain their families, outfit themselves for the logging season, or celebrate Christmas. Then, during the timber harvest, employers sold their workers exorbitantly priced supplies. As a result, workers often began and ended the logging season indebted to their employers. The Masters and Servants Act prescribed public whipping as punishment for workers who broke their contracts and abandoned their debts to work for someone else (Grant 1976:51–52; Bolland 1988:159).

Several waves of immigration also occurred during the nineteenth century. Even prior to emancipation, woodcutters had sought wage laborers to augment the work performed by slaves. As early as 1802, Garifuna, then referred to as "Black Caribs," were hired to cut mahogany in the south. The Garifuna had originated in the eastern Caribbean, where indigenous Caribs had incorporated Africans into their society.[5] The Caribs put up fierce resistance to British efforts to colonize their land. After several decades of such resistance, the British defeated the Caribs militarily; subsequently, the British classified the Caribs into two color categories: lighter-skinned individuals classified as "yellow" Caribs were returned to St. Vincent; darker-skinned individuals categorized as "black" Caribs—perceived by the British as more threatening—were deported to the island of Roatan, off the coast of Honduras (Gonzalez 1988:23). Most abandoned Roatan to establish settlements along the coasts of Honduras and Guatemala. Some made their way to Belize, where slaveholders were divided over their presence: some slaveholders eagerly hired the newly arrived Caribs for forestry work, while others warned that they might lead a slave insurrection (Burdon 1934:60–61; Shoman 1994:74).

After emancipation, in spite of the measures taken to ensure that freed slaves would provide an adequate and pliant postemancipation labor supply for the forestry industry, employers complained of labor scarcity. Forestry barons increasingly sought out Garifuna labor, and in 1865 they imported a small number of indentured workers from China, Barbados, and Jamaica.[6] Those from Jamaica included both blacks and East Indians (Shoman 1994:87).[7]

However, by far the largest influx of immigrants, one that more than doubled the population of Belize, began in 1847, when a rebellion by indigenous peoples in the Yucatan peninsula of Mexico sent waves of refugees across the border into northern Belize. The refugees included a small number of elites of putatively "pure" Spanish descent; groups of Maya who wanted to avoid being drawn into the war; and members of the intermediate "Mestizo" strata, a term that designated mixed indigenous and Spanish descent (Cal 1991:217). The refugees' arrival marked the first significant Spanish presence in Belize. Most of the refugees were classified as "aliens" by colonial elites and prohibited from owning land in Belize; only the wealthiest were permitted to become naturalized British subjects and purchase land (Judd 1989). Spanish elites with capital established the first commercial agricultural enterprises in Belize, initiating a brief sugar boom from the 1860s to the 1880s. The majority of immigrants from Yucatan combined subsistence agriculture with wage labor on the plantations or in the forestry industry. While immigrant elites attempted to recreate the three-tiered society of Yucatan, drawing economic and social boundaries to distinguish among whites, mestizos, and Indians, British colonial officials and the English-speaking settler elite lumped them into two categories: "Yucatecans" and "Indians." The boundary between Spanish and Mestizo categories appears to have blurred early on, with most adopting the self-designation "Spanish" to distinguish themselves from both Indians and English speakers (Judd 1989).

Late in the nineteenth century, increasing appropriations of Indian land and labor in Guatemala led Mopan and Kekchi Maya to migrate into the southern and western districts of Belize, beyond the reach of the Guatemalan state (Gregory 1984:1; Thompson 1988:23). Around the turn of the century, a short-lived banana boom in southern Belize attracted additional immigrants from Central America and Jamaica (Shoman 1994:88). At the same time, rising U.S. demand for chicle, the base for chewing gum, set off a chicle boom in Belize. Many of the wealthier Spanish/Yucatecan immigrants became chicle contractors, along with a number of turn-of-the-century immigrants of Middle Eastern origin. Chicle collection itself mobilized a predominantly Mayan labor force from both Belizean and Guatemalan territories.

If Anglophone elites were pleased that their labor supply had expanded through these various streams of immigration over the nineteenth century, they were somewhat apprehensive that Spanish immigrants, whom they perceived to exercise significant influence over other refugees from Yucatan, might pose a potential threat to Anglophone dominance in Belize. In an effort to legitimize and perpetuate their continued dominance, English-speaking whites attempted to forge a "native," or "Creole," identity (the word *creole* is derived from the Spanish term *criollo*, meaning local or native) that encompassed the entire Anglophone population, recruiting "whites and blacks," or "Africans and all who speak the English language" (Grant 1976:54). Together with Creoles of color, they fashioned a Belizean origin myth based on the last Spanish attack on the settlement, a 1798 conflict known as the Battle of St. George's Caye. During the battle, masters and slaves were said to have fought "shoulder to shoulder" against the better-armed Spanish warships, ultimately driving them "with disgrace" from Belizean waters (Burdon 1934:212). The Baymen who fought the battle claimed, "We have rendered the galling yoke of Slavery so light and easy as to animate our Negroes to a gallant defence of their Masters, by whose sides they fought with the most determined bravery and fidelity" (Burdon 1931:272). The battle's resurrection and celebration a century later saluted the bravery of both slaves and masters; asserted their loyalty to Belize and to one another; and credited them both with wresting control of Belizean territory, once and for all, from Spanish invaders. The institution of a holiday commemorating the battle on its centenary affirmed native status for persons of all colors who claimed descent from participants in the battle, defining them as real—founding—Belizeans.

In contrast, Anglophones portrayed the immigrant "Spanish" population as cowardly and treacherous. Colonial reports complained that Yucatecans had refused to serve in a volunteer force for the defense of the northern town of Corozal. The Yucatecans were accused of abandoning the town and fleeing in the face of Indian attacks; a few were accused of selling gunpowder to the Indians (Burdon 1935:199, 208, 320–21). English speakers interpreted such conduct as proof that the Yucatecans were not loyal to Belize and could not be relied on to defend the colony against invasion, in contrast to the Baymen's valiant defense at the Battle of St. George's Caye. These nineteenth-century distinctions—between Creoles/natives and immigrants, between Anglophones and Spanish speakers, between loyalty to Belize and treacherous self-interest—build on seventeenth- and eighteenth-century conflicts between Britain and Spain. Similar distinctions reappear again in twentieth-century conflicts.

Anglophone "natives" also sought to legitimize their dominance by claiming adherence to British culture, which they deemed superior to Spanish culture (Judd 1989). Creoles of African descent were able to use this hierarchical ordering of cultures to invert the color hierarchy, asserting superiority over the less "civilized"—but lighter-skinned—Spanish by virtue of their association with British culture (Ashdown 1979:17). However, while some embraced this opportunity, the construction of a broad Creole category that crossed color and class distinctions did not necessarily imply harmony or unity across those distinctions: while employers invoked the loyalty of the Baymen's slaves in the 1798 battle as a model for worker-employer relations in the present (Shoman 1994:128), the poorest segments of the population rioted in 1884 and 1919 to protest racial discrimination and poverty (Ashdown 1979, 1985, 1986). Many natives of African descent also enthusiastically embraced Garveyism, forming a branch of the Universal Negro Improvement Association in 1920 (Bolland 1988:179).

The consolidation of British political and economic control also contributed to the emergence of a Creole, or native, identity. As British naval power eclipsed that of Spain, Britain had begun to exert more control over Belize during the early nineteenth century. However, after Central America became independent in 1821, Guatemala challenged Britain's claim to Belize, asserting that it had inherited ownership of Belize from Spain. The British government concluded a treaty with Guatemala in 1859, in which Guatemala withdrew its claim to the territory of Belize in exchange for British construction of a road connecting Guatemala City to the Caribbean coast. The treaty paved the way for Britain to officially name Belize a colony in 1862. When Belize was made a Crown Colony in 1871, its traditional elected governing body was replaced with a council whose members were appointed by the colonial governor. As the British government subsequently consolidated its rule over Belize, British companies consolidated their control over the Belizean economy. The largest, the British Honduras Company, acquired more than half of all privately held land in Belize and dominated the Belizean political economy over the following century (Bolland 1977:183–84, 193; Bolland and Shoman 1977). As British control over the colony expanded during the nineteenth century, so did discontent with British rule; thus English-speaking residents born in Belize and increasingly subordinate to British interests also began to assert native status to distinguish themselves from the British officials and merchants whose dominance they resented (Judd 1989:113). This motivation for the construction of native identity also carried over into twentieth-century struggles, as a basis for the nationalist movement.

Emergence of an Independence Movement

As the diverse populations that had immigrated during the 1800s became incorporated into the colonial labor regime of the "forestocracy," the majority found themselves in parallel economic circumstances: "they were powerless, were kept in debt to their employers, were prevented from owning and controlling their own land, and were excluded from participating in politics and trade" (Wilk 1986:75). Employers continued to use the advance and truck systems to maintain their workforce through constant indebtedness. The Masters and Servants Act, which declared a worker's breach of contract a criminal offense, was strictly enforced throughout this period, although the punishment prescribed for workers who broke their contracts was amended from whipping to twenty-eight days' imprisonment with hard labor (Grant 1976:51–52; Bolland 1988:159, 163). Workers' shared grievances gave rise to organizing during the 1930s and 1940s.

The Belize settlement had been established in the 1600s to satisfy the demand of metropolitan markets for tropical forest products. Still reliant on timber exports in the twentieth century, the Belizean economy remained highly susceptible to fluctuations in metropolitan markets and international trade. Thus, the depression of the 1930s in the developed countries crippled the forestry industry and eroded already poor living conditions in Belize. Many formerly seasonal workers became unemployed for longer and longer stretches of time. The situation deteriorated further after a hurricane devastated the colony in 1931. When Britain forced Belize to submit its treasury to Britain's control as a condition for granting a loan to rebuild, anticolonial sentiments began to build among both elites and the homeless, jobless poor. In 1934, the poor of Belize City, the colony's largest urban center, organized the Labourers and Unemployed Association (LUA). The LUA used petitions, marches, boycotts, strikes, and mass meetings to press for relief programs, more employment, higher wages, and access to health care and housing. LUA leaders linked labor issues to an attack on colonialism, blaming both colonial officials and the merchant elite for the "poverty and injustice" experienced by the working poor and unemployed. The LUA also took its struggle beyond Belize City to the districts, organizing the Mayan and Mestizo laborers in the north and west and Garifuna along the south coast (Bolland 1988:176).

In response to similar labor disturbances throughout the Caribbean during this period, Britain decided to legalize trade unions; thus, Britain forced the Legislative Council in Belize to legalize trade unions in 1941 and to re-

peal the Masters and Servants Act in 1943 (Bolland 1988:164). Former leaders of the LUA, which had disintegrated once part of its demands had been
met with work programs, had already begun organizing a union, with branches
in Stann Creek, Corozal, and San Ignacio. This organization transformed itself into the General Workers Union (GWU), a colonywide organization of
wage laborers that blamed their impoverishment on the collusion of British
colonialism with the London-based companies that controlled the Belizean
economy (Bolland 1987:9; 1988:178). With its anticolonial stance and its
membership that crossed racial and regional boundaries, the GWU provided
the foundation on which middle-class activists would forge an independence
movement a decade later.

As the working classes became increasingly organized and ever more
vocal in their opposition to colonial political and economic policies, local elites
also increasingly found themselves at odds with the colonial government.
Both banana and chicle production, initiated toward the turn of the century,
were geared toward U.S. markets; increasing quantities of Belizean mahogany
were also being exported to the United States. Tensions rose between the
capitalists whose primary trade links were to U.S. markets and the British
companies that controlled much of the colony's land and shaped colonial
policies to suit their needs. The former group increasingly referred to themselves as "natives."

In this context of rising anticolonial sentiment, a British decision to de-
value the Belizean currency in 1949 galvanized broad opposition to colonial
rule. The devaluation further eroded the purchasing power of the poor and
punished local elites with trade ties to the United States, while it benefited
British timber and import firms (Bolland 1991:94–95). In response, a group
of young, middle-class Creoles from Belize City launched the first Belizean
political party, the pro-independence Peoples United Party (PUP). The General Workers Union threw its support behind the PUP, and party leaders quickly
co-opted and took control of the GWU, appropriating the union's organization
in the out-districts to broaden the party's political base beyond Belize City.

Though various efforts had been made to configure a sense of nativeness
during the colonial period, the constitution of a Belizean nation became imperative only with the emergence of this independence movement in the 1950s.
Since the invention of nationalism during the eighteenth and nineteenth centuries, Anderson asserts, the nation has become "the most universally legitimate value in the political life of our time" (Anderson 1991:3). Only a nation
could demand—and justify—the creation of a sovereign state in a global

order organized on the basis of nation-states. Hence, the independence movement in Belize was required to rally a nation on whose behalf it could speak. As they worked to construct and mobilize a Belizean nation and legitimize their demands for an independent Belizean state, PUP leaders deployed a developmentalist rhetoric. They also pressed for an expanded definition of democracy that challenged the legitimacy of both colonial rule and limitations on electoral participation.

Leaders of the independence movement drew on emerging transnational discourses that prescribed economic development—defined and measured in terms of the growth of *national* economies—as the means for ameliorating poverty in the Third World. Nationalist leaders took up the antithesis between poverty and economic growth posed by emerging discourses of development to indict British colonial rule: they argued that British colonial rule had immiserated the colony's population and prevented true economic development; while a few colonials had accumulated great wealth, Belizeans were kept in poverty. As the devaluation had clearly demonstrated, British firms ran the colony in their own interests. As a result, Belizean nationalists argued, the creation of an independent state was necessary for the economic development of the nation. This argument paralleled Chatterjee's description of the assertions advanced by the Indian nationalist movement, insofar as the nationalists' critique of colonialism was largely *economic.* Their economic critique of colonialism "was the foundation from which a positive content was supplied for the independent national state": an independent state "represented the only legitimate form of exercise of power because it was a necessary condition for the development of the nation" (Chatterjee 1993:203).

In addition to this developmentalist ideology, the nationalists also championed "democracy," another multivalent concept whose meaning has been variously defined (Hall 1983; Laclau 1977). Clearly, economic elites in Belize who defined British colonial rule as "more democratic and just" than Spanish colonial rule had a somewhat different perspective on democracy—and a different agenda for it—than nationalist leaders who demanded universal suffrage and the right to elect political leaders (Shoman 1994:145). At the time when the nationalist movement emerged, the colony's Legislative Council had come to comprise a mix of appointed, ex officio, and elected members.[8] However, property requirements for either candidacy or the franchise excluded most of the colony's people; only 1.8 percent of the population were registered voters (Dobson 1973:305). The PUP defined its vision of democracy in terms of two criteria: the right to self-government that would enable the sovereign Belizean nation to chart its own destiny, and universal adult suffrage that would enable all Belizeans to have an equal say in shaping their future. Indeed, the PUP dates the beginning of democracy in Belize to the beginning of universal suffrage in 1954. It has referred to Belize's achievement of national independence and subsequent pursuit of national development as a "peaceful, democratic revolution."

The PUP also deployed an inclusive, pluralist strategy to construct and mobilize a Belizean nation. Confronted with a linguistically and culturally diverse population in which no single category represented an absolute majority, PUP leaders used the GWU's organization in the districts to incorporate Spanish, Garifuna, and Mayan communities into what had begun as an urban, primarily Creole, movement. However, the PUP's efforts to incorporate Maya and Spanish/Mestizos into the nationalist movement—along with its opposition to participation in the proposed West Indies Federation and its goal of integrating Belize into Central American political and economic networks—were taken by some Creoles as signs of a "pro-Central American orientation" that threatened to marginalize Blacks.[9] Guatemala had renewed its claim to Belize after the British failed to build the road agreed to in the 1859 treaty. Some Creoles feared that an independent Belize would be rapidly recolonized by Guatemala. They feared the impact this might have on Belizeans of African descent in particular, noting that Guatemala's Indian and Black populations were subordinate to Spanish/Mestizo control. Thus, shortly after the PUP's emergence, loyalists who favored continued British rule formed the National Party to counter the PUP's call for independence. Its membership comprised primarily middle-class Creole civil servants who defined Guatemala, not Britain, as the real enemy of Belizeans. Its leaders accused the PUP of racial prejudice. The PUP, they asserted, was trying to "stir up dissension among people of Negro extraction here so that people of non-Negro extraction may some day control our affairs." They charged that the PUP aimed "to build a non-Negro majority to lead the country into Guatemala as a department of that republic" (Shoman 1979:66).

Though the opposition party's charge of racial prejudice failed to persuade most Creole PUP followers, in 1956 tensions between the pro–Central American orientation of George Price and the pro–West Indian orientation of other PUP leaders split the independence movement itself. PUP leaders Leigh Richardson and Philip Goldson feared that an independent Belize would be vulnerable to recolonization by Guatemala; they believed the brightest prospects for Belize's future lay in federation with other West Indian colonies, which the British were actively promoting. George Price rejected the West Indies Federation as a British colonial project and argued that Belize should look to Central America and the United States for its future (Shoman 1987b:23–24). This issue split the party in 1956, when Richardson and Goldson left the PUP, taking the General Workers Union with them. Price maintained control of the PUP. Others who remained in the party founded the Christian Democratic Union (CDU), which subsequently reorganized many of the GWU's members; the CDU allied itself with George Price and the PUP (Shoman 1987b:24–25). Richardson and Goldson formed a third political party, but eventually allied themselves with the National Party.

In spite of these defections, the PUP's inclusion of the colony's distinct populations, together with its developmentalist rhetoric that emphasized the economic subordination they all shared, propelled the party to power. In 1954, when Britain granted to Belize universal adult suffrage and a Legislative Assembly whose majority would be elected, the PUP won the elections; in 1964, when Belize obtained internal self-rule, the PUP again won the elections and took control of most state functions.

Once in power, the new PUP government embraced the premises of development discourse promoted by the United States and international institutions such as the World Bank, the IMF, and United Nations agencies. Anthropologists (Escobar 1995; Esteva 1992; Ferguson 1990) and economists (Meier 1984; Rostow 1984) have analyzed the emergence of the concept of "economic development" following World War II, suggesting that U.S. concern that former colonies would fall under Communist domination combined with a "spirit of policy-optimism" derived from the success of economic planning during the war to generate new theories and practices around the concept of economic development.[10] The economists and policymakers who elaborated development discourse in the postwar period defined goals, prescribed strategies for their achievement, and devised evaluative measures for determining the relative success or failure of nations' development efforts. Diagnosing poverty as the "problem," development discourse prescribed economic growth as the solution and identified capital for investment as the key factor needed to stimulate growth (Escobar 1995). Relative poverty or prosperity among countries came to be summarized in the measure of annual per capita income, and increase in per capita GNP became the primary measure for development success.[11] Development discourse acquired material force and became institutionalized through the creation of international and national agencies to implement and manage development. Indeed, bodies such as the

IMF and the World Bank, and bilateral programs sponsored by the U.S. Agency for International Development (USAID) or the Colonial Development Corporation (later the Commonwealth Development Corporation, CDC), have not only planned and promoted development interventions; they have also worked to ensure that "developing" countries comply with the goals, strategies, and measures delimited by development discourse.[12]

Indeed, if the PUP had urged Belizeans in 1950 to "unite and organize ourselves . . . to present a solid front against the possible invasion of any exploiting capital" (Shoman 1994:170), by the time the party took control of the apparatus of self-government it had begun to espouse "wise capitalism" and employers' "right to reasonable profits" (Shoman 1994:186). The PUP government's 1965 electoral manifesto invoked the work of the pioneering U.S. development economist W. W. Rostow, whose 1960 *The Stages of Economic Growth: A Non-Communist Manifesto* prescribed large infusions of capital from abroad to jump-start the economic growth process in less developed economies, beginning cycles of increased production and further investment that would eventually lead to an economic takeoff and subsequent self-sustaining economic growth. The PUP prophesied that, by following this prescription, Belize would soon "take off to a prosperous economy" and reach the "plateau of plenty" (Shoman 1994:185).

By this time agriculture had displaced the forestry industry as Belize's primary export earner. After a brief boom in the late 1800s, sugar production had been revived in 1935, when Belize was still a colony, with the establishment of a factory in the northern town of Corozal. The factory was initially supplied by a handful of Mestizo-owned estates, but, by 1944, predominantly Mayan small farmers were allowed to deliver cane to the factory as well (Shoman 1994:193). In 1953 a Jamaican company purchased the factory and began to acquire increasing amounts of land in Corozal District on which it established plantations. During the 1950s, the PUP had supported the increasingly militant wage laborers and *milperos* (subsistence farmers) of the north, who opposed the Jamaican company's expansion program and demanded that the government make land available to workers and peasants to enable them to become cane farmers themselves, rather than farmworkers. After coming to power, the PUP adjusted its development priorities to encourage *both* smallholder and plantation production of sugar cane; while it facilitated the acquisition of land for cane cultivation by Mayan and Mestizo workers and farmers, it also apportioned land to the British transnational Tate and Lyle, which had purchased the cane processing facilities in 1963 (Shoman

1994:195). The government was able to pursue this dual strategy because less than 15 percent of the land in Belize that was suitable for agriculture was under cultivation. With huge expanses of land under forest cover, the government sought to expand the national economy by converting more Belizean land to agricultural export production. To this end, the government acquired land from absentee landholders for distribution to Belizeans and leased parcels of state-owned land to both Belizean smallholders and transnational capitalists. Once the leased land had been developed to the satisfaction of the state, the leaseholder could apply to purchase the parcel. Indeed, with so much "idle" land available, the government also allocated large parcels to Mennonite settlers to begin to produce food for the domestic economy, in an effort to decrease the amount of food Belize imported.

With the sugar industry in the north expanding under the control of the British transnational, the PUP government espoused such foreign investment as the means for development and sought to attract more of it to further expand the Belizean economy. At the same time, its provision of land to smallholder cane producers had resulted in the emergence by 1967 of more than one thousand such producers. Incomes and standards of living were on the rise throughout the two northern districts of Belize. As former wage laborers and milperos became cash crop producers, many of these upwardly mobile Maya adopted Spanish/Mestizo identities (Birdwell-Pheasant 1985; Brockmann 1977, 1985; Henderson 1990; Wilk 1986). Not surprisingly, these smallholder cane farmers voted overwhelmingly for the PUP.

As it pursued the developmentalist vision it had used to justify its push for independence, the PUP also reinforced its pluralist configuration of the nation by introducing symbolic shifts that displaced Creoles from the primary position in Belizean history that celebration of the Battle of St. George's Caye had accorded them. Moving to anchor the Belizean nation in antiquity and strengthen its hold on the disputed territory it claimed, the PUP emphasized Belize's Mayan roots: the Belizean capital was moved from the Creole stronghold of Belize City to Belmopan, a new town in the interior named for the Mopan Maya; and the new government buildings in Belmopan were designed to resemble an ancient Mayan plaza. Further, the creation of holidays honoring Spanish and Garifuna transformed St. George's Caye Day into one among several national holidays.

A decade later, new challenges to the PUP's agenda emerged. Inspired by the Black Power movement in the United States and other anticolonial, antiracist struggles in the Third World, young Creoles frustrated by the PUP's failure to deliver development to the urban poor and critical of what they defined as PUP attempts to "Mayanize" Belize (through its emphasis on Mayan history, the construction of the new capital, and its openness toward Central America) organized the United Black Association for Development (UBAD) in 1969. UBAD promoted Black consciousness, celebrated what it defined as African or Black culture, and demanded that African and Afro-Belizean history be taught in Belizean schools. The movement incorporated both Creoles from Belize City and Garifuna from Dangriga, invoking a shared African heritage and constructing a new Afro-Belizean identity to forge bonds between them. (As UBAD linked Creole identity to Blackness, Whites distanced themselves from the Creole category; Judd 1989). A second organization, the People's Action Committee, also emerged in 1969. Its organizers, Mestizo Lionel del Valle and Assad Shoman and Said Musa of Palestinian-Belizean families, had just returned from university studies abroad, where they had been inspired by the critiques of both colonialism and dominant forms of "dependent capitalist development" generated by Third World intellectuals. Rejecting Belize's continued colonization and the PUP's pursuit of "dependent capitalism," the PAC took up the cause of Belizean wageworkers and milperos from the north, calling for the appropriation of Belizean land from its foreign owners and its redistribution to Belizeans (Grant 1976:272; Shoman 1994:205).

UBAD and the PAC soon merged. Defining colonialism as "a total system of foreign domination embracing the economic and cultural as well as political life of a society," they called for an attack on colonialism on all three fronts (Shoman 1994:204). However, the alliance was beset by internal tensions between UBAD's cultural goals and the PAC's political-economic agenda, and between the PAC's focus on rural Mayan and Mestizo (or "Spanish") peasants and UBAD's focus on urban Blacks in Belize City and Dangriga. Many were also frightened by the "communist" label that had been applied to PAC organizers (Grant 1976:272; Shoman 1994:208). As a result, the alliance soon dissolved. Subsequently, two former PAC leaders, Shoman and Musa, joined the PUP government, becoming the party's left wing. UBAD briefly formed an alliance with the opposition party, rooted in racial issues. After an electoral loss, UBAD also disintegrated, though its newspaper, the *Amandala,* continued to publish and has since become the most widely read weekly in Belize.[13]

As this brief summation of Belizean history makes clear, market forces, social movements, and discourses originating outside of Belize have significantly shaped Belizean politics and social mobilizations. As shifts in external markets generated changed economic conditions to which Belizeans were forced to respond, discourses of development, dependency, and Black Power provided tools that different groups of Belizeans adopted and adapted to their own ends. Pursuing this theme, the rest of this chapter explores how the government has deployed three key transnational discourses—of development, nation, and democracy—to mediate pressures from Belizeans and from abroad.

Official Discourses on Development, Nation, and Democracy

After winning internal self-government, the PUP continued to push for full independence. All that stood in the way now was the Guatemalan claim, which Guatemala had dramatized several times by mobilizing troops on the border and threatening to invade. The Peoples United Party worked to build international support for Belizean independence at the same time that it sought a settlement with Guatemala (former PAC leader Assad Shoman, now incorporated into the PUP, was central to these efforts). The new PUP Left lobbied hard among developing nations within the Commonwealth, the Non-Aligned Movement, and the UN, winning increasing support from newly independent states who supported the developmentalist rationale for Belizean independence. The number of votes in favor of the annual UN resolution calling for Belizean independence grew each year (Shoman 1992). In 1981 the PUP government was an approving witness as Britain and Guatemala signed a document called the Heads of Agreement, which was to serve as the basis for future treaty negotiations. However, the opposition United Democratic Party (UDP) and the civil servants' union rejected the agreement as concessionary to Guatemala. Angry protests erupted in the streets of Belize City, leaving four people dead. In their wake, the PUP backed down on its support for the Heads of Agreement and sought a British defense guarantee instead. By this time, overwhelming support for Belizean independence among UN member states, with the United States voting in favor for the first time in 1980, brought increasing pressure on Britain to facilitate Belizean independence. Britain responded with a defense guarantee, and, subsequently, Belize declared its independence on September 21, 1981, with British troops still patrolling its boundaries.[14]

In postcolonial Belize the definition of goals, the prescription of policies, and the elaboration of identities have revolved around three key concepts that circulate internationally: development, nation, and democracy. The governments of "developed" nations have sought to impose particular meanings on these terms. However, while Belizean government officials have drawn heavily on the dominant meanings assigned to these terms in international arenas, they have simultaneously rearticulated them to define a distinctly Belizean set of interests and identities. Below, I explore the official discourses that constitute the Belizean nation and its links to development and democracy. During the time I conducted much of the research for this study, these official state discourses were widely disseminated in Belize through the media. The government of Belize controlled national-level radio broadcasting, probably the most important source of communication across the nation as a whole. Each political party also controlled its own newspaper. The state and the parties that compete to control it used these channels to mediate ideas and prescriptions that originated outside of Belize for their Belizean audience. In addition, many Belizeans received U.S. perspectives on world events directly through pirated signals from the major U.S. networks and a Voice of America transmitter that broadcast from southern Belize.

Development

Kaufman suggests that development discourse "has become one of the binding forces that holds the global system together," shaping the ways governments and international organizations interrelate (Kaufman 1997:107). Certainly, Belizean development policies have closely reflected the definitions of development that international lending institutions have enforced coercively. The PUP embraced developmentalism from its inception, pursuing economic growth through a development strategy based on the expansion of sugar production for export. This strategy aimed to boost Belize's GDP, the benchmark for development success, while the hard currency generated by sugar exports would help to pay for the imports on which Belizeans depended. In addition, sugar cultivation was seen as a means to make more productive use of Belizean lands, at the same time that it provided opportunities for Belizean workers and farmers to raise their incomes (and perhaps move out of the working class altogether).

During the 1970s the PUP's development strategy appeared to be a success both politically and economically, as increases in foreign exchange earnings underwrote increased government investment in infrastructure and other public spending. However, the national economy was becoming increasingly dependent on sugar exports. When Belize finally achieved formal independence in 1981, instead of the increased development the PUP had argued that independence would bring, a drop in sugar prices and a reduction in the sugar quota extended to Belize by the United States led to shrinkage rather than expansion in the Belizean economy in 1982 and 1983. One of the two sugar factories closed in 1985. Weakening terms of trade aggravated Belize's trade and budget deficits: having borrowed to cover its deficits and finance its development aspirations, the government now lacked sufficient foreign currency to service its debts. By 1984 Belize was forced by the IMF to adopt an austerity plan in exchange for loans to continue to service its debts. The austerity measures, which included an unpopular tax increase and large cuts in government spending, contributed to a victory by the UDP in the 1984 elections, ending twenty years of PUP rule.

Declaring itself "unabashedly pro-American," the new UDP government pursued policies that reflected the incentives offered and disciplinary measures deployed by the United States and the IMF. The United States had suddenly become very interested in Belize as part of its larger response to political-economic upheavals that characterized the circum-Caribbean region during the first years of Belizean independence. In the Caribbean, the revolutionary "New Jewel" movement came to power in Grenada in 1979, and the governments of Jamaica and Guyana had embraced socialism. In Central America, a 1979 revolution brought the Sandinistas to power in Nicaragua, and revolutionary movements were gaining strength in Guatemala and El Salvador. The U.S. government interpreted these events as challenges to U.S. dominance in the region. In response, the Caribbean Basin Initiative (CBI) was launched to reassert U.S. influence over Central America and the Caribbean. The CBI posited two challenges facing the United States in the region to its south: "rescuing the hemisphere's troubled economies and establishing principles of political legitimacy" (NBCCA 1984:4). A bipartisan commission established by U.S. president Reagan to study the region's "problems" and recommend solutions reported:

> The hemisphere is challenged both economically and politically. . . . First, the commanding economic issue in all of Latin America is the impoverishment of its people. . . . The contraction of the hemisphere's economies, and the impoverishment of its people, must be reversed. Real growth must be restored. . . . Second, the political challenge in the hemisphere centers on the legitimacy of government. . . . Powerful forces are on the march in nearly every country of the hemisphere, testing how nations shall be organized and by what processes authority shall be established

and legitimized. Who shall govern and under what forms are the central issues in the process of change now under way in country after country throughout Latin America and the Caribbean. . . . [W]e must do all we can to nurture democracy in this hemisphere. (NBCCA 1984:11–12)

The report causally linked economic and political practice, suggesting that capitalist economic development and democracy mutually reinforced one another, as did their opposites, communism and totalitarianism (Medina 1998).

To "rescue the hemisphere's troubled economies," the CBI prescribed economic growth: increased opportunities for capital accumulation would spur investment in productive capacity, which would create economic growth. Economic growth would reverse the impoverishment of Latin American peoples through job creation and the downward trickle of wealth. Accordingly, the CBI's legislative centerpiece, the Caribbean Basin Economic Recovery Act (CBERA), aimed to expand Caribbean countries' production of exports by according them privileged access to U.S. markets. The legislation eliminated U.S. import tariffs for some goods produced in the Caribbean Basin, including citrus products. This strategy would also tie Central American and Caribbean countries more closely to the United States economically and politically, while increasing export earnings would enable debt-burdened countries in the region to continue payments to foreign creditors (Deere et al. 1990). Accompanying the CBI, the U.S. presence in Belize swelled to unprecedented proportions during the 1980s: U.S. embassy staff expanded from 7 in 1981 to 47 in 1985, USAID took on a major role in restructuring the Belizean economy along neoliberal lines, and the United States began training both the Belize Defense Force and aspiring Belizean entrepreneurs (Shoman 1994:233).

In a five-year development plan largely dictated by the IMF and USAID, the UDP government assigned top priority to the expansion of exports, at the same time that it curtailed price supports for the production of domestic staples (Shoman 1994:233). In accord with IMF and USAID specifications, the government sought to diversify its agricultural exports away from nearly complete dependence on sugar by encouraging the expansion of citrus and banana cultivation, crops that enjoyed protected markets through the Caribbean Basin Initiative and the Commonwealth, respectively.[15] The British Commonwealth Development Corporation and the World Bank made funding available for citrus expansion. The expansion of banana production was predicated on the privatization of what had been government-owned plantations.

The Inter-American Development Bank subsequently funded expansion of banana production by the private entrepreneurs who purchased the plantations. This strategy aimed to increase per capita GDP, decrease the trade deficit by boosting exports, and earn foreign currency to pay creditors, at the same time that it streamlined the government and encouraged private entrepreneurship.

Thus, the PUP and the UDP have largely shared a single development strategy, shaped and in large part funded by external donors. However, development discourse in Belize reflects not only *coercion* applied by more powerful states and their proxies, but a *belief* in international models and definitions of development. The PUP took a developmentalist orientation early on, pursuing foreign investment and export expansion; the UDP promoted this strategy even more aggressively. Though they may quibble over the details, neither party challenges the basic tenets of international development discourse, its definitions, strategies, and measures. For its part, the United States has also made clear the high price countries would pay for significant deviations: armed invasions—either by the United States itself or by troops financed and trained by the United States—restored Grenada and Nicaragua to international development orthodoxy.

In support of its export-led development strategy, the government of Belize—under either party—has encouraged investment by offering tax and tariff concessions to investors and working to keep wages low. The government has recommended that Belizeans seek benefits from the economic development process by investing in export agriculture, such as citrus production, rather than seeking wage increases (Ministry of Foreign Affairs and Economic Development 1985:41; Moberg 1992). Agro-industrial and other export producers demonstrated their clout by winning exclusion for their workers from minimum wage laws established in 1992: while minimum wages were set at BZ$2.25 an hour for manual workers, they were restricted to BZ$2.00 an hour for workers in export industries (Shoman 1994:242).[16] An additional measure the government has taken to maintain downward pressure on wages is support for the use of immigrant labor from Central America, especially in the agro-industries that have driven Belizean economic expansion.

The government's export-led development program has been successful, as success is defined by international elites: in 1990, as per capita GDP rose to BZ$2,500, a USAID representative echoed the development rhetoric of the 1960s by declaring Belize "close to the take-off point" for self-sustaining economic growth. However, despite economic growth, unemployment was estimated at 20 percent, wages lagged behind the rising cost of living, and an estimated 23 percent of the population lived in poverty (Shoman 1994:245; SPEAR 1990:18). In measuring the success of this development strategy, many Belizeans have "voted with their feet," with tens of thousands emigrating to the United States in search of employment opportunities. The remittances sent to relatives by Belizeans working in the United States have, in turn, become a significant source of foreign exchange, representing 12–15 percent of the GDP, and a safety valve for rising social pressures (SPEAR 1990:25).

The Nation

Official Belizean discourses on the nation intersect with development policies and discourse in multiple ways. In defining who should belong to the nation, they designate who should *benefit from* national economic development and whose *participation in* the process of national development should be facilitated by the state's provision of resources. Official Belizean discourses of nation assign places in the nation on the basis of collective ethnic belonging to a multiethnic Belizean nation or individual belonging on the basis of contributions to national development.

During the colonial period, when differences among Belizeans were conceptualized primarily in racial terms, the PUP used a multiracial strategy in its construction of a Belizean nation. Later, as U.S. academics began to utilize the concept of ethnicity in the 1960s and 1970s, subnational difference in Belize began to be reconceptualized as *ethnic* and *cultural* rather than racial—both by academics from abroad who studied Belize and by Belizean nation-builders themselves. Thus, in postcolonial Belize the idea of culture took center stage in official constructions of difference and sameness, with ethnic and cultural affiliations replacing racial terminology (see Medina 1997a). PUP governments consistently defined Belize as a multiethnic "haven of cultural pluralism," recognizing several ethnic categories as collective members of the nation. The largest categories—Creole, Spanish/Mestizo, Garifuna, and Mopan and Kekchi Maya—have been cast as its most central members, and thus as the most legitimate beneficiaries of national development (see table 1). These categories are recognized as contributors to an emergent, still-in-production Belizean culture.[17] Smaller categories—White, Lebanese, Chinese, Indian, and Mennonite—are more tenuously tied to the

Table 1 Ethnic Classification of Belizean Population, 1991

Ethnic Category	% of Population
Mestizo	43.6
Creole	29.8
Garifuna	6.6
Kekchi Maya	4.3
Mopan Maya	3.7
Other Maya	3.1
Indian	3.5
German/Dutch Mennonite	3.1
White	0.8
Chinese	0.4
Syrian	0.1
Other	1.0
Not stated/don't know	0.0

Source: CSO 1992.

Belizean nation, officially recognized as part of the nation's diversity but less celebrated as contributors to national culture.[18] While the multiethnic nation was initially a PUP project, the opposition party also came to define the nation in pluralist terms. By 1984, when the UDP won national elections for the first time, it had broadened its appeal beyond its Creole base to incorporate constituents from all ethnic categories who had become disaffected with the PUP.

If official discourse defines Belize as a unique nation on the basis of its particular configuration of ethnic diversity, it defines Belize as an *exemplary* nation on the basis of its celebration and validation of ethnic difference: "As a Caribbean nation in Central America our country serves as a bridge and a haven of cultural pluralism, a model that acknowledges the value of the diverse cultural heritages that constitute Belize and provide its unique national identity. We must preserve this uniqueness" (PUP 1989). Diversity is thus defined as an asset; its acceptance by Belizeans makes their country a model for other nations to emulate.

However, tensions among ethnic categories often complicate the happy visions of Belizean nationhood espoused by the government. For example, the geographic concentration of ethnic groups has created a link between regionalism and racialism such that the direction of development funds to one district rather than another has been perceived as favoritism toward one group or discrimination against others. In spite of official designation of differences among Belizeans as ethnic, criticisms made in the context of regional competition more often define perceived favoritism or discrimination in racial terms. Thus, the government's investment in an extensive roads program in the northern sugar districts, where the population is predominantly Mestizo and Mayan, and its location of family planning clinics in Belize City, Dangriga, and Punta Gorda, all areas with large Black populations, have both been interpreted by Garifuna residents of Dangriga as evidence of government anti-Black racism. The recent proliferation of ethnic organizations reflects competition among ethnic groups to claim honored positions in the nation and capture resources for development.

Although the official nationalist project defines Belize's constituent ethnic groups as equal and integral parts of the nation, many Belizeans disagree about the equivalence of different ethnic groups' contributions to the nation and their appropriate places in the nation. Since a place of honor in the nation is understood to confer rights and resources on its holder, competition among Belize's constituent groups has resulted in attempts by some groups to link their own racial and ethnic identities preferentially to the nation. Such an agenda is being pursued most avidly by Creoles and Garifuna fearful of their possible subordination to the Spanish under a regime of "Latin domination." Such concerns have been fueled for decades by Guatemala's claim to Belize and its oft-repeated threat to invade. The Guatemalan state's violent oppression of its indigenous population and the social and economic marginalization of Guatemala's Black population have been noted in Belize as examples of what an invasion might bring. As a result, Guatemala's threats have been experienced by Creole and Garifuna Belizeans in racial terms: a former UBAD leader asserts, "what the Guatemalan claim always does, when it flares up, is make Black Belizeans acutely conscious of the colour of their skin, because Guatemala is such a racist society" (*Amandala,* editorial, 22 Nov. 1991). But if some Blacks have expressed fear that a Guatemalan invasion would push them to the bottom of a racial hierarchy dominated by the Spanish,[19] they have also expressed suspicions that Spanish Belizeans might support the imposition of such a regime, which would elevate their status. Thus, some Creoles and Garifuna have questioned the loyalty of Spanish Belizeans to the Belizean nation.

While the threatened military invasion has not occurred, the immigration of tens of thousands of Central Americans, the bulk of them Guatemalans, to Belize during its first decade of independence has been interpreted by many Creoles and Garifuna as a *non*military invasion. The civil wars that wracked Guatemala and El Salvador in the 1980s pushed hundreds of thousands of their citizens to flee. Estimates of the number of Central Americans who immigrated to Belize during this decade ranged from forty thousand to sixty thousand (Stone 1990:102); the 1991 census counted 25,548 foreign-born individuals, a figure that represented 13.8 percent of the Belizean population. Three-quarters of the foreign born were from Central America, primarily Guatemala; 10 percent were from Mexico.

This immigration exacerbated already high rates of unemployment, estimated at 20 percent nationally, and complemented the government's efforts to maintain downward pressure on wages in order to attract investment. In turn, increased unemployment and stagnant wages fueled already high rates of Belizean migration to the United States, estimated to be as high as sixty thousand to seventy thousand (Vernon 1990:6). While most of the immigrants have been classified as Spanish, urban Creoles made up a large proportion of Belizean immigrants to the United States (Vernon 1990). Together, these population movements generated a sense among Creoles and Garifuna that the ethnic balance between Afro-Caribbean and Central American segments of the Belizean population was shifting. The 1991 census was perceived as confirmation of these concerns: the 1980 census had counted 40 percent of the population as Creole and 33 percent as Mestizo (Spanish); the 1991 census classified 44 per cent of the population as Mestizo, while the number of persons classified as either Creole or Garifuna totaled only 36 percent (CSO 1992).

As Afro-Belizeans saw themselves becoming a minority in Belize in relation to the Spanish category, many began to fear the imposition of Latin domination in Belize *without* a military invasion. In 1987, a government-appointed Immigration Advisory Committee warned, "[Immigrants] could acquire increasing proportions of the nation's economic and political power. History provides us with lessons when immigrants become so dominant over the native population. Two examples that readily come to mind are South Africa and Israel. . . . [Immigration policy should therefore] focus on the immigration of persons with man-power skills that Belize needs [and] an ethnic identity that could assimilate into the national fabric" (Immigration Advisory Committee 1987, cited in "Riding High on the 'Aliens' Bandwagon," *SPEARhead* June–August 1987). The extreme examples chosen as lessons, in which immigrant populations have subjugated large, racially defined native populations, indicate the danger that Afro-Belizeans perceive in Central American immigration. Apprehension about their potential future subordination to a "Spanish" majority spurred attempts by Creole and Garifuna leaders to (re)construct and solidify an Afro-Belizean racial identity that could unify and mobilize members of both ethnic categories as a counterweight to the growing number of Spanish. The 1990s witnessed Afro-Belizean summits and the formation of a nationwide Afro-Belizean Committee to work toward the goal of unifying all persons of African ancestry in Belize.

Concerns about Spanish immigration and the potential for future Latin domination intensified Creole and Garifuna suspicions about the interests and identities of all Spanish-speakers in Belize. Unable—perhaps unwilling— to readily distinguish Belizean-born Spanish from Central American immigrants, some Creole and Garifuna Belizeans began to challenge the Belizeanness of all unknown Spanish people with whom they interacted, referring to or directly addressing Spanish individuals as "aliens." The right of Spanish people to be physically present or to occupy public space in Belize has been challenged by Afro-Belizean demands that they "Go home!" and threats to expel them from bars and bus seats. Further, because of the blurred boundary between Spanish and Mayan categories (as a result of shifts from Mayan to Spanish self-identities in northern and western Belize), Afro-Belizeans have also applied the "alien" label to people who identify themselves as Maya. Implicit in such challenges is the assertion that only Blacks can automatically be taken as Belizeans. This marks the emergence—or re-emergence—of an Afro-Belizean discourse that defines Belizeans as Black and Spanish as aliens, marginalizing Spanish Belizeans from a racialized Belizean nation.[20]

This discourse portrays Spanish "aliens" not only as *non*-Belizean, but also as *un*-Belizean. Stereotyped as violent and lawless, prone to murder and mayhem, in contrast to peaceful, democratic Belizeans, Central American immigrants are defined as "too different" culturally to be integrated into the Belizean nation; their presence threatens the very integrity of the nation and the peaceful, democratic practices that are its hallmark and claim to international honor and legitimacy. When the Immigration Advisory Committee expressed concern about the nature of recent immigration and called for limiting immigration to persons who have "an ethnic identity which could assimilate into the national fabric," the implication was that Spanish immigrants could not be assimilated into the national fabric; rather, they threatened to unravel that fabric. However, while the immigrants have been defined as too *culturally* different to fit into the Belizean nation and its peaceful, democratic system, they have been identified as aliens on a *racial* basis according to physical appearance.

Official multiethnic constructions of the Belizean nation are challenged by discourses that racialize the nation as Black and exclude Spanish people as probable aliens. Further, although both the UDP and the PUP promote the official multiethnic construction of the Belizean nation, and each courts constituencies that cross racial-ethnic categories, each has also sought to use these racial tensions to its advantage. Though both parties have authorized the use of foreign laborers in Belize, the UDP newspaper has sounded alarms about aliens committing crimes, usurping land, being registered to vote by the PUP, and conducting themselves in an un-Belizean manner, while the PUP's slogan in its successful 1989 election bid to regain control of government was "Belizeans First."

Beyond espousing collective ethnic belonging to a multiethnic Belizean nation, the Belizean state has defined a second avenue for national belonging based on contributions to "national development." In keeping with economic development policies that aim to attract and facilitate investment in export production, official rhetoric extols capitalist entrepreneurs as the most significant contributors to national economic development and equates the concerns of investors with the interests of the nation as a whole. For example, the minister of labor explained in a 1990 radio interview that, in spite of 20 percent unemployment, the government must allow investors to import labor in order to "make a success . . . out of [their] investment," because "without the foreign input of labor, many of our industries would naturally die. Therefore, *Belize* would lose a lot" (emphasis added). Here, the minister equated the success of Belize with the success of its investors. In establishing investment as an exemplary contribution to the nation, the government has extended economic citizenship to entrepreneurs, granting Belizean passports to foreigners who invest at least BZ$25,000 in Belize. Conversely, wage labor has not been defined as a contribution to national economic development; instead, jobs have been counted among the benefits provided by investors/economic development.

This second official avenue to national belonging offers a place of honor in the nation to both foreign investors and Belizean economic elites not tightly tied to the nation in ethnic terms. In general, ethnic designation and economic position do not overlap neatly for the larger ethnic categories: the majority of each of the largest ethnic categories are wage laborers or small-scale farmers or both, though some members of these categories are included among political and economic elites. The White category represents the closest correlation between ethnic designation and economic position, since Whites—especially in the expanded sense suggested by Judd (1992) that incorporates wealthy Spanish and Arabs—control significant portions of the Belizean economy and Belizean territory. Thus their status as contributors to national economic development provides a place in the nation to Whites only tenuously connected to the nation in ethnic terms. However, this official discourse on national belonging has also been challenged: the *Amandala* newspaper has been especially vociferous in decrying what it has called the "sale" of Belizean citizenship.

Democracy

During the 1980s, Belizean democracy discourse became as integrally linked with the U.S. Caribbean Basin Initiative as its development policies. After attaining independence, the Belizean government continued efforts to negotiate a resolution with Guatemala, but it also redoubled efforts to retain international support for its independent status and territorial integrity. In a 1985 speech, Prime Minister Esquivel emphasized, "We must reflect the reality of Belize in our relations with the world outside our border, consciously acknowledging that the claim of a neighbouring state to our land, a claim which made precarious the timing our independence, is still unresolved. We must remember that we need more than ever the goodwill and the understanding of friendly nations in our search for an honorable solution to this problem which continues to threaten our viability" (prime minister's 1985 Independence Day Message, quoted in Fernandez 1989:91). The dominant role played by the United States in the hemisphere, and its close relations with Guatemala, made continued support from the United States particularly crucial to Belizean security after independence. In addition, the United States exercised influence over the direction of international development funds for which Belize now competed, and it had become Belize's largest trading partner; by the 1980s the United States consistently accounted for 50 percent or more of both Belizean exports and imports (CSO 1994:86; World Bank 1984:14, 77). Hence U.S. prescriptions for the region powerfully shaped emerging political-economic visions in Belize. The CBI's explicit linkage of economic development and democracy resonated with and reinforced their linkage in Belize, where the notion of democracy became central to the Belizean state's self-portrayal.

Belizean democracy discourse was elaborated in two directions: one directed outward to the international community, the other inward to Belizean citizens. In courting U.S. political and economic support during the 1980s, Belizean political leaders adopted the U.S. CBI's definition of democracy in terms of civilian leadership elected in "free and fair" multiparty political contests (NBCCA 1984:5; Medina 1998).[21] Belizean officials portrayed their country as a bastion of democracy still threatened by the turmoil of its less democratic neighbors. Government officials validated Belize's democratic status by invoking its history of government by elected civilians, with two major political parties peacefully alternating in power in accord with election results. They contrasted the peaceful stability of Belize with the strife of its Central American neighbors—especially Guatemala—in order to define Belize as an exemplary nation; in so doing, they worked to legitimize Belizean sovereignty and attract foreign aid and investment.

Belizean political leaders argued that the destiny of Belize was crucial to the United States and the West in the context of the cold war. In 1986, the prime minister warned that if developing countries such as Belize fail, "the consequence will be the erosion of public confidence in our Western economic philosophy, a turning away from our traditional beliefs, and a collapse of freedom and peace. This is not a simple matter of economies, it is a battle to determine . . . [whose] philosophy will survive, that of Thomas Jefferson or that of Karl Marx" (Prime Minister Esquivel, Commencement Address, 1986, quoted in Fernandez 1989:100).

Indeed, during the 1980s Belizean electoral democracy was noticed and praised by the U.S. government. Following 1984 elections in Belize, the U.S. Department of State congratulated Belizeans "for their firm commitment to the democratic process. The election was conducted in the peaceful and democratic manner which has characterized Belize's electoral history. The elections in Belize serve as a further reminder of the vitality of democracy and the powerful trend toward its growth and stability which is evident in this hemisphere" (Fernandez 1989:75). Thus the political comportment of Belize helped to legitimize its very existence. In this context, official discourse elevated a love of democracy to the level of a Belizean national trait: government officials identified a love of peace and a high regard for democracy as core values that characterized all *true* Belizeans and unified them across racial-ethnic divides, even as it distinguished Belizeans from their "violence-prone," "despotic" Central American neighbors.

While the government of newly independent Belize adopted the central tenets of U.S. discourse on democracy, it also infused democracy with localized meanings that articulate with development and nationalist policies and discourses in multiple ways. A second, more particularly Belizean discourse on democracy was elaborated within the domestic political arena. This localized variant emerged from nationalist demands for universal suffrage as a first step toward self-determination: democracy was defined as the rule of the majority, a majority Belizeans referred to collectively in generic terms as the "small man." Belizeans defined representative democracy as a fair system because it allowed the "small man" majority to shape government policies in their favor (Medina 1990). National leaders argued that the incorporation of the "small man" into the political process and economic development was the key to sustaining peace and democracy: "We want to protect the little man, . . . to help him, . . . to bring him in [to the development process]. . . . That's the only way we are going to have stability in our country. We need to learn from the lessons around us. Why is there civil war in El Salvador? Why is there guerrilla fighting in Guatemala? Why are guerrilla insurgents beginning in Honduras? Because the little man, the majority—and the little man is the majority of the people—were neglected. . . . [W]e are fighting for democracy" (speech by Prime Minister George C. Price at a Citrus Growers Association meeting, November 1989).

Thus, the Belizean government's articulation of development and democracy discourses for a domestic audience revolved around the "small man," whose desire to be integrated into and to benefit from the economic development process must be accommodated in order to maintain his faith in the political system. Each Belizean political party has invoked this local version of democracy discourse to legitimize its own policies as representative of the interests of the majority and to revile the policies of its opponent as benefiting primarily elites.[22] As we will see in later chapters, this version of democracy discourse has also been used by voters to shape the government's development policies.

The "small man" has been at the center of Belizean democracy discourse since the PUP positioned itself as his champion in the 1950s. And beginning with internal self-government in 1964, the PUP government sought to bring the "small man" into the development process, facilitating the incorporation of smallholders into commercial sugar production alongside plantation production by the transnational Tate and Lyle (Jones 1971). Aiming to broaden its popular support while it expanded export production, the party's portrayal of itself as the champion of the "small man" and his integration into the development process laid the foundation for Belizean democracy discourse. Later, when its debt crisis prompted efforts to diversify the country's export base through the expansion of citrus and banana production, the Belizean government again incorporated both large- and small-scale producers into expansion programs in the citrus industry (this time, in response to small growers' public invocation of Belizean democracy discourse to demand resources for investment, as chapter 3 will demonstrate). In the banana industry, the U.S.-based Inter-American Foundation helped to underwrite participation by smallholders (Shaw 1988).

Today each party competes to define itself as the true champion of the "small man," while both pursue development policies that disproportionately benefit wealthy investors in export production. These disjunctions reveal contradictions between the state's claims to legitimacy on the basis of its adherence to the procedural forms of representative government and those based on its pursuit of an economic development program on behalf of the nation. Chatterjee has noted a similar disjunction in the Indian case:

> The former connected . . . the legal-political sovereignty of the state with the sovereignty of the people. The latter connected the sovereign powers of the state directly with the economic well being of the people. The two connections did not necessarily have the same implications for a state trying to determine how to use its sovereign powers. What the people were able to express through the representative mechanisms of the political process as their will was not necessarily what was good for their economic well being; what the state thought important for the economic development of the nation was not necessarily what would be ratified through the representative mechanism. The two criteria of representativeness, and hence of legitimacy, could well produce contradictory implications for state policy. (Chatterjee 1993:203–4)

Indeed, in Belize the placement of the "small man" at the center of democracy articulates awkwardly with efforts to keep wages low and the equation of investors' interests with those of the nation. The ambiguity of the "small man" category has provided the tactical space in which this contradiction has been "managed." Democracy discourse does not specify which class positions qualify one as a member of the "small man" majority. While most

Belizeans place themselves in the vague "small man" category, in practice "small men" *investors* in agro-export production have most successfully won government recognition of their invocations of "small man" status and used it to shape policies. As investors—albeit small scale—they count as contributors to national development, and their demands are not perceived as inimical to the government's overall development strategy. Workers, whose demands threaten a development project that relies on keeping wages low, have been less successful in positioning themselves as the "small men" whose interests democracy champions.

In part, wage laborers' inability to gain recognition and wield power as "small men" stems from the government's authorization of the use of immigrant labor in the agro-export industries that have constituted the engine of Belizean economic growth, and the government's subsequent designation of all agricultural workers in general as immigrants. Although agriculture accounts for 16 percent of the jobs in Belize (CSO 1992), the government complains that Belizeans are reluctant to seek work in agriculture.[23] As a result, the government (under either political party) has authorized the importation of labor from neighboring Mexico, Guatemala, and Honduras for the agricultural industries that have driven Belizean export expansion since the 1960s, echoing the arguments of cane, banana, and citrus growers and processors that these industries would die without foreign labor. In deploying this strategy, the government of Belize and Belizean agricultural export producers took advantage of the civil wars that wracked Guatemala and El Salvador in the 1980s and pushed hundreds of thousands of their citizens to flee, wars fueled in part by parallel—but more repressive—efforts by their governments to facilitate investment and increase export production by suppressing wages.

Further, the government's portrayal of agricultural workers—the largest sector of the Belizean labor force—as aliens excludes them from the benefits of *Belizean* development and democracy. Although the government does not collect documentation to account for the actual percentage of agricultural workers who are unnaturalized immigrants, in official documents and speeches to constituents, government officials assert that agricultural workers—who are predominantly Spanish—are foreigners.[24] For example, a UDP five-year development plan predicted that most of the jobs created through expansion of the citrus industry would be taken by immigrants and recommended that more Belizeans should become citrus farmers, "so as to avoid the untenable situation of a massive expansion of production without any significant employment of Belizeans" (Ministry of Foreign Affairs and Economic Development 1985:41). In a 1990 radio interview, the minister of labor rationalized the employment of foreign workers by making explicit the government's commitment to help investors get the most for their money: "[T]he investor, the person who is spending his dollars, his hard-earned dollars . . . makes an assessment of the output of the Belizean worker and the output of the refugee or the foreign worker. . . . The person who is spending wants to get the best for his dollar spent. And in many occasions it is reported to me, officially and unofficially, that the foreign labor produces more than the Belizean worker."[25]

Defining Belize's predominantly Spanish agricultural workers as foreign marginalizes them from the Belizean nation and the right to share in its development and democracy. While citizenship has been granted to investors as a token of appreciation for their contribution to national development, allegedly "alien" agricultural workers are neither invited into the nation nor seen as contributing to it. At the same time, the designation of predominantly Spanish agricultural workers as aliens plays into long-standing racial-ethnic tensions between Creole and Spanish Belizeans and meshes with Afro-Belizean discourses that challenge the Belizeanness of *all* Spanish.

Official Belizean discourses on development, nation, and democracy reflect both the priorities of foreign governments and multilateral institutions and the aspirations of Belizeans, as the two have interacted over time. They generate constellations of identities and interests, with membership in the Belizean nation and concern for its sovereignty and its development at their center. These official discourses intersect, folding back on one another in multiple ways. Some are mutually supportive; others provide potentially contradictory frameworks for interpretation and action. The definitions and measures associated with development support nation-building activities, insofar as both the economy and the development process are conceptualized as national in scope. Democracy discourse and the practice of democracy in Belize reinforce the explicitly multiethnic construction of the Belizean nation by offering representation to all ethnic categories. Indeed, both major political parties court constituents from all racial-ethnic categories and run candidates affiliated with each of the major racial-ethnic groups (Bolland 1991:104–5). Further, positing the love of democracy as a trait that binds together all true Belizeans mitigates the dangers posed by ethnic differences and potential ethnic divisiveness. Both nationalist and democracy discourses legitimize state development policies, taken on behalf of the nation and, by definition, in its best interests.

But at the same time, the subject positions posited by development, nationalist, and democracy discourses can collide awkwardly. For instance, the celebration of investors as contributors to national economic development and the equation of the nation's interests with those of investors articulates uncomfortably with the centrality that democracy discourse accords to the small man. The drive to keep wages low contradicts the imperative of democracy discourse to allow the small man majority to shape government policies in "his" interests. The identification of all Spanish agricultural workers as aliens marginalizes some Spanish Belizeans from participation in development, nation, or democracy. Thus, official discourses generate complex and refractive subjectivities. However, the effectiveness of these discourses in shaping identities, alliances, and, ultimately, development trajectories must be sought in actual historical processes.

3 Citrus History
The Strategic Negotiation of Foreign and Local Interests

This chapter explores the historical development of the Belizean citrus industry and the way its trajectory has been shaped by the agendas of local, national, and international players. The first half of the chapter focuses on the political organization and mobilization of citrus farmers in confrontations with the processing companies and the government. This history demonstrates how citrus farmers have appropriated official democracy and development discourses for their own ends. The second half examines the history of labor organizing in the industry. It explores how workers have been mobilized as collective actors, around what identities, and in pursuit of what agendas; and it places these mobilizations in the context of wider political processes in Belize and beyond.

This chapter provides abundant evidence of the Belizean citrus industry's dependence on external forces. A small and relatively high-cost producer, the Belizean industry must compete with much larger producers of frozen concentrate juices, Brazil and Florida. Brazil alone accounts for nearly two-thirds of world trade in processed citrus products (FAO 1991). In contrast, Belize accounts for less than 0.2 percent of world citrus production. As the world leader in frozen concentrate orange juice exports, Brazil can essentially set world prices to reflect its production costs, while Belize, a higher-cost producer, is unable to affect international prices. Consequently, Belize has always relied on access to protected markets in order to profitably produce and export citrus products, making the Belizean industry dependent on metropolitan markets and the trade policies that regulate foreign access to them. International—and especially U.S.—discourses on development and democracy and the institutions established to shape political activity in developing countries have also influenced both farmer and labor segments of the industry. International union confederations sponsored by the United States channel resources to unions that cooperate in implementing U.S. visions for development and democracy, while Belizeans report CIA surveillance of noncooperative unions.

However, the chapter also demonstrates some of the ways Belizeans exercise agency, mobilizing and maneuvering to influence the actions and policies of foreign governments, agencies, and organizations and to capture the resources they offer. They also work to influence the actions and policies of the Belizean government and the political parties that vie for control of the government. They struggle for control of the Citrus Growers Association or the union in order to shape the goals these organizations will pursue. And they negotiate alliances within and across such organizations, as well as national, regional, and ethnic affiliations.

Early Citrus Production

The citrus industry in Belize began with fifteen acres planted in the Stann Creek Valley in 1913, at a time when bananas dominated agricultural cultivation in that area, the result of a turn-of-the-century banana boom (Bowman 1955:1; Moberg 1997). At the time, there were no roads in this southern district, but the government had recently subsidized the building of a railway line that connected upper Stann Creek Valley to the coast, with the aim of facilitating commercial agriculture. Subsequently, United Fruit had established a banana plantation at Middlesex in the upper valley, but disease wiped out its operations there within only a few years. As banana production declined due to disease and subsequent disinvestment, a group of about a dozen local merchants who had begun to plant citrus pooled their fruit, established a packing shed, and began to export fresh grapefruit to England. The citrus produced in the Stann Creek Valley won awards in London, attracting the attention of the Spencer family, which already owned extensive citrus holdings in Jamaica. The Spencers acquired the United Fruit Company's land at Middlesex in 1931 and replaced the large banana acreage with citrus to establish the largest citrus operation in Belize. Later, the Spencers acquired the fruit packing operation initiated by the smaller farmers and opened a factory where grapefruit sections were canned.

Citrus production in Belize expanded after World War II, as a result of a program initiated by the British government to provide orange juice to British schoolchildren. Britain planned to purchase the juice from its Caribbean possessions. Hence, the Spencer brothers, who acquired a second parcel of land at Pomona in 1948, established a juice processing plant to supply the British program, establishing the Citrus Company of British Honduras. As citrus cultivation in the valley began to expand in response to this opportunity, the British Colonial Development Corporation bought the area around Alta Vista and replaced its bananas with citrus.

The prices that growers were offered for their fruit were quite low. Further, since the factory gave priority to fruit from its own groves, it often could not accept all of the growers' fruit for processing.[1] Seeking to improve the situation, the largest grower, George Rowan, launched efforts to attract a second processing company to establish operations in the Stann Creek Valley, in order to increase processing capacity and encourage competition for growers' fruit. In 1962, North American investors bought the Commonwealth Development Corporation's citrus holdings at Alta Vista and established a second processing plant, which was purchased by Nestlé (the Switzerland-based transnational) in 1978. The expanded market for growers' fruit provided by the addition of a second factory prompted further citrus planting, and the government encouraged citrus farmers to sell fruit to both companies in order to promote and maintain competition between them (White 1968:90). However, fruit prices remained low. Most of the fruit the companies processed came from their own orchards, and the Citrus Company coerced many growers into delivering their fruit to that company, even though its prices were lower than those offered by its new competitor. Since only the Citrus Company processed grapefruit, the company required grapefruit growers to sign contracts for orange deliveries before it would accept their grapefruit (White 1968). In 1968, only 26 of 124 growers had no grapefruit and could thus risk not signing a contract for oranges with the Citrus Company. During this same year, the Citrus Company offered $0.85 to $0.95 for each box of oranges, while its competitor offered $1.25. Since it cost approximately $0.80 for smallholders to produce a box of oranges, they were just breaking even if they sold their fruit to the Citrus Company. Large growers could realize profits even at this price, because they achieved higher yields using more intensive methods, but only a handful of growers fell into this category (White 1968:88). Eventually, the second company began to process grapefruit.

Citrus Growers' Mobilization

After Belize obtained self-government in 1964, the government conducted an inquiry into the industry that resulted in the drafting and enactment of the Citrus Ordinance in 1967. Through the ordinance, the state granted itself regulatory powers over the industry in accord with its claimed responsibility for the nation's economic development. The ordinance established a Citrus Control Board, comprising representatives of processors, growers, and government, along with three members from outside the industry, to arbitrate disputes between processors and growers. Although growers had formed an association much earlier, the Citrus Ordinance also formally sanctioned the Citrus Growers Association, charged with pursuing "growers' interests." The ordinance required all who delivered fruit for processing to become a member of the CGA and pay a cess to finance its operation. This requirement obligated the two processing companies to become members, since they each owned orchards, but their membership in the CGA complicated the issue of what constituted "growers' interests." The largest private grower and CGA leader, George Rowan, had insisted on an additional clause in the ordinance that required the CGA board of directors to account for 15 percent of the industry's total production among themselves. The PUP minister with responsibility for the industry had insisted that the CGA have a one-man, one-vote rule, in accord with the party's championing of democracy. Rowan explained in an interview why he had opposed this principle: "That won't work. . . . How would you like your yardman telling you what to do? You need to provide for large grower leadership." The 15 percent rule represented a compromise that would ensure Rowan a position on the board, since his 600-acre holding dwarfed the acreages of all other private growers. The next largest grower had 91 acres of citrus (White 1968).

Although the ordinance had sanctioned a formal framework for the negotiation of prices to growers, the processors continued to dictate fruit prices to growers. At the prices offered by the citrus companies at that time, 85 to 90 cents per box of fruit, only farmers with more than seventy acres could operate at a profit (White 1968:35). But, aside from the two companies, only three farmers owned more than seventy acres, and three other growers owned around fifty acres each. Most of these farmers belonged to white merchant families of Dangriga. The vast majority of citrus farmers—just over one hundred—had much smaller holdings, and citrus farmers generally divided themselves into two categories: large and small. A 1968 study noted that, since "small producers are most affected by the high cost of production and low prices," they were also "the most vocal in demanding higher prices by the companies" (White 1968:85). One citrus farmer recalled: "Growers voiced objections to the way prices were arrived at"; when the CGA leadership—with George Rowan as chair—did nothing to change the system, "we knew we had to change the management committee." Many farmers were suspicious about the control larger producers exercised over the CGA: some wondered if large growers might be receiving higher prices for their own fruit. During the mid-1970s growers registered a vote of no confidence in George Rowan's leadership at a CGA meeting and replaced him as chair of the CGA board of directors with another large producer. However, when a letter written to the processors by the new chair of the association—exempting the companies from making further payments to growers for a previous crop season—came to light, growers considered this proof that the CGA's directors were not doing all they could to get higher prices for growers' fruit. Angry farmers voted to remove the new CGA chair and elected Oliver Hassan, a grower with thirty-five acres, to replace him.

The new leadership demanded that fruit prices be negotiated, as the ordinance required. The processing companies ignored the growers' demand and refused to meet with them. The growers met again and agreed not to reap their fruit until the processors came to the negotiating table. However, the processors still refused to negotiate. Small growers turned next to the government, demanding that it enforce the Citrus Ordinance. Farmers demonstrated with placards in the streets of Dangriga and traveled to the capital to lobby the minister of trade and Prime Minister George Price. They also enlisted the support of the citrus workers union, which sent its own delegation to the capital to ask the government to intervene and resolve the impasse. After three months of deadlock, the prime minister directed the Citrus Control Board chair to settle the dispute according to the provisions of the Citrus Ordinance. Thus, the dispute was sent to the board, where members representing the CGA, the government, and business people from outside the citrus industry voted together to force the citrus companies to the negotiating table. Citrus growers had launched their first coordinated action in deciding collectively not to harvest their fruit until the processors negotiated prices with them. Their continued campaign forced the government to implement the Citrus Ordinance, which provided a larger role for the growers association than it had previously played. The government's intervention reinforced the legitimacy of its claims to represent the interests of the "small man" and to act as the catalyst for economic development. It also reinforced smallholder citrus farmers' sense that they were an important part of the "small man" category at the center of official democracy discourse.

Energized by its initial success, the CGA demanded that the Citrus Control Board develop a price formula to set citrus prices more fairly. The government complied, and the implementation of the formula immediately increased fruit prices. However, the growers were suspicious of the figures the companies provided for the price calculations; they pushed further, demanding a Control Board investigation into the processors' books to ascertain whether or not correct figures were being used in the formula. The auditor appointed by the Control Board discovered "misallocations" and "questionable areas" in the processors' accounting that confirmed growers' suspicions. The Control Board recalculated prices with the corrected figures and directed the companies to make additional payments to growers.

The increasingly active CGA also intervened when the Citrus Company of Belize suffered financial difficulties in the mid-1970s. The company lost $1.7 million in one year alone, and farmers became worried that the company might close, leaving the other company with a monopoly. To prevent this, the CGA lobbied the government to facilitate the company's reorganization and continued operation. In response, the government agreed to guarantee $800,000 worth of loans for the company; it required that the company take on an equivalent amount in loans in order to continue operating.

A "Growers' Factory"

The Citrus Company of Belize was still in a weak financial state when a group of citrus growers and businessmen negotiated to purchase the company for $5 million in 1983. The new shareholders were led by Arthur Rowan (George Rowan's son), the owner of the largest private citrus orchards; Richard Porter, a white Jamaican who had migrated to Belize during the Manley era, bringing substantial capital with him that he invested in establishing a citrus estate, as well as other business ventures in Belize and the circum-Caribbean; and the Cooperative Citrus Growers Association of Trinidad, which controlled 50 percent of the company's shares. Several other large-scale citrus producers also bought shares in the company. The citrus producers who formed the core of the Belizean investors proclaimed their company a "grow-ers' factory." Emphasizing that "we are growers," the investors promised to use the company to obtain the highest possible fruit prices for all growers. By casting their enterprise as a growers' factory, they hoped to win the backing of both citrus growers and the government, which would be reflected in in-creased fruit deliveries and tax and tariff concessions.

At the time of the company's sale, the industry was again locked in con-troversy over the imposition of a new price formula. Growers believed the new formula was fairer, but the processing companies refused to implement it. During the previous harvest season, much of the grapefruit crop had dropped from the trees and rotted while processors and growers wrangled over the new price formula. The companies had finally agreed to use the formula, in amended form, for only one year. However, after the group of citrus growers had negotiated the purchase of the Citrus Company early in the 1983/84 harvest season, the Citrus Company broke ranks with Belize Foods and an-nounced that it would comply with the new price formula. The Citrus Company's acceptance of the new formula led to an immediate jump in the prices growers received for their fruit at that company and legitimized the new owners' definition of their company as a growers' factory. In response, independent growers shipped the bulk of the fruit produced that year to the Citrus Company. Many growers supported the growers' factory idea, and the government followed suit, granting CCB a development concession and au-thorizing the quasi-government development bank, the Development Finance Corporation, to underwrite a quarter million dollars' worth of shares to be made available for small growers to purchase. The CGA itself bought shares in order to gain access to the company's financial statements. After the sale was concluded, the new shareholders painted "Grower Owned and Operated: Da Fu We" (This is for us; it's ours) in large letters on the exterior wall of the factory. Their symbolic use of the Creole language emphasized that the com-pany was now Belizean and belonged not just to "the big money men," but to all growers.[2]

Few growers, however, actually invested in shares in the new company. Some large growers were wary of investing in an enterprise they would not control, and few small growers purchased shares from the block of shares being held for them. The company's failure to extend the deadline for the purchase of shares from that block and contradictory rumors about the fate of the remaining shares made small growers suspicious of CCB's "growers' factory" rhetoric. Later, CCB's prices dropped, disagreements among large-grower shareholders led some large growers to resign from CCB's board and/ or sell their shares, and the remaining shareholders converted the enterprise from a public to a private company, confirming small growers' suspicions. While the majority of growers ultimately came to disbelieve CCB's "growers' factory" rhetoric, the sale of CCB did produce an important change in the industry: it initiated the division of large growers into competing shareholder and nonshareholder factions that would become significant in the future.

The Citrus Boom

Citrus production had actually declined during the 1970s, as low prices led growers to minimize farm expenses by cutting maintenance of their groves. Growers began to reinvest in their groves in response to rising prices in the late 1970s, and in 1979 the managing director of the Citrus Company of Belize and Arthur Rowan, who had taken over the family citrus business from his father and was serving as chairman of the CGA, contacted the Commonwealth Development Corporation of the United Kingdom to request funds to rehabilitate their badly neglected orchards. A team dispatched by the CDC to evaluate the Belizean industry recommended that the production of existing citrus holdings be increased as rapidly as possible by giving top priority to rehabilitating neglected groves. This prioritization would have directed most of the funds toward the program initiators, owners of the largest orchards in Belize. The CDC report also recommended the creation of a new citrus estate, arguing that large-scale investment would increase production more rapidly and efficiently than smallholder investment (Tout et al. 1979).

In 1980, the Belizean government was asked to guarantee a loan from the CDC to finance the implementation of the report's recommendations. News of the proposed program was leaked to small growers, who were immediately suspicious of the secrecy in which the study and negotiations had been carried out. While the program initiators argued that their plan would benefit *all* growers by providing money for all to rehabilitate their orchards, small growers were outraged that the plan's priorities would have directed most of the money to large growers. At this time, there were 24 growers in the industry who owned more than fifty acres in citrus (6.7 percent of all private growers) out of a total CGA membership of 361. Together, these growers accounted for 45 percent of the total acreage in the industry. (The Citrus Company of Belize accounted for 17 percent of the total citrus acreage, Belize Food Products 14 percent.) The increase in the number of large growers reflects expan-

Table 2 Distribution of Citrus Acreages, 1985

Size of Holdings (Acres)	Number of Growers	% of All Growers	Total Acres	% of All Acres
1–5	160	44	459	4
6–10	92	26	710	6
11–20	55	15	810	7
21–30	18	5	519	4
31–40	5	1	179	1
41–50	5	1	243	2
>51	26	7	9,626	77
Total	361	100	12,546	100
CCB	1	—	2,193	17
BFP	1	—	1,766	14
Total processors	2	<1	3,959	32

Source: CGA 1985.

sion by some families that had owned citrus holdings for many years, planting by processing company administrators, and investment by a few Jamaican Whites who left Jamaica and migrated to Belize as part of the capital flight that characterized Michael Manley's administration during the mid-1970s (including Richard Porter and Bill Williston). However, 92 percent of the growers owned fewer than fifty acres of citrus, and fully 70 percent of the CGA's membership owned ten acres or less (see table 2).

Large growers who had been left out of the negotiations, led by Oliver Hassan (who by this time had significantly expanded his citrus holdings), aligned themselves with the smaller farmers. They called a special meeting of the CGA, where farmers expressed indignation that the government appeared to be favoring large growers over smaller producers. They passed a resolution demanding that the loan funds be directed toward the "small man" majority instead, to finance *expansion* of their citrus holdings. Following the meeting, a CGA delegation carried the resolution to the capital to make their case to the prime minister. Embarrassed by small growers' accusations of government favoritism toward large growers, the government agreed to incorporate CGA directors into negotiations with representatives from the Belizean government, the Commonwealth Development Corporation, and the

Development Finance Corporation. During negotiations that stretched over more than a year, small growers made repeated attempts to limit large growers' access to the loan funds, while the CDC opposed such exclusions, arguing that they would slow the program and jeopardize its goal of strengthening the citrus industry. Ultimately, the government agreed to guarantee the loan from the CDC on two conditions: expansion was to be given priority over rehabilitation, and the funds were to be directed toward small growers rather than a new citrus estate, the CDC's recommendations about efficiency notwithstanding.

However, despite the small growers' success in reshaping the loan's priorities, fruit prices were too low and interest rates too high to entice small growers to apply for the funds, until two dramatic changes occurred in international frozen concentrate orange juice markets. First, a series of freezes in Florida in the early 1980s transformed the United States from a net exporter of citrus products into a net importer of frozen concentrate orange juice. Brazil became the major supplier to the United States, followed by Mexico, the third largest producer of frozen juice concentrate (Barham 1992; Brown 1987:12). The second significant change was wrought by the elimination of tariffs on citrus products imported into the United States from Caribbean Basin countries under the Caribbean Basin Initiative. At the urging of the Florida citrus growers lobby, the United States had imposed tariffs on imported frozen concentrate orange juice in the 1950s, amounting on average to 40 percent of Florida citrus production costs (Barham 1992:845). The tariffs protected the U.S. domestic industry and pushed citrus prices on the U.S. market higher than world market prices. Prior to this time, Belize had difficulty selling its citrus products in the United States and had depended on protected marketing agreements to sell its frozen concentrate in Europe and the Caribbean. Although the Florida citrus lobby pressured the U.S. Congress to exclude citrus imports from Caribbean Basin Initiative trade legislation, they were unsuccessful. Hence, the CBI opened the lucrative U.S. market to citrus from Belize and other Caribbean producers. Now Belize was able to market its frozen concentrate for just under the Brazilian price and still turn a profit. As a result, the proportion of Belizean citrus products sold in the United States jumped to 60 percent, though Belizean frozen concentrate orange juice imports still accounted for less than 1 percent of the concentrated orange juice sold on the U.S. market (Barham 1992:845; Central Bank of Belize 1990).

Preferential access to the U.S. market for Belizean citrus resulted in a jump in the prices offered for oranges in Belize from $6.85 per box in 1982/

Table 3 Fruit Prices ($/box), 1970/71–1990/91

Crop Year	CCB Orange	BFP Orange	CCB Grapefruit	BFP Grapefruit
1970/71	1.15	1.25		
1971/72	1.25	5.00		
1972/73	0.75	1.80		
1973/74	1.70	1.80		
1974/75	1.50	1.25		
1975/76	1.67	1.25		
1976/77	2.37	2.54	1.96	1.92
1977/78	4.61	6.01	3.01	2.53
1978/79	5.73	5.73	3.09	3.09
1979/80	5.98	6.01	4.62	4.59
1980/81	4.40	4.81	3.69	4.07
1981/82	4.46	4.46	2.95	2.95
1982/83	6.18	6.85	3.11	2.08
1983/84	10.65	10.75	2.75	2.85
1984/85	12.22	12.22	3.83	3.94
1985/86	6.81	10.00	5.05	5.05
1986/87	11.32	12.06	7.64	7.98
1987/88	12.25	12.21	7.53	8.08
1988/89	12.35	12.35	6.46	6.46
1989/90	13.60	13.96	7.30	6.15
1990/91	10.58	10.58	5.84	5.84

Source: CGA 1991, 1981; figures supplied by companies.

83 to $10.75 per box in 1983/84 (see table 3). The higher fruit prices stimulated investment in citrus, and many growers began to apply for the CDC loan monies to rehabilitate or expand their groves. By 1990, the total acreage in citrus had grown from nine thousand to twenty-five thousand (CGA 1990:12). Production of citrus, which had reached one million boxes in 1963/64, rose to two million in 1986/87 and three million in 1991/92. Citrus's share of national export earnings rose from 8 percent in 1980 to 18 percent in 1989 (Central Bank of Belize 1991:31).

Nearly one-quarter of the CGA's members funded expansion through the CDC loan program. Eighty-four percent of the participants began with fewer than twenty acres, the size defined by the Ministry of Agriculture and Industry as an "economic acreage" (DFC 1989). Forty-five percent of the participants began with 5 acres or fewer and expanded an average of three acres; 31.5 percent began with six to ten acres and expanded an average of eight acres; and 7.1 percent began with eleven to twenty acres and expanded an average of eleven acres (DFC 1989). In the random sample of citrus growers interviewed in 1989, 73 percent had expanded their citrus holdings recently, either with or without CDC loan money, and 77 percent planned to expand more in the near future. While smallholders had enlarged their citrus holdings to take advantage of the boom, larger producers had expanded even more rapidly, with many of them more than doubling their acreages.[3] The increase in acreage under citrus also reflects an increase in the number of individuals who cultivated citrus: CGA membership rose from 361 in 1985 to over 600 in 1994. In 1990, 22 percent of the workers included in random samples from the unionized labor force in the industry had also begun planting citrus. Citrus expansion during this boom period also drew other districts into the industry, as increasing amounts of citrus were planted in Cayo District, and citrus cultivation was initiated in far southern Toledo District. As it had earlier in northern Belize in the sugar industry, the government facilitated the tremendous expansion of citrus production by providing state-owned land on lease to both large and small investors.[4] During this period of expansion, the number of growers with more than fifty acres more than doubled.

The breakdown of cooperation between the processors, the expansion of independent growers' citrus holdings, and access to higher prices provided by the Caribbean Basin Initiative led to a price war between the companies in 1984 that resulted in record prices for fruit (see table 3). During the following two harvests, three large growers kept the price war going by pooling their fruit and asking the processors to bid on it. The prices they received—which exceeded those dictated by the price formula—were extended to all growers who delivered fruit to the winning company.

As the citrus boom continued, a second loan program was launched with a 1988 World Bank offer of a million dollar loan to develop one thousand acres of new citrus in Belize. The World Bank's priority was further diversification of the national economy away from dependence on sugar. The Belizean government, concerned with portraying itself as a champion of the "small man" rather than provoking another embarrassing confrontation with small farmers, negotiated an agreement with the World Bank that would direct the program toward smallholders; the government proposed funding five hundred acres of new citrus holdings in twenty-acre blocks and five hundred acres in five-acre blocks in order to encourage small growers to expand up to the twenty-acre level designated as economically viable (World Bank 1988:13). However, officials at the Development Finance Corporation, which was to administer the loan, recommended that the bulk of the funds be loaned to one or two large growers to expand several hundred acres each, asserting that it would be "much more efficient to fund a couple of large projects that will have the same overall effect." In suggesting that loaning the funds to large growers would "have the same overall effect," DFC officers referred to the program's impact on citrus production and export earnings rather than its possible impact on political-economic relations in southern Belize. Through several years of negotiations leading up to the program's implementation, the government, concerned to increase production while maintaining the political support of the majority of farmers, insisted that the program be directed toward small farmers. The final agreement allocated funds to both small and large farmers, and, again, the government made land available to both small and large growers to facilitate expansion.

The Caribbean Basin Initiative and the favored access to the U.S. market that it provided had an explosive impact on Belizean citrus: access to higher prices available in the United States spurred a boom in Belizean citrus production. Moreover, the CBI's emphasis on linking democracy to development resonated with and reinforced their linkage in official Belizean discourses, which underwrote an important role for smallholders in the citrus industry's expansion. Small growers publicly invoked "small man" status and used it to force the government to respond to their interests. Government support for large-scale agro-export investors significantly expanded export production; support for small-scale producers achieved relatively small increases in production, but it reinforced Belizean discourse on democracy that requires government policies to benefit the "small man." While supporting only large-scale investors would have made the drive to increase export production more efficient, the allocation of some resources to small producers facilitated the achievement of both goals established by the CBI: economic growth and stable democracy. Government provision of land and credit to small growers legitimized official development policies and gave a material reality to Belizean democracy discourse by providing material gains for "small men." The linkage of development and democracy in Belizean government discourse and policies helped to construct an alliance of small and large agro-export producers in support of the dominant export-led development strategy.

Counting on Coke: The Real Thing?

The Caribbean Basin Initiative that had ignited the citrus boom had a life span of twelve years. Belizeans in the citrus belt, who had experienced boom and bust cycles in the past with export crops such as starch, bananas, and citrus, wanted this boom to last. Thus, the Citrus Growers Association and the processors began to press for an extension of the program beyond its 1996 expiration date. They lobbied Belizean government officials to press the U.S. ambassador on the industry's behalf, emphasizing the importance of the CBI to the prosperity of the Belizean citrus industry, and the importance of Belizean peace and prosperity to U.S. geopolitical interests in Central America and the Caribbean. The CGA also established contacts with officials from Florida Citrus Mutual, the organization that represented Florida citrus growers. The Belizean CGA worked to persuade Florida Citrus Mutual not to oppose extension of the tariff exemptions on Caribbean citrus, arguing that Caribbean citrus production was too small to pose a threat to the Florida industry. However, during the mid-1980s, CGA officials' highest hopes for extending the tariff exemptions revolved around Coca-Cola Foods' plans to invest in citrus in Belize, a result of the Caribbean Basin Initiative.

Coca-Cola Foods' Minute Maid subsidiary in Florida had suffered substantial losses in freezes in the early 1980s. In 1985 Coca-Cola purchased 193,600 acres in northwestern Belize and announced plans to replace its Florida losses with citrus development in Belize.[5] The Belizean government was eager to facilitate such investment, amid projections that Coke's investment could spur the creation of a whole new citrus industry in sugar-depressed northern Belize.[6] In fact, the government was so eager to see Coca-Cola invest that it bypassed the legal safeguards meant to ensure the land's development in such transactions with foreigners. Belizean citrus growers and processors were eager to see Coca-Cola invest as well: they hoped Coke would use its influence to persuade the U.S. Congress to extend the Caribbean Basin Initiative's tariff exemptions.

However, Coke faced opposition to its proposed project on several fronts. Within Belize, Coca-Cola encountered resistance to some of its demands from the CGA. In addition to the usual exemptions on taxes and duties, Coke also wanted to rewrite the Citrus Ordinance to exempt itself from the law's provisions. CGA officials feared that such revisions would make it possible for Belize Food Products and the Citrus Company of Belize to eventually exempt themselves from the ordinance as well. The revision would have weakened the ordinance, which had provided the legal foundation for growers' increased power in the industry. Thus, the CGA sent a delegation to inform Prime Minister Manuel Esquivel of their opposition to any exemptions from or amendments to the ordinance, warning that if the CGA suffered economically, the United Democratic Party would suffer politically. At the same time, however, the delegation emphasized that the CGA did not oppose other concessions and would like to see Coke invest.

Meanwhile, in the United States, Florida citrus growers lobbied successfully to prevent Coca-Cola from obtaining low-cost OPIC (Overseas Private Investment Corporation) risk insurance for its Belizean holdings. In Europe, the environmentalist group Friends of the Earth launched an international campaign in January 1987 opposing Coca-Cola's plans to clear Belizean rain forest for citrus planting. The group staged protests in Stockholm and occupied a Coca-Cola bottling plant in Hamburg to pressure Coke into abandoning its project ("Coca-Cola Shows Caution on Timetable for Citrus Scheme," *Caribbean Insight,* April 1987). In addition to political opposition to Coca-Cola's plans on multiple fronts, world prices for citrus concentrate began to fall, making it potentially less expensive for Coca-Cola to purchase citrus concentrate than to produce it. As a result of this combination of factors, in October 1987 Coke suspended its project in Belize. To defuse environmentalist opposition, the company has since divested itself of its holdings in Belize. When Coke decided against developing citrus in Belize, there was little the government of Belize could do, having bypassed the laws intended to ensure that the land would be developed in its haste to conclude a deal with Coca-Cola. However, Belizean citrus producers were heartened when, even without pressure from Coke, the U.S. Congress voted to extend the CBI agreement in 1990.

Labor Organization and Union Representation

If citrus farmers' decisions and their political mobilizations have been shaped through interaction with larger national and international forces, so has the mobilization of wage laborers in the citrus industry. The following summary of labor history in the industry draws on archival research, secondary sources, and interviews with union leaders and politicians involved in labor organizing (and reorganizing) in the industry over the last half century. Rather than presenting a picture of workers as a homogeneous collective actor with a homogeneous set of interests, this kaleidoscopic history of union activity in the industry reveals the extremely contested and conflictual nature of efforts to organize, mobilize, and represent wage laborers. Wage laborers and those who would lead them have often accorded significance to ethnic and regional distinctions and competition as they have mobilized. Competition among Belizean political parties has also played a key role in shaping union organizing efforts. In a broader context, the U.S. government's cold war preoccupations and policies have also played an important role in shaping both union activity and Belizean political parties' efforts to intervene with workers.

Wage laborers in Stann Creek District began to be organized by Belize's first labor union, the General Workers Union, during that union's earliest days in the 1940s. A decade later, the GWU threw its support behind the nationalists who formed the Peoples United Party in 1950, and PUP leaders capitalized on that support by gaining control of the GWU and using its structure to incorporate wage laborers into the core of the independence movement. The PUP attempted to mobilize workers as loyal constituents of the party that stood for Belizean independence, as it sought to represent those workers in both economic and political arenas. However, for the PUP the political arena quickly assumed greater importance than the workplace (Shoman 1987a). Indeed, missing from accounts of the events described below, whether the accounts derive from secondary or archival sources or interviews, is discussion of workers' concerns with the conditions of their employment and pay. The co-optation of the GWU by the PUP set a precedent for relations between political parties and organized labor that the PUP and later its opponents would pursue across decades.

The monolithic nature of the GWU itself as representative of workers' voices was challenged in 1950 when some workers in Stann Creek District broke away from the GWU and formed the British Honduran Development Union. The new BHDU was led by a local Garifuna man, Catarino Benguche, who "believed that 'Dangriga had a unique constituency with unique needs'" (Shoman 1987a:8). Ninety-five percent of the BHDU's members were Garifuna, and their secession from the GWU was perceived to be motivated by "ethnic considerations," including a lack of trust between Garifuna and Creoles in the GWU and a sense that workers from Stann Creek (a district associated with the Garifuna) were sending too much money to the national union in Belize City (a Creole stronghold) (Shoman 1987a:8).

The GWU and the BHDU began to compete with one another to recruit members in the citrus industry; they also competed over external affiliations. The General Workers Union was already affiliated with the International Confederation of Free Trade Unions (ICFTU), an anticommunist union confederation launched by the United States as a counter to socialist labor organizing. Such international affiliations were important as a source of training opportunities and financial support for Belizean unions, and the GWU blocked the BHDU's entrance into that confederation, depriving its rival of such opportunities (Labour Department 1956–57:9).

According to former GWU leader Nicholas Pollard, while Benguche focused the BHDU's attention on the Stann Creek waterfront, Pollard worked to strengthen support for the GWU among citrus workers in the Stann Creek Valley. For its part, the Citrus Company refused to recognize either union. Finally, in 1952, the GWU called a one-day general strike throughout the colony to protest the lack of progress in negotiations over wages with the colonial government and big employers, and the Stann Creek branch of the GWU voted to continue the strike until the Citrus Company recognized their union. The managing director of the Citrus Company negotiated with the striking workers, resulting in the GWU and the Citrus Company signing the first collective bargaining agreement in Belize. The agreement provided for increased hourly and piece rates and annual bonuses (Pollard 1986:4–5).

However, in 1955 the Citrus Company refused to negotiate a new contract with the GWU, which was demanding 20 percent wage increases, a union shop, and improved benefits. The GWU responded with another strike in February 1956 to force the company to the negotiating table. The General Workers Union asked the British Honduran Development Union to support the strike, offering in exchange to recommend the BHDU for membership in the International Confederation of Free Trade Unions. The BHDU refused, and the strike ended in two days. Immediately following the strike, the GWU and the BHDU negotiated an agreement to support one another's strikes in the future, on the condition that the GWU recommend the BHDU's affiliation with the international confederation. In July 1956 the ICFTU accepted the BHDU, and the two unions began to cooperate locally: the GWU represented most workers in the orchards and factories, while the BHDU and the GWU alternated in supplying workers on the Dangriga waterfront (Labour Department 1956–57).

However, inter-union relations turned conflictual once again, after the Peoples United Party split later in the year. Though George Price retained control of the PUP, the leaders of the breakaway faction took the GWU with them when they left. Loyalists to Price and the PUP founded the Christian Democratic Union (CDU) and subsequently launched a campaign to oust the

General Workers Union from workplaces and reorganize GWU members into the CDU. In Stann Creek, the Citrus Company continued to acknowledge the GWU as the primary union in the citrus industry. However, the CDU successfully reorganized some citrus workers away from the Stann Creek branch of the GWU, including workers at the plant where fruit was prepared and packed for shipping. Citrus workers who joined the CDU carried out a series of strikes and public demonstrations to demand recognition for their union, as well as a share of waterfront work for its members. The Labour Department responded by drafting a plan that established conditions for a representational poll to be conducted in the industry. However, the BHDU and the GWU rejected the plan, and no poll was conducted (Labour Department 1956–57:11).

Competition among the three rival unions in the citrus industry continued until 1958, when a visiting representative from the ICFTU urged unionists in Belize to establish "lines of demarcation" in the citrus industry. The resulting agreement allocated field workers to the General Workers Union, factory workers to the Christian Democratic Union, and the waterfront to the British Honduran Development Union (Labour Department 1958:10; 1960:17).

In 1960, the GWU, with branches throughout Belize, and the BHDU, based in Stann Creek District, decided to amalgamate to form the General Workers Development Union (GWDU). However, the GWDU's representation of citrus field workers was soon challenged by the CDU, after field workers at the citrus company's Middlesex estate launched a wildcat strike to demand an increase in their piece rate. The strike took the GWDU by surprise: the union's leader acknowledged that he had been unaware of the grievances that led to the strike. A representational dispute ensued, when the GWDU attempted to represent the Middlesex workers in negotiations with the Citrus Company. To resolve the dispute, the GWDU, the CDU, and the company asked the Labour Department to conduct a poll of workers in all sectors of the industry. The CDU won the poll and became the sole union representative for all citrus workers (Labour Department 1960:17–18).

Though the PUP-affiliated CDU had triumphed in the citrus industry, by this time the union was in decline nationally. Its national leader, Nicholas Pollard, had come into conflict with George Price, and Price had subsequently edged him out of the union in 1958. Pollard responded by establishing another union based in Belize City, the Christian Workers Union (CWU), which began to draw membership out of the PUP-affiliated Christian Democratic Union. In 1961, with the Christian Democratic Union in disarray, the Peoples United Party sought to renew its trade union support by creating regional unions under the patronage of PUP district representatives (Shoman 1987a:6). With this impetus, the Northern Cane Workers Union and the Cayo Labour Union were registered in 1961, and the Southern Christian Union (SCU), which incorporated the citrus workers who had belonged to the PUP-affiliated Christian Democratic Union, was registered in 1963. Pollard's Belize City-based Christian Workers Union later allied itself with the three PUP-affiliated regional unions to create the National Federation of Christian Trade Unions. This Belizean federation became affiliated externally with the International Federation of Christian Trade Unions, another explicitly anticommunist union federation. Competition between the Christian unions and the General Workers Development Union was fierce throughout Belize: Labour Department reports for the period describe them as "archrivals" (Labour Department 1965: 22).

Increasing Labor Militancy: The United General Workers Union

In the citrus industry, the politics of the PUP-affiliated Southern Christian Union took a new turn in the 1970s. In 1975, Mishek Mawema, a Dangriga schoolteacher originally from Zimbabwe, was elected to head the SCU. Under his leadership, the union grew more demanding and expanded its political agenda. In 1975 the SCU began a membership drive that increased its membership threefold and expanded beyond the citrus industry to the banana plantations of southern Stann Creek District (Shoman 1987a:13); in 1976 it signed an improved severance agreement with the citrus companies; in 1977 it obtained wage increases of over 18 percent (Tout et al. 1979:2). Since the high cost of keeping a ship in port made the citrus companies most vulnerable to labor strikes or slowdowns on the waterfront, the union effectively used collective action on the waterfront to press for higher wages and benefits in all parts of the industry. In response, the processing companies made concessions to waterfront workers that were not extended to workers in other areas: it allowed the union itself control over hiring, job assignments, and the assignment of work shifts on the waterfront.

Union politics in Belize had always been implicated in politics that extended beyond the workplace, including struggles between Belizean political parties and the cold war conflicts that gave rise to the international labor confederations that offered training and resources. However, under Mawema's leadership, the SCU made this extended terrain of union politics more explicit by adopting an adamant pro-independence political agenda. Mawema appropriated the PUP's developmentalist rationale for Belizean independence, but he pushed the argument much further, deploying the "development of underdevelopment" critique of dependent capitalist development being elaborated at the time by Third World scholars. "Development," he argued, "entails the reversal of those forces which caused our underdevelopment in the first place and created cultural, political, and economic dependence" (Shoman 1987a:15). Blaming both colonialism *and capitalism* for Belizean underdevelopment, he argued that development required both political independence and "the rejection of capitalism" (quoted in Shoman 1987a:15). Putting this argument into action, the SCU defied both Belizean and U.S. governments by abandoning its affiliation with the explicitly anticommunist International Federation of Christian Trade Unions and affiliating with the socialist World Federation of Trade Unions. As the WFTU made available new sources of training, SCU members began to attend seminars in Cuba, Prague, and Moscow.

At the same time, young leaders in the Orange Walk and Belize City branches of the General Workers Development Union became more militant as well, mobilizing around both workplace issues and an expanded pro-independence political agenda (Shoman 1987a:14). GWDU leaders called on the PUP to declare Belizean independence. They publicly proclaimed solidarity with the Sandinistas in Nicaragua (who themselves supported Belizean independence) and with leftist guerrilla movements gaining strength in Guatemala and El Salvador (Shoman 1987a:17).

The shared political goals of SCU and GWDU leaders led the formerly rival unions to initiate cooperative efforts. The largely Spanish-speaking Orange Walk branch of the GWDU began to participate jointly in seminars with the Garifuna-dominated citrus union, and the two began to discuss the possibility of amalgamation. However, while the activist leaders of the Belize City and Orange Walk branches of the GWDU shared many goals with the SCU, the Corozal branch of the GWDU was led by a traditional PUP loyalist who believed that "unions should not meddle in politics" (Shoman 1987a:14). The Corozal branch only reluctantly approved a plan for the GWDU to amalgamate with the SCU, after the Orange Walk and Belize City GWDU branches and the SCU acceded to its demand to maintain some traditional leaders among the new union's officers. Thus, in August 1979, the Southern Christian Union of Stann Creek and the General Workers Development Union, active in Orange Walk, Corozal, and Belize Districts, amalgamated to form the United General Workers Union (UGWU). The UGWU became the largest union in

Belize, with an estimated five thousand to six thousand members in key industries such as sugar, citrus, and electricity.

The UGWU under Attack

The size and strength of the United General Workers Union, its militant working class and nationalist agendas that extended well beyond workplace issues, its affiliation with the socialist World Federation of Trade Unions, and
its support for leftist movements in neighboring Central American countries
worried other Belizean unions as well as both Belizean and U.S. governments.
UGWU leaders in Dangriga report that Americans they believe worked for
the CIA investigated their activities and travels, and union leaders from northern Belize assert that the United States directed Prime Minister Price to
destroy the UGWU (Shoman 1987a:24–25).[7] The U.S. embassy official in
charge of labor matters in Belize in 1985 unambiguously labeled the Dangriga
UGWU branch leader a communist, the most dangerous label one could at-
tach to anyone in the Central America of the 1980s. With the 1979 Sandinista
victory in Nicaragua, escalating civil wars in El Salvador and Guatemala, and
U.S. president Reagan's cold war rhetoric, Belizeans were caught up in
regionwide fears about falling under communist domination or antagonizing
the United States and having to pay the consequences.

The UGWU's attempt to break with traditional union-political party relations and "chart an independent course" also earned it the enmity of both
political parties in Belize and the unions aligned with each of them (Shoman
1987a:25). Although the UGWU's call for immediate political independence
reflected the PUP's central political commitment, the powerful right wing of
the PUP regarded both the union's external relations and its internal strength
as dangerous. Its socialist affiliations and rhetoric set the union in opposition
to the PUP's agenda for Belizean development and threatened to attract U.S.
displeasure. UGWU leaders also suggest that the PUP Right feared the UGWU
might turn itself into a political party that could threaten the PUP's hold on
power and usurp its claim to be the sole representative of nationalist, pro-
independence sentiments. At the same time, the small left wing of the PUP
(Shoman and Musa, of the former People's Action Committee) supported the
UGWU and in turn received strong backing from the union.

The UGWU was also beset with internal conflicts, as leaders of its Corozal
branch continued to express opposition to the union's socialist affiliations
and agenda (Shoman 1987a:18). Conflicts also flared over power sharing

between the Orange Walk and Corozal branches. The cumulative tensions between the two branches came to a head during contract negotiations with the sugar company, when members from Corozal attempted to oust the Orange Walk leadership. When the attempt failed, the Corozal branch, along with dissidents from Orange Walk, seceded from the union. Politically conservative PUP representatives from Corozal and Orange Walk intervened to help the workers organize a new union, the Belize Workers Union, playing on regional and ethnic competition for power within the UGWU and applying the feared label of "communist" to the UGWU leadership to rally support for the new union (Shoman 1987a:18–20).[8] Supported by the PUP representatives of the two northern districts, the Corozal workers demanded that the Labour Department conduct a single representational poll for both Corozal and Orange Walk Districts, over the protests of the PUP left and the UGWU leadership (Shoman 1987a:21). The single poll allowed the larger number of workers at the older, less mechanized Corozal plant to pull both branches out of the UGWU. This cut out the financial heart of the UGWU and the largest part of its membership; it left the militant Orange Walk leadership with neither a constituency nor jobs. During the same period, workers of the Belize Electricity Board also broke away from the UGWU to form a separate union under the patronage of another right-wing PUP minister.[9]

In this manner, by the time Belize declared its independence in 1981, the UGWU had been reduced to a fraction of its earlier strength, and Stann Creek District workers had become its largest branch. Mawema, the maverick leader of the Dangriga branch, left Belize to return to Zimbabwe, leaving questions among his supporters about whether he was deported or left freely. In 1982, the Citrus Company closed its grapefruit sections canning plant, throwing its large female labor force out of work. In 1985 the UDP government sold the government-owned banana farms in south Stann Creek District to private owners, and the Dangriga UGWU lost the banana workers in the transition. By 1986 the Dangriga branch itself confronted tensions among its members along a number of fault lines, as we will see in chapter 5.

This historical accounting demonstrates that labor organizing and reorganizing in Belize generally and in the citrus industry specifically have been powerfully shaped by political rivalries both within the Belizean national arena and beyond it in international arenas during the cold war. Further, charismatic leaders, such as Price and Pollard, cultivated loyalty to themselves among workers they sought to lead, and both the workers and politicians who sought to mobilize wage laborers attempted to recruit them into competing versions of Belizean nationalism and competing visions for development. Intertwined ethnic and regional affiliations were sometimes attributed importance by union leaders and their followers, as was the case when Catarino Benguche mobilized some citrus workers as Garifuna ethnics with primary loyalties to their home district.

Shifting Associations: Racial-Ethnic, Gender, and National Typing of Work

If the associations that bound citrus workers to unions, to political parties, or to national and international union confederations have shifted kaleidoscopically over the last five decades, so have the associations between particular jobs in the industry and the kinds of people believed suited to perform them. Specifically, the ethnic, gender, and national associations of work in the citrus industry have shifted in relation to the kinds of work required and the kinds of people available to perform that work. Many of the major industries in Belize—forestry, sugar, citrus, and chicle—have been seasonal. Their seasons overlapped to a large extent, creating competition for labor during the peak season for cane cutting, citrus harvesting, chicle tapping, and logging, and producing high unemployment during the off, or "mauger," season. Logging, cane cutting, and chicle collecting were defined as masculine activities, but reaping citrus appears not to have been gendered in decades past. Many growers and workers reported that women worked seasonally in the citrus industry, picking fruit alongside men. Early on, many Garifuna from Dangriga were employed in the citrus industry, along with Jamaican immigrants and others who lived in the Stann Creek Valley or in villages along the southern coast. When the industry expanded in the 1950s, the Citrus Company began to recruit workers from Cayo and Toledo Districts to meet its labor needs (White 1968:59).

While reaping was not a gendered task, factory work *was* gendered. When Belize was shipping fresh fruit or canned grapefruit sections overseas, women wrapped and packed fresh fruit or peeled, sectioned, and canned grapefruit. Indeed, the majority of the Citrus Company's factory workforce were women who worked in the grapefruit canning plant: the plant was not automated, and women were considered "better workers at the tedious tasks of peeling, cutting, and packing" (White 1968:94). The women canners received less pay than male factory workers: for peeling the fruit, cutting it up, and packing the sections in cans, women received twenty to forty cents per hour in

Table 4 Birthplace of Valley Workers

Birthplace	Number	%
Stann Creek District	12	25
Cayo District	10	21
Corozal District	0	0
Orange Walk District	1	2
Toledo District	6	13
Belize District	3	6
Guatemala	13	27
Honduras	1	2
El Salvador	2	4
Total	48	100

Source: Random sample of BWU.

1968, while men employed in menial tasks and monitoring the automated process of juice production were paid forty-five to fifty cents per hour (White 1968:94). According to women who used to work in the canning plant, most of its employees were Garifuna. When the union was insufficiently attentive to their concerns, they launched wildcat strikes to force negotiations with both management and the union leadership to address those concerns.

The composition of the citrus labor force and the typing of citrus work has shifted in recent decades, as new sources of labor have become available and new products and technologies have been adopted. The processing companies had complained for decades about labor shortages at harvest time, and Labour Department reports indicate that the citrus companies were importing workers from Guatemala as early as the 1960s (Labour Department 1968). With the expansion of citrus in the 1980s, they asserted even greater shortages of labor and an increased need for foreign workers, in spite of an unemployment rate of 23.7 percent in Stann Creek District. Simultaneously, escalating political-economic violence in Guatemala and El Salvador led tens of thousands of Guatemalans and Salvadorans to emigrate to Belize. The increased availability of male workers from those countries, especially Guatemala, contributed to the redefinition of orchard work in both gender and ethnic terms (see table 4). From a midcentury labor force that appears to have comprised both men and women, at least half local Garifuna and Creoles from Stann Creek District, orchard work has been masculinized and re-ethnicized, becoming perceived as the appropriate domain of immigrant "Spanish" men. Now Garifuna, who say that they or their parents used to work for the companies, complain that the jobs that still exist have been taken by "aliens," who accept lower wages and poorer working conditions than Belizeans. However, it is impossible to accurately determine the number of immigrant laborers employed in the citrus industry. Employers may not apply for permits for short-term workers, and Labour Department records of permits issued are inconclusive; they lump all agricultural workers together, and some entries refer to "additional lists" not included in the ledger.

At the same time, the transition to production of frozen concentrated orange and grapefruit juice involved sophisticated new machinery that required little labor compared to earlier canning operations. The labor-intensive grapefruit canning operation at the Citrus Company of Belize was closed in 1982, decreasing the number of factory jobs available, especially for women. The highly mechanized process of producing frozen concentrate orange juice came to be monitored by small shifts consisting entirely of men. These changes contributed to the emergence or strengthening of a male breadwinner model in the citrus industry, as better paying, full-time jobs were increasingly masculinized.

As this chapter indicates, the citrus industry's overall trajectory reflects efforts to construct and define collective interests across local, national, regional, and even global contexts. The industry's history reveals a multitude of competing efforts to mobilize collective agents under diverse, often opposing banners. In the process, citrus farmers and workers in the industry have been both agents and subjects of competing constructions; they have not historically constituted unitary collective actors that persisted across time. Farmers have sometimes acted as "citrus farmers," but they have often mobilized along narrower affiliations based on differences in acreages or shareholder/nonshareholder status. Workers have engaged in collective action along lines of gender (women canning factory workers' wildcat strikes), ethnicity (the creation of the Garifuna majority BHDU), political party affiliation, and political stances on independence or socialism.

4 Citrus Workers
Segmentation and Solidarities

While chapters 2 and 3 presented a number of discourses, official and unofficial, that have sought to "position" wage laborers, this chapter draws on narratives collected through ethnographic interviews and participant observation to explore how eight workers in the industry measure such official and unofficial discourses against their daily practices in an ethnic- and gender-segmented labor force. Their accounts demonstrate how they position themselves in relation to the ways they are positioned by others, situating them simultaneously as agents and subjects. The multifaceted identities that result provide the potential for alliances in several directions or schisms along a number of fault lines, including gender, ethnicity, nationality, work area, job title, or place of residence.

Aurelio Pech

Aurelio Pech worked as a reaper in the Citrus Company's orchards at Middlesex, climbing a ladder to pick the ripe fruits and toss them to the ground, where he would later scoop them into bags. Aurelio worked in a crew whose members he described as Spanish and Mayan men. A captain circulated in the groves to see that Aurelio and his coworkers picked only the ripe fruit, but the captain did not have to enforce productivity: since reapers were paid seventy cents for each bag of fruit they picked, the wage system itself pushed them to work quickly in order to make money. Aurelio estimated that he reaped about forty bags a day during the height of the season.

A young man of nineteen years, Aurelio migrated to Stann Creek District seasonally from the village of Bullet Tree Falls in Cayo District of western Belize. His income helped to support his parents and younger siblings in Bullet Tree. After finishing primary school, Aurelio had worked with his father on the family's small plot of agricultural land in Bullet Tree. But by the age of seventeen, Aurelio decided he wanted to earn his own money: "I wanted to make some money, so I had to leave the village, because there is no work there." His first paying job, on a citrus farm in Cayo District, was close enough to home that he was able to live at his parents' house and commute to work every day. But the farm manager sometimes laid him off for a week or two. A friend who worked at the Citrus Company offered to help Aurelio get steadier work at the company, so Aurelio traveled with him to CCB's Middlesex operations and began picking oranges. Soon, Aurelio helped his older brother get a job at Middlesex, and the two of them had now worked there for three harvests.

During the workweek, Aurelio shared a two-room section in a workers' barracks with his brother and two other young, single men from villages in Cayo District. The barracks consisted of long rows of rooms, divided into two-room sections. A door on one side and a window on the other provided light until the sun set and oil lamps were lit. Each section of barracks had its own cook shed behind it where workers prepared their meals over wood fires. The door to Aurelio's living quarters was adorned with a warning in Spanish: "Enter with caution." With some embarrassment, he attributed the crude drawings of naked women on the Masonite walls to previous occupants of the room. In the evenings, Aurelio and his roommates relaxed in their hammocks and talked, argued, or teased one another in Spanish. Though all were Belizean, not all were comfortable speaking English or Creole. Aurelio explained that he spoke only a little English, "because I didn't really like going to school." This was not a problem on the job, since most people in his work crew spoke Spanish, including the captain.

When I asked Aurelio about his ethnicity, he expressed uncertainty. His parents were Mayan, he said, but he was unsure of his own identity. His parents spoke Mayan, as well as Spanish and a little bit of English. But Aurelio did not speak Mayan: "I could understand what they tell me, but I can't speak it," he explained. He believed this disqualified him from claiming a Mayan identity. However, although he was most comfortable speaking Spanish, he was not certain this was sufficient to make him ethnically Spanish. Aurelio's uncertainty over how to locate himself ethnically reflected the boundary blurring that has occurred between Spanish and Mayan categories in northern and western Belize over the last century.[1]

Every other Friday, workers received small envelopes with two weeks' pay in cash at midday, and work stopped until the following Monday morning. On these weekends Aurelio rode the bus to Cayo to visit his family and take them money. The bus company that served Cayo District sent two empty buses down to the Stann Creek Valley each payday to transport Cayo workers and their pay back to their homes, returning them to Stann Creek District on Sunday evening. When there was no longer enough fruit left in the orchards to allow him to earn good money, Aurelio returned to Bullet Tree to work with his father on the farm until the next harvest.

Aurelio was a participant in what has become a gendered rite of passage into adulthood for young men in Cayo District. In order to establish independence from their parents, earn money for their own purposes, and support their families, young men leave the district to search for work in other regions of Belize where work is more plentiful. Even once they have established their adulthood and begun families of their own, the lack of employment opportunities in Cayo District pushes many working-age men to seek employment in other districts.[2] This rite of passage is gendered: I neither met nor heard about any young women migrants from Cayo working in the citrus industry, though there were young women from Guatemala and Honduras. In some respects, Aurelio's pattern of employment reflected the pattern the government claimed was typical for agricultural workers, involving migration to Stann Creek during the harvest and then a return home. However, since his home was in Belize, he also contradicted the government's official portrayal of migrant agricultural workers as non-Belizean. Indeed, within the random sample of valley workers, no non-Belizean men practiced the seasonal cycle of migration that the government imagined for them; instead, immigrant workers came to stay.

Hugo Sanchez

Hugo Sanchez was one of these immigrants. Like Aurelio, Hugo worked as a reaper in the Citrus Company's orchards. But at age thirty-four, with family responsibilities, Sanchez worked all year round in the groves. He counted on the company to hire him for maintenance work in the orchards during the mauger season between harvests. On the day we first visited him, during the height of the harvest, he had picked fifty bags of oranges, working from seven in the morning until two in the afternoon. Like Aurelio, Hugo worked in a large crew comprising primarily Spanish-speaking men under the supervision of a Spanish-speaking captain. Though the crew included Belizeans and immigrants, communicating in Spanish while they worked enacted a degree of commonality.

When the harvest finished, most of the men in Hugo's crew were assigned maintenance work in the groves on a contract or piecework basis, chopping the grass or "bush" underneath the trees. Piece rates were sometimes negotiable, he explained. Although the companies and the union had agreed on a set rate per tree for chopping, the companies sometimes lowered the rate, arguing that the bush was not very high; or workers sometimes demanded a higher rate, because the bush was high or the trees were on a steep hillside. Because workers shared information among themselves about piece rates, immigrants like Hugo quickly learned to gauge the appropriate price for different kinds of work.

Although Hugo's crew tried to persuade the captain to pay them what they considered a fair wage, he seldom acceded to their demands. Then workers had two options: accept what the company offered, or refuse to work and wait for a union official to negotiate with the company on their behalf. For example, once the company assigned Hugo's crew work in an orchard nearly six miles from Pomona, offering them twenty cents for each tree they circled. Knowing the trees in that orchard were further apart than average, the workers felt that twenty cents was too little. Moreover, the company was not providing transportation, so they would have to walk the six miles. Most of them, including Hugo, decided to go home instead of taking the work. As they walked back to their homes in Pomona, they encountered a union leader and explained their problem to him. The union leader took up their case with management and struck an agreement for thirty cents a tree and transport to the work site. But, Hugo complained, union officers were usually very slow in pursuing orchard workers' demands, so his crew was seldom this successful in renegotiating pay rates.

Hugo was born in Jutiapa, Guatemala, where he lived half his life. But the land in Jutiapa is exhausted, he said, nothing grows there any more. When he was fifteen his family moved to Peten, where they obtained twenty-five hectares of land. However, the escalation of armed conflict between the

Guatemalan army and guerrilla forces in Peten during the 1980s made it difficult to work the land. "The land is rich in Peten," Hugo said. "Anything can grow. The problem in Peten is that people are caught between the army and the guerrillas. . . . It was dangerous to go to your fields." Some people from his village were killed: "Sometimes we would all go to sleep at night, and in the morning someone would be dead." As a result, his family decided to sell their land and move to Melchor, the town at the Belizean border, when Hugo was in his early twenties.

There was little employment available in Melchor, and Hugo had heard people say that Belize was a good place to work. So he obtained a passport and crossed the border, asking Belizean immigration officials for a tourist visa. "If you say you are coming as a tourist, they want to see that you have enough dollars to spend as a tourist in Belize." But that isn't a problem, he explained. "There are guys at the border who rent money for 10 percent. If you need to show five hundred dollars, you pay them fifty dollars and they loan you the five hundred dollars. You show it to the guy at immigration, and the guy who rented you the money is waiting for you outside, watching for when you come out, to get his money back." Hugo found work in the citrus industry, picking oranges during the harvest, but he quickly tired of the work and migrated to northern Belize to cut sugar cane. That work was heavier and dirtier than reaping oranges, so he stayed only a month and then returned to Guatemala, where he got a job felling mahogany. When the citrus harvest began the next year, he decided to look for work again in the Stann Creek Valley. He found a job with a private grower, who laid him off after two months. Then Hugo sought more stable work as a reaper at the Citrus Company and discovered that the company paid better than the private grower. His previous employer had paid him forty cents for each bag of oranges; the union rate at the company was seventy cents a bag. But, he reasoned, "newcomers don't know what wages normally are here, and they think they're earning a lot. When I first came," he recalled, "I earned fourteen dollars a day, and I felt rich."

The ease with which Hugo entered Belize and found work—twice—reveals both the Belizean government's inability to police its borders and its intention to satisfy agro-export producers who argue that foreign labor is necessary for the operation of the agro-industries that have dominated Belizean development efforts. Hugo was one of the tens of thousands of Central Americans who migrated to Belize during the 1980s to escape escalating political violence in Central America and its economic consequences. The arrival of

Hugo and others like him contributed to the redefinition of orchard work, particularly reaping, from an activity performed by both men and women and by Garifuna and Creoles from Stann Creek District, into a masculine activity appropriately performed by "Spanish" immigrants. As immigrants swelled the number of people available for work in expanding Belizean agro-industries, the government repeatedly defined agricultural laborers *as* immigrants, asserting that virtually no Belizeans performed agricultural labor. However, if the government described agricultural workers as migrants who came to Belize only for the harvest season, Hugo confounded this assertion. Hugo, like most Central American workers interviewed, was an *immigrant* rather than a migrant.

Hugo had met his wife, Olivia, while working in Pomona. Her family had migrated to Belize from Honduras some twelve years earlier to work in the banana industry of southern Stann Creek District. Olivia had traveled alone to Pomona, where she found work as a domestic with the wife of a company manager. When she and Hugo began a family, she quit her job. They had three children, the youngest still a baby and the oldest looking forward to kindergarten. In addition to providing for his wife and children, Hugo still supported his parents as well, traveling to Melchor every few weeks to take them money.

Hugo and his family lived in a small two-room house in the company camp at Pomona, where class difference and hierarchy were sculpted into the landscape. The camp was divided into halves by Stann Creek Valley Road. The factory and the houses of administrators and supervisory personnel, all enclosed by a fence, occupied one side of the road, where indoor plumbing and electricity—even fans and air-conditioning—were standard features. On the other side of the road, workers inhabited rows of small two-room houses or barracks, each with its cook shed behind it. Some evenings, when the biting insects were especially ferocious, Olivia closed the screenless windows to protect the baby from bites. Closed up in their stifling living quarters, she then fanned the baby—too hot to sleep—with a piece of cardboard. One evening, as rainwater dripped through the roof of their cook shed into pots Olivia had placed strategically on the floor, she complained about the company's unwillingness to repair workers' houses. Her husband interjected: "They are always building new houses inside the compound, but they are only for the bosses! They said they were going to get a new light plant and put light over on this side," he continued. "They did get a new generator, but they are using it on the other side. They have four generators over there. They have enough

Workers' housing in a company camp.

electricity to give us light, but they don't want to. They treat us like dirt."

"The water is another problem," Olivia added. Workers in the camp had to haul water in buckets from standpipes by the roadside to cook, wash clothes, or bathe. "The pipes are very rusty, and sometimes the water is very dirty. Our water comes from the river, but the bosses' water comes from somewhere else, and it's very clean. Besides, only a trickle of water comes out of the faucet, so sometimes I have to fight with other women in camp for water; it takes a long time to fill a bucket, and each one wants to fill three or four buckets before the next person can use the water."

Hugo and Olivia—like many other workers interviewed—read the camp's physical layout as an expression of their employer's contempt for them, and an effort to make obvious a class hierarchy in which workers are positioned as less valuable and employers as more valuable. Indeed, workers who lived in the camps complained as frequently about the way they were treated outside of work as they did about problems that arose on the job. The distinctions between "this side" and "that side" were manifestly clear. Hugo argued: "Here, although we are the ones who make the product, they don't look out for us. We maintain them, but they don't do anything for us."

But if Hugo felt the company did not look out for the workers, Olivia pointed out that it did watch them. She referred to "company spies" who kept

Fruit selectors at a factory.

an eye on people's activities in the camp. If anyone is causing problems, they report you to the boss, she explained, and if you are guilty they make you leave. Thus, workers who lived in the company camps found themselves constantly under the scrutiny of their employers. Men drinking in the Pomona Club, a bar owned by the general manager's wife, would pass a warning quickly from table to table—"Aguas, aguas"—when one of the bosses approached. At Pomona, even watching television emphasized to workers their employer's pervasive control over their lives. Although Hugo and Olivia did not have electricity, they owned a small black and white television powered by a car battery. When the battery ran low, Hugo carried it across the road and paid five dollars to have the company recharge it. They accessed a television signal through the largesse of their employer. The general manager of the Citrus Company of Belize had purchased a satellite dish years ago. He transmitted its signal down the valley, sharing the programs free of charge. Hugo and his family took advantage of this favor, but this required that they watch what the manager wanted to watch. For example, one evening we encountered Hugo and his family sitting in the dark watching a mystery thriller. The older children exchanged nervous glances as ominous music swelled to signal impending danger to the movie's hero. Then, the programming abruptly switched to a Chicago Cubs game.[3]

Making drums at the factory.

If the physical organization of the camp at Pomona reinforced and magnified class difference and class tensions, Hugo recalled that in the past it had also manifested tensions between Spanish and Blacks. "All the Spanish lived in Spanishtown, on the other side of the football field, and only Blacks [morenos] lived in the main part of the camp. They would always try to make us feel inferior—as if, because we were not from here and we didn't speak English, they are better than us. Before, the Caribs [Garifuna] didn't let Spanish people live in Pomona. The place on the other side of the football field was for them. But now Pomona is all mixed, with Blacks and Spanish, [morenos y hispanos], living together." Again, "here" and "there" organized space and hierarchy to divide "us" from "them."

During this time, there had been a great deal of tension between Spanish and Blacks in Pomona. "They used to have dances in the bar every payday. But every dance ended in a fight between the Blacks and us [los morenos y nosotros]. In every dance, there were Black and Spanish men and Black and Spanish women, and everybody danced with everybody. But after people had drunk a few beers, someone would start a fight, and then everyone would join in. It always turned into a big brawl, so they finally stopped having the dances." In this example, though people mixed, crossing boundaries at the beginning of the dance, by the time the dance concluded people had chosen—or been

Runners hooking drums to the winch on the waterfront.

placed on—ethnically defined sides in the brawl: the "blacks" versus "us,"
the "Spanish."

Even as he recalled these tensions, Hugo positioned himself in the Spanish category, clear that this is where the Blacks had located him. But he
added: "Now we don't have problems in Pomona. We're used to each other.
Now they're used to having us here." Indeed, as a result of Central American
immigration into Belize and internal migration within Belize, people classified
as Spanish now constituted the majority of Pomona's residents. By this time,
Hugo had also learned to speak some English, enough to understand directions and make some jokes with English- or Creole-speaking neighbors. "But,"
he was quick to point out, "there are still a lot of problems when you go into
Dangriga or take the bus." As Pomona had once "belonged to" Blacks,
Dangriga, the nearest town, still did, from his perspective.

Hugo's perception that Garifuna people asserted ownership of particular
places in Dangriga resonated with a recent experience my husband had had,
and he recounted to Hugo the story. Unaware of such putative ownership, he
had gone into a bar on Dangriga's main street at the invitation of a Spanish
Belizean acquaintance. The bar was full of Garifuna men drinking bitters.
When my husband and his friend ordered beers and began to converse in
Spanish, some of the Garifuna men became angry and interrupted them, ad-

monishing them that no one was allowed to speak Spanish in this bar, only Creole or Garifuna. Others shouted their agreement and demanded that my husband and his friend leave: "We don't want any Spanish here," they insisted. The Creole owner advised my husband not to pay attention to the men, but several continued to insist that the two Spanish men should leave.

Then, one of our Garifuna neighbors came to my husband's defense, identifying Chema as his neighbor, and asserting that he was a good person. "Besides," he added, "he doesn't work in the citrus groves. If you pick a fight with him, you'll be starting a fight with me too," he warned. A second Garifuna man, who my husband had never met, also came to his defense, and the angry men returned to their drinks and dominoes. The neighbor's plea in my husband's favor—that he was not employed in the citrus industry—underscores the element of economic competition that drives ethnic conflicts in Stann Creek District.

Hugo was not surprised by my husband's story: such encounters were to be expected by Guatemalans who imposed on Garifuna spaces. He identified the bus as another locus of conflict over ethnic and national control of public space. "They [the Garifuna] don't want us to sit down on the bus or to lean against them while we stand. The Garifuna think the buses belong to them," Hugo asserted, "even though the owner of the bus line is not Garifuna." Indeed, bus trips between Dangriga and Belize City, via the capital, Belmopan, routinely involved rituals of hostility in which participants struggled over the right to occupy space in Belize. Most Garifuna boarded the bus at the station, either in Dangriga or in Belize City, claiming seats at the beginning of the trip. When the bus reached Belmopan, passengers would step down to buy tamales, and people waiting for the bus in Belmopan—perceived as Central American "aliens" by Garifuna passengers—would rush to occupy their empty seats. When the Garifuna passengers returned to reclaim their seats, the newcomers would brace themselves, along with their supplies and children, in the aisle. Sometimes Garifuna loudly passed comments to the driver, suggesting that he not allow aliens or *paisas* to board the bus. Often, when the people in the aisles leaned on or brushed against a seat, its occupant turned to glare at the offender. The atmosphere on the bus grew tense, as the people jammed into the aisle tried not to touch any Garifuna and invite insult, or as one purposely leaned on a seat to annoy its occupant. When the "Spanish" got off the bus at Middlesex, Alta Vista, and Pomona, Garifuna assumptions about aliens taking the jobs in the valley that formerly belonged to their parents—and the increasing competition for jobs in the district—were affirmed.

Hugo explained the meaning of the word *paisa:* Blacks in Dangriga, or in Belize generally, "use the word *paisa* [a shortened form of *paisano*] to insult us, but among ourselves it's not an insult." Indeed, Spanish-speaking immigrants—especially Guatemalans—often used the term *paisano,* meaning compatriot in Spanish, to address people from their region of origin. However, Hugo continued, in Belize "they call people who can't speak English 'paisa.' It's not really an insult, it just means someone who is not from here. But, you can tell by the way they say it that they *mean* it as an insult!" Indeed, labeling someone as "not from here" challenged their access to rights and resources in Belize. Belizeans tended to use one of several synonyms, considered to reflect varying degrees of politeness, to label people they perceived as foreign workers. "Refugee" was used as the most polite way of referring to immigrants, its legal-technical meaning in international arenas set aside. "Immigrants" was less polite, followed by the most frequently used term, "alien." "Paisa" was used in the least polite circumstances. As Hugo noted, the derogatory nature of the term derived from its deployment, rather than its Spanish meaning.

Hugo's comments reflected the recognition that he was being positioned by Afro-Belizeans as Spanish and alien, a paisano who did not belong in Belize. But as he adopted those identities—as Spanish or Guatemalan/paisano—he attempted to attribute positive meaning to those labels. Hugo defended his presence in Belize, arguing, "Belizeans don't want to work. They want to earn more and work less." He explained: "People in Dangriga have a lot of relatives in the United States, and that's why they are lazy: their relatives maintain them; they send them checks from the States. The company couldn't do anything without foreigners," he argued. "We work very hard for little money, which Belizeans wouldn't do."

Elena Contreras

Elena Contreras was a single parent, with sole responsibility for her five children. One of few women employed in the citrus industry, she counted herself as lucky: "I can make twenty-five, thirty-five dollars a day picking oranges. There's nowhere else I can make that much money," she explained. Elena's assertions reflected a gendered division of labor, in which employers would not hire women to perform many jobs, and jobs typed as "women's work," primarily domestic labor, paid extremely low wages. Elena made what she considered good money picking oranges precisely because it was *not* women's work.

Elena was born in the Peten region of Guatemala, where her father farmed and her mother worked as a domestic. Elena began wage labor as a domestic at the age of fourteen, and a few years later she began a family with a man from the same village. They had six children together, but his heavy drinking led to their separation.

On her own with six small children, Elena found a job in a small restaurant. But her meager wages were insufficient to stave off her children's hunger, and she lost one child to illness during those difficult years. "Sometimes when I think of all the suffering I've endured to raise my children by myself, I cry," she said. "I remember when my husband left, and Arturo was just a baby. How he cried, because he wanted bread with his coffee! At night I would lie down beside him and tell him 'Tomorrow I'm not going to be able to give you bread, but you're not going to cry. [No vayas a llorar.] Don't cry.'" Her tone of voice revealed that this was more a plea than an order. "But the next day, when I gave him his coffee, he always cried, because he wanted bread. He had become accustomed to having bread every day, but I didn't have money to buy it now." Desperate to increase her earnings, she consulted a neighbor who had worked in Belize. With his advice, she left her children in her mother's care and traveled to Pomona at the beginning of the harvest. She found work picking oranges for much higher wages than she had earned in Guatemala: "In Guatemala a woman earns sixty quetzals [about BZ$24] a month," she said; "I can make that in one day here."

After securing one of the two-room houses in the company camp at Pomona, Elena brought her children to Belize. Each day during harvest seasons, she would leave home early in the morning in order to begin picking fruit as soon as it was light. "I worked from four in the morning sometimes until five in the evening in order to make enough money. All by myself I picked the fruit and filled the sacks. I would hang one sack around my shoulders and pull a second one like an ant carries its things, dragging it along behind me." A small woman, Elena described some types of work in the orchards as a "torment." For example, once her crew was spreading lime in an orchard where the grass was up to her shoulders. Unable to see where she was putting her feet, Elena fell into a hole. As she fell, she lost her grip on the bucket of lime she was carrying, spilling most of its contents in her face. The lime she inhaled made her nose bleed for days, and the doctor she consulted was concerned that it might have damaged her lungs. "The union fights against this," she said, "when they send us to work where the grass is high. But," she added, "if I say that the workers should stop, that we should not go into the orchard until the grass has been chopped, the boss comes around and asks 'Who stopped you?' 'It was so-and-so,' they say, and then the company will fire me. Because even if I'm doing it for the good of everyone, afterwards, the others don't support you."

While Elena worked, she left her oldest daughter in charge of her younger siblings. "At midday I would sit down to eat my cold tortilla, thinking about whether my children had eaten, if they were fighting, if something might have happened to them, because I couldn't be with them. I had to leave them alone all day, and I always worried about them." But Elena needed to try to earn enough money during the six- to eight-month harvest to see her family through the mauger season that would follow.

As the harvest concluded each year, Elena would hope to be given maintenance work in the groves, reminding her crew captain of her years of service to the company. However, though the company had sometimes given her work between harvests, Elena had gone as long as three months without work. One year she had been promised work spreading fertilizer after the harvest, but when she arrived to begin work the captain told her they had decided not to hire any women. "He told me that if the company gave me work spreading fertilizer, they would have to give work to all the other women—everybody's wives—as well. 'No,' I said, 'there are very few women who actually work for the company full time. You should give them—the employees—work. You wouldn't have to give all the housewives work.' But they wouldn't listen." In this exchange, Elena struggled to position herself as a worker, an employee, in contrast to housewives who do not work for wages. However, the company positioned her as a woman, explicitly defining women as housewives and men as wageworkers and legitimate breadwinners. According to this logic, when work was scarce, men should be given priority as breadwinners on whom their families depend.[4]

Unable to get "men's work" for herself during times such as this, Elena had been forced to seek domestic employment to make ends meet. "But, I can make thirty-five dollars a day reaping; you can't make anywhere near that working as a domestic," she complained, citing the case of a Guatemalan friend who was earning only forty dollars a week as a domestic, working fourteen hours a day, Monday through Saturday. Elena was thus acutely aware of the ways gender was materialized in work opportunities and pay, even as she helped to reproduce gender relations and meanings by assigning domestic responsibilities to her daughters. In contrast, when Elena's oldest son left school at the age of thirteen, he began to help her reap, boosting her earnings. Two years later, he began to work on his own account. Now that he was earning his own money, he gave Elena about fifty dollars a week, though he kept most of his pay for himself. At seventeen, he was becoming a man, an expensive endeavor that involved buying rounds of drinks at the Club.

Having lived for a number of years in Belize, Elena said she had learned enough English to "understand when the Blacks are insulting me." However, Elena spoke Spanish in most of her everyday interactions with her children, coworkers, and neighbors in the camp. Their use of Spanish drew a circle that included Spanish-speaking Belizeans, Guatemalans, Salvadorans, and Hondurans, while it excluded Belizeans who did not speak Spanish. Within this circle, Elena adjusted the terms she used to address people to assert greater solidarity with some Spanish speakers than with others. Workers from Guatemala or El Salvador often used the pronoun *vos* (very informal "you") rather than *usted* (formal "you") or *tu* (informal "you") with family members and trusted friends and neighbors.[5] Their reciprocal use of *vos* simultaneously expressed and built trust and familiarity. It also connoted equality or sameness. Using *vos* across class lines or in a relationship that was not egalitarian and based on mutual trust would be considered an abuse. For example, recounting a conversation she had had with a friend in the camp, Elena said, "Y yo le dije, 'Lo que vos debés de hacer . . .' " ("And I told her, 'What you [*vos*] ought to do is . . . '"). She interrupted herself to explain why she had used the term *vos:* "You see, she's a paisano." Being paisanos implied a reason both for using *vos* and for giving the woman advice: mutual trust, or *confianza.* Indeed, Elena's closest friends were all paisanos from Guatemala; most were also from Peten. Among them, their use of *vos* connoted a commitment to share resources with one another when needed, and Elena regularly gave advice and material assistance to several other women from the Peten, counseling them in their dealings with men or sharing food and clothing with them. Although they had not known one another before migrating to Belize, their provision of mutual assistance to one another made material a shared identity as paisanos in the positive sense.

However, Elena's expectations of confianza and mutual assistance did not extend automatically to all Guatemalans, and those friends she called *vos* sometimes betrayed her trust (a fact made more painful by the presumed confianza that their mutual use of *vos* signified). And beyond the category of paisanos, Elena's relations with Spanish Belizeans or Salvadoran and Honduran immigrants lacked the trust required for the use of *vos.* Indeed, Elena and her family held many of the same negative stereotypes about Salvadorans that Belizeans did.

Although Elena's closest relationships were with Guatemalan paisanos, she was by now firmly established in Belize, with no intention of returning to live in Guatemala. She had furnished her small house in Pomona with a gas stove, a table and stools, and beds with mattresses. This was her home, unlike the barracks of the migrant men from Cayo, whose real homes were elsewhere. She had also spent more than a year and over one thousand dollars to obtain Belizean residency, including the cost of medical examinations, police certifications, and trips to the capital to move the process along.

Pedro Ruiz

Pedro Ruiz worked as a sideman in a three-man crew that transported fruit from the orchards to the factory at Belize Food Products. Pedro and another sideman hoisted the sacks of fruit left by reapers and emptied them into a trailer. When the trailer was full, they rode with the tractor driver to the factory to unload the fruit onto a conveyor belt that carried it past fruit selectors and into storage bins. He worked hard to maximize his earnings during the harvest, when he could earn two or three hundred dollars a week. "It takes us about twenty minutes to load the fruit," he estimated, and "when we are working close to the factory, we can make twelve or thirteen trips a day. We make $3.75 for each trip, so the faster we work and the more trips we make, the more money we earn." After the harvest, he was usually assigned day work, earning just $23.85 a day, or about $115 a week. "That is very little to maintain my family. It's not enough. That's why I take the opportunity to earn as much as I can during the harvest, when there is overtime and a lot of work."

Compared to orchard or factory workers, transport workers such as Pedro exercised greater autonomy in their work. They were more mobile and less heavily supervised than most workers; the tractor driver himself reported the number of trips and the number of hours his crew should be paid. Thus drivers and sidemen were disciplined primarily by the contract rate at which they were paid.

Pedro's wife, Rosario, also worked Monday through Thursday as a domestic. She earned $12.50 a day, half of what her husband earned for day work. "It's not much," she said, "but I worked for years in Guatemala and never made more than thirty quetzals a month," about one-quarter of her wages in Belize. In the morning, before leaving for her paid job, she filled a washtub with soapy water to soak the family's clothes. Then she walked the four miles to work, where she cleaned, cooked, washed clothes, and ironed. After walking back home in the evening, she washed her own family's clothes, while her daughters cooked the evening meal.

Both Pedro and Rosario were born in Guatemala, in the department of Zacapa. Pedro's parents owned land in Zacapa, but it was not enough to support their children's families when they began to marry. After Pedro and Rosario married, they moved to the Guatemalan Peten, where Pedro acquired land to establish his own farm. Though the farm provided for many of their subsistence needs, to meet their cash requirements Pedro worked in the bush as a *chiclero,* tapping sapodilla trees to collect the chewing gum base chicle. He lived in the forest for most of the week, leaving Rosario alone on the farm. Pedro heard from a friend that he could earn more money in Belize, and he decided to explore the opportunities Belize offered. He found work in the Citrus Company's orchards at Middlesex and soon brought his wife and their new baby to Belize. That was eighteen years ago.

After working at Middlesex for six years, Pedro worked for a couple of private growers for four years before starting a job at Belize Foods, where he had been for eight years at the time we met him. By this time, Pedro had obtained Belizean residency, making all of the necessary trips to Belmopan to file the paperwork: health certificates, letters from upstanding Belizean citizens vouching for his good character, police records, and a multitude of fees. He had also applied to the government for a piece of lease land, and in 1982 he was allotted a thirty-five-acre block at a rent of one dollar a year. The land was located three-quarters of a mile away from Stann Creek Valley Road, "to the back," behind an already established farm at the roadside. As soon as he was able to build a small two-room house of rough wood planks and a cook shed of palmettos, he moved his family to the farm. By this time, they had had eight children; seven were still alive. Their oldest son, age nineteen, worked for a private citrus farmer. Their oldest daughter had married and was living with her husband and baby in Melchor. A sixteen-year-old son and a fifteen-year-old daughter attended high school in Dangriga, getting up at four in the morning to catch the bus to school. The three youngest, a son age five and two daughters aged eight and eleven, attended primary school in the valley.

Once Pedro had obtained the parcel of land, each year he cleared a small piece with axe and machete, burned it, planted a crop of corn, and then set out citrus seedlings. By 1989, he had planted ten acres and was still expanding. However, the expenses of maintaining the family, especially the cost of keeping two children in high school, left Pedro with insufficient income to purchase the inputs recommended by the CGA for citrus production. As a result, Pedro had 5-year-old trees that hardly produced fruit, because he was unable to apply fertilizer or lime.

In addition to their wage-paying jobs and citrus, the family grew corn to meet household consumption needs and cultivated a variety of fruit trees both for home consumption and for sale in company camps or in Dangriga. They also raised chickens, ducks, and turkeys.

Like many workers who plant citrus, Pedro Ruiz viewed his farm as a ticket out of the working class for the future. Though part of his motivation for beginning a farm was to have something secure when he gets too old to work for wages, he also saw the farm as the beginning of new possibilities for his family. "The problem," he said, "is that I have a job that pays very little, especially when I have such a large family. So I can't give them everything they want. But I tell them in a few years, when the citrus is bearing, then I will be able to buy them nice shoes and other things they want. . . . So I tell them that if they have to do some chopping on the farm, they should do it with love, because although they don't have everything they want now, in a few years I will be able to give them the things they need with money from the farm. It's the farm that will provide those things for them."

Farm ownership, made possible for workers because government land was still available on lease, offered workers the possibility of decreasing their dependence on the companies in the present—through subsistence cultivation and a place to build a house—and the possibility of leaving the working class altogether in the future—through investment in citrus. That this altered their perception of where their interests lay is illustrated by Pedro Ruiz's reaction to the news that Belize Food Products, where he worked, might close down (see chapter 7): "But CCB would not be able to accept all of the fruit produced in the valley. It's too much for CCB to handle alone!" he exclaimed with alarm. "Fruit prices would drop!"

"Wouldn't you lose your job too?" I asked him. Yes, that was also true, he conceded, though it seemed to be a secondary concern.

Pedro and his family performed most of the farmwork themselves on weekends and evenings: the whole family reaped, and Pedro and his older sons struggled to keep up with the machete work. However, Pedro's own wagework left him with insufficient time to maintain his farm. When time was running short before the onset of the rains, he compensated for his own lack of time by paying Guatemalans to clear the piece of land he wanted to plant next. He hired Guatemalans, he explained, because they charged two hundred dollars per manzana, while Belizeans charged three hundred to three hundred fifty dollars per manzana. Later, he hired two men to plant corn for him, because he was too busy at work to do it himself. In this practice, Pedro resembled seven other workers in the random sample of citrus workers, who hired labor on their farms to clear land or maintain their orchards. Most of them hired Guatemalans, arguing that Belizeans were too expensive. Thus, on their farms, workers took advantage of the downward pressure on wages exerted by the continual flow of immigrants that may have hurt them in the workplace. In this way, farming introduced multiple and contradictory pressures into the construction of a worker's class identity and interests; Pedro was simultaneously a wage laborer (desirous of higher wages), a farmer (concerned about citrus prices), and an employer (looking for cheap labor).

By the time we met them, Pedro and Rosario had become established in Belize and had no desire to return to Guatemala. The children, all but the oldest born in Belize, saw themselves as Belizean. Though Pedro and Rosario had both obtained Belizean residency, they were less certain about their national identities. Legal residents of Belize, they were still citizens of Guatemala. And though they had lived in Belize for eighteen years, they realized that many people still considered them aliens.

Pedro emphasized that he wanted his son to go to school, even though he could use his help on the farm, because he did not want him to be limited to machete work. He did not want his children to have to do the kind of hard work he had done all his life. The children had also embraced this goal, which reflected the messages they received as they passed through the Belizean education system: office work is modern and prestigious; agricultural work is backward, dirty, and not appropriate for Belizeans (Rutheiser 1990). While Pedro and Rosario hoped their children would do better economically, they also believed in the dignity of their own hard work, and this produced some tension. For example, when Pedro and Rosario were both given month-long "vacations" during the mauger season, most of which would be unpaid, Rosario became concerned about the family's lack of income. She suggested to her teenaged daughter, on vacation from high school, that she look for a temporary job. Her daughter Amalia, who was studying in a secretarial track, responded, "I'm not going to get a job until I can get one as a secretary in an office." She continued, "When I graduated from primary school, the principal told us 'If I see any of you working in someone else's house or picking oranges, I'm going to drag you out of there, because you're too smart to work at those kinds of jobs' [los voy a sacar de ahi, porque ustedes no son tontos para tener un trabajo de tonto]. Jobs like chopping and farming are for foreigners. Belizeans work in offices." Amalia's tone and expression indicated that she was joking, baiting her mother. But Rosario was visibly agitated by her daughter's comments. She was proud of her daughter's scholastic accomplishments, and the family sacrificed to pay for her education precisely so that she would have options other than the domestic and agricultural work her parents performed. Yet Rosario was unwilling to see her own hard work diminished, and she did not appreciate being derided as a Guatemalan, fit only for "trabajos de tonto" by her Belizean daughter. Rosario replied sharply, "Just remember how your father and I pay for your schooling." The ambiguity of Pedro's class positioning was replicated in the ambiguity of his family's national affiliations and the valuations attached to them. Pedro and Rosario had positive views of the rural, agricultural life they had carved out in Belize, though they hoped their children would do better. Their children shared this hope, having learned in the Belizean school system to evaluate rurality and agriculture unfavorably and to associate them with foreigners.

Silvio Vasquez

Silvio Vasquez worked in the factory at the Citrus Company of Belize. The process of extracting and concentrating the juice was highly mechanized; workers like Silvio monitored the machines and provided occasional cleaning and repairs.

Factory work was shift work, performed for an hourly wage, and each factory had two shifts that alternated working night and day every two weeks. The town shift from the coastal town of Dangriga comprised primarily Creole and Garifuna men, who were transported up the valley to work and back to town after their shift. Silvio belonged to the valley shift that included Spanish, Creole, and Garifuna workers who lived in the company camp at Pomona. Members of this ethnically diverse crew used Creole to communicate with one another on the job. The valley shift was perpetually on call, responding to the factory's whistle signals: four short blasts called them in to work, one blast told them to stay home.

When the quantity of fruit coming into the factory was moderate, each crew worked a nine-hour shift. But at the height of the harvest, they began ten-, twelve-, or sometimes fourteen-hour shifts, alternating night and day every two weeks. As the harvest wound down, the factories moved to only one shift, and the night shift might be out of work for two weeks. For this reason, Silvio liked the long shifts during the season's peak: they provided the opportunity to earn overtime that could compensate for the lack of work later on. His normal wage rate was $2.90 an hour, but he got an extra five cents when he worked at night. Night work was harder, he explained, "and they don't want to see anybody nodding off." To keep workers alert, especially on the night shift, a "watchimán" circulated around the factory to monitor them: "If the watchimán catches you sleeping, he takes out his book and writes 'so and so is sleeping at such and such an hour, on such and such a day.' And he gives that book to the boss, and he makes a report to the managers. Then the manager calls you in to ask why you were sleeping."

Silvio was born and raised in the village of Benque Viejo del Carmen in Cayo District, adjacent to the Guatemalan border. His mother was from a Benque family, his father from the Guatemalan Peten. Both died when Silvio was small, and an aunt and uncle raised him. At the age of twelve he began to work with his uncle collecting chicle, a job he continued for decades. During the six-month chicle season, he lived in camps in the forest for one or two months at a time, with twenty-five to thirty other men. Every month or two, he visited his family in Benque. However, eventually the market for chicle disappeared; so Silvio, by then in his forties, migrated south with some friends to look for work in Pomona. Initially, he was hired to do machete work in the groves at the Citrus Company. After several years, he was offered the opportunity to move into factory work. At the age of fifty he was happy to have found work that did not require as much physical exertion as machete work. Silvio usually worked all year round with the company, doing repair work around the factory during the mauger season.

Although his wife had visited Pomona when he first began to work for the company, she did not like the camp. Since they already owned a small house in Benque, she continued to live there, along with their youngest son, who was finishing high school. Silvio traveled to Benque to see them every Friday evening. Another worker from Benque had recently purchased a van, and he transported about ten workers from Pomona to Benque on Fridays and back to Pomona on Monday mornings, leaving at three in the morning to arrive in Pomona in time for work.

Monday through Friday, Silvio shared quarters in the men's barracks at Pomona with another *benqueño*. He spent most of his evenings with fellow benqueños, who congregated on benches near the cooking shed of one of the migrants to talk about events at work, in the camp, or at home. Indeed, although they spent most of every week in Pomona, they still lived in Benque in many respects; Benque was home. Though most of them spoke some English or Creole, they usually conversed in Spanish, rehashing the soccer match played in Cayo the previous weekend, telling stories, or discussing events at the Citrus Company. Although workers from other places drifted in and out of these nightly conversations, benqueños formed their core. Indeed, a Guatemalan living in the barracks once commented that the benqueños did not associate much with other workers. "The benqueños are very distinct. After work, they go straight back to their rooms to talk with other benqueños. They almost never talk to the Blacks; they don't have any kind of relations with them, like we do." Indeed, workers from Benque saw themselves as different from both immigrants and their Afro-Belizean compatriots: "People from Benque are different from people from other parts of Belize. The others, the Blacks, like to dance in the street. We don't do that. We're more tranquil." In Benque, Silvio clarified, "almost everyone is Spanish." In the relationships he put into practice almost every evening, Silvio positioned himself as benqueño, a place-specific designation that located him as both Belizean and Spanish, even as it distanced him from both the majority of Belizeans and the majority of Spanish speakers.

The evening conversations among benqueños in Pomona revealed that they routinely lived their lives across both sides of the Belize-Guatemalan border. They talked comparatively about the cost of food and medical care on each side of the border, and they described weekend visits to relatives who lived on the Guatemalan side. Silvio had two sisters on the Guatemalan side, whose families he visited regularly. The most extreme case involved another benqueño worker, whose family moved back and forth across the Belize-Guatemalan border daily, as a strategy for maximizing both their purchasing power and their educational assets. This worker had been born in Melchor, on the Guatemalan side of the border. But, he claimed, his parents registered his birth in Belize, in Benque, making him a Belizean. His wife was from Guatemala, and they had six children: three were Guatemalan, and three were Belizean. In 1989 his wife and children were living in Melchor, because everything was cheaper on the Guatemalan side, due to the mid-1980s devaluations of the Guatemalan currency. However, their children crossed the border every day to attend school in Belize, because he believed that it would be beneficial to them to speak English. If Stann Creek natives saw the spatial and social boundaries between Guatemala and Belize, or between Guatemalans and Belizeans, as rigid barriers, to benqueños from western Cayo District those boundaries appeared more fluid and permeable.

The Benque workers' evening conversations often turned to rumors about the progress of negotiations, as the union and the company negotiated a new contract. One worker, frustrated with the slow pace of the contract talks, complained, "Although it's the workers who make their money for them, the owners don't want to give us a raise. They think we're not worth anything." When I mentioned that I had heard the union was negotiating for electricity for Pomona as part of the agreement, the men laughed. "It's the same old thing," Silvio said. "They always offer us electricity, but they never really give it to us. They've even sent people over to measure where posts should go. But they say they don't have enough wire. That's what they say. But on the other side they're always putting in more wire, more lights. For that side, they have wire. Only for here they don't."

They contrasted the darkness in which they congregated nightly to the luxuries enjoyed by their supervisors and bosses who lived inside the factory compound on the other side of the road. Like Hugo Sanchez, they read the camp layout as a clear statement about class differences between management and workers and positioned themselves accordingly. However, they also recognized that they could not count on solidarity from all of their coworkers in the camp. One explained that "the people who live inside the compound are the captains, the people who supervise us."

"How do they get to be captains?" my husband asked, "because they have worked here a long time?"

"No," responded another. "Here they don't promote you for your work, but rather for this," he said, pointing to his tongue. "People who talk a lot, who tell the bosses everything that goes on, get promoted to be captains."

Stanley Rivers

Stanley Rivers worked at Belize Food Products as part of a four-man crew that transferred frozen juice concentrate from big cooling tanks into drums for storage and transport. He earned an hourly wage of $2.65, and, like Silvio

Vasquez, he liked the twelve-hour shifts that allowed him to earn overtime. "What you're working for now is basic hunger," he said. "With a little bit more that you earn, that's a little more food." Further, "since workers receive a 4 percent bonus at the end of the crop," he reasoned, "it pays twice to make a lot of overtime." During the mauger season, he was usually laid off for about a month before being called back for cleaning or maintenance work in the factory. Stan had been working at Belize Foods for twelve years, beginning as a fruit selector when he was seventeen.

Rivers was part of the town shift; the company transported his crew of Garifuna and Creole men from Dangriga to and from the factory daily. Stan had lived in Dangriga all his life. He owned the small wooden house where he, his wife Valerie, and their four small children lived. The house had electricity and a faucet in the yard, which meant that Valerie did not have to fight for water, as women in Pomona sometimes did. Their access to electricity enabled them to enjoy luxuries not available to workers in the company camps, including electrical lights and a color television hooked up to cable. Stan and his wife identified themselves as Garifuna. However, though they had grown up speaking the Garifuna language, they spoke Creole at home with their children.

Stan was currently the only wage earner in the family, though Valerie had worked in the grapefruit canning plant at Pomona until it closed. During nearly every visit, she was at the stove, making flour tortillas for Stan's lunch the next day. Stan expressed concern that the "starvation wages" workers earned and the competition for jobs in Stann Creek District had inhibited workers' collective action. Pressed by their families' needs and the competition for jobs that resulted from the district's high unemployment rate, Stan echoed Elena Contreras's complaint that workers often refrained from demanding that the companies live up to their contract obligations—or supporting coworkers who did make such demands—in order to avoid getting fired. "If you want to protest something the company is doing that's wrong, they say 'I don't want to do this, because I have children.'" For example, he explained, the company used to transport workers in a truck whose canvas top was old and rotten. "When it rained, we always got wet. We complained, but the company never did anything. One rainy day, I decided 'this truck is not fit for us to ride!'" He lobbied his coworkers not to ride the truck the next day to protest its condition. Although all agreed to the boycott, the next morning some of the other workers did ride the truck, and Rivers's supervisors reprimanded him for his role as instigator of the protest. Listening to the story, Valerie nodded her head and added, "The workers don't back you up. They want to cooperate when they don't see the bossman, but as they see the bossman, they get frightened. They say 'I need to feed my children. If I don't give my wife money, she will leave me.' So they won't back you up. They're afraid."

The competition for work in Stann Creek District was integrally linked to interethnic relations in Belize and concerns about Central American immigration. As a native of Dangriga who worked in the valley, Rivers felt a personal stake in the debate over whether or not Belizeans were willing to work in agro-industries. Many different kinds of people insisted that Dangrigans would not work in the valley. A government labor officer noted that, while Belize Foods employed primarily Belizeans, CCB employed a large number of foreign workers, claiming that nationals were not interested in agricultural work. One CCB administrator "lamented" this, asserting that immigrants "work much better than the Belizeans, unfortunately." Another argued that in order to get Dangrigans to do reaping, "first you must bring the tree to town."

In contrast, Stan Rivers argued that there *were* reapers from Dangriga working at Belize Foods. If the company paid more, he suggested, there would be a lot more reapers from town. But he also asserted that the companies were reluctant to hire people from town. Many other people from Dangriga shared Stan's sentiment. In Stann Creek District unemployment stood at 23.7 percent, and fully 46 percent of the employed population worked less than full time and were considered underemployed (CSO 1984). Competition for work had been exacerbated during the 1980s by migration into the district.

Rivers commended BFP for being "willing enough to hire Belizeans." But, he said, "I've heard management from the other company say they will use whoever pushes harder. And those Salvadorans will work really hard, because they really need the job, the money. They have a lot of children. And they want to show the boss that they can do the job. So they will really push." Valerie added, "Those Salvadorans come from a hard place, so they feel like they're earning a lot in Belize, like they have it good here. But they do things that Belizeans wouldn't do—they work in conditions that a Belizean won't. Like me," she said. "I can't get a job, because I will always tell the bossman, 'No push me around. I know my rights.'" Her husband agreed, but, he added, "you can't really blame the Salvadorans, because Belizeans are going to the States to work too. But there, there is more industry, more factories. Here there are only two factories, so there is not much jobs. So if the Salvadorans take them, then what will we do?"

Here, Stan Rivers and his wife blurred the boundaries between Spanish and immigrant workers, classifying the majority of orchard workers as immigrants, or Salvadorans. Stan shifted back and forth between the argument that "the companies don't want to hire people from town" and the argument that "if they paid more, people from town would be more interested in working at the companies." These are not necessarily contradictory statements: wages have been depressed through the companies' hiring of immigrant workers and workers from other districts of Belize; the enlargement of the labor pool through Central American immigration had exerted downward pressure on wages in the citrus industry and contributed to high unemployment rates in Stann Creek District. As Stan pointed out, these circumstances made it difficult to mobilize workers for collective action in pursuit of their rights. Workers felt their jobs were not secure, and alternative employment was not readily available.

Charles Nuñez

Charles Nuñez[6] worked as a truckman on the waterfront. Drums of concentrate were trucked from the factories to the pier near Dangriga. Then each drum, weighing just over five hundred pounds, passed through the hands of the whole waterfront work gang, comprising about twenty-two men. Truckmen like Charles tipped each drum on its rim and rolled it to the edge of the truck and onto a ramp. "It's an art," he asserted, to be able to maneuver five-hundred-pound drums safely. He worked five years as a truckman before perfecting the technique required to roll the drums without getting wet or injured. "Do you know how many others we've tried to train as truckmen?" he asked. "But they always ask to do something else, because they can't do it. It's hard work, and, until you get the technique, you strain yourself a lot."

Once the drums were positioned on the ramp, runners slid the drums down the ramp and eased them onto dollies. Other runners wheeled them to the edge of the pier and attached them to the winch line. The winchman hoisted the drums and lowered them into the ship's hold, where the stevedores unhooked and stowed them. The checker recorded the amount of cargo handled and compiled records at the end of the shift to determine how much workers should be paid. A union foreman supervised the work, and a union representative formed part of each gang to handle on-the-spot negotiations with the company representative. Another waterfront worker provided an example of such on-the-spot negotiation:

> It might start to rain during a shift. The company rep might tell us "I want my cargo to move." "Yeah," we say, "but it's raining." The company rep and the union rep discuss it. Let's say we've already been working eight hours, so we're getting time and a half. When it starts to rain, the union rep sits down with the company rep to see if he could get us double time for working in the rain. If the company rep tells us he could pay us double time, we say, "Let's go, let's make some money!" And they write it down in black and white and the foreman signs it and the company rep signs it, and we start work. If not, we'll just sit down and wait for the rain to stop.

Waterfront workers' wage rates varied depending on their positions. The foreman earned the most, followed by the winchmen, checker, and union rep, who all earned the same amount. Truckmen and stevedores earned slightly lower wages, and runners made the least. However, since their pay was based on the amount of cargo they loaded collectively, workers could maximize everyone's pay by cooperating to work quickly. Workers reported making anywhere from $240 for a twelve-hour shift to $300, $400, or $500 for longer shifts or work in the rain that may be paid double time. Thus a single shift on the waterfront paid as much as or more than an orchard or factory worker earns in a week. However, stevedores generally worked only once—perhaps twice—a month during the citrus harvest. Thus, although they earned much more than other workers per shift, they did not necessarily earn more than other workers over the course of a whole harvest season, especially because there were few jobs available in Dangriga to supplement their waterfront incomes.

Charles described the waterfront workforce as "lone brethren," all Garifuna men. Though most were natives of Stann Creek District, where Belize's Garifuna population is most concentrated, Charles had been born in Guatemala to a Guatemalan mother and a Honduran father, both Garifuna. His mother had moved the family to Belize when Charles was small. However, because Charles was Garifuna, his coworkers counted him as a "brother" rather than an alien, despite his Guatemalan birth. During their waterfront shifts, workers conveyed information to one another, gave instructions, conversed, and joked in Garifuna, speaking English only when they needed to communicate with the company representative supervising the process. Thus they ethnicized their cooperation, positioning themselves simultaneously as waterfront workers and Garifuna in opposition to the company representative who could not understand their language. Waterfront work was also clearly gendered: the show of strength involved in moving the drums connoted masculinity, while the relatively high pay that dockworkers earned solidified their positions as breadwinners. For example, Charles was proud to have built a house for his family with his waterfront earnings. Another waterfront worker expressed pride that his wife did not work outside their home: "She doesn't need to," he said, "because she has a good husband who provides for her."

As we saw in chapter 3, the union had attained a great deal of control over work on the waterfront as a result of the strategic position of the waterfront in the production and export of frozen citrus juice concentrate: it decided who worked on the waterfront, when they worked, and what job they would be assigned. But Charles pointed out a number of ways in which the union's control of the waterfront created tensions within the union. For example, Charles would have liked to move into a less strenuous job that paid higher wages than his position as a truckman. Waterfront work takes a heavy toll on your body, he emphasized. He compared himself to several men who had recently been retired from the waterfront, although they were decades away from retirement age. These "young old men" were not physically able to continue the strenuous work required on the waterfront. Charles himself complained of a recurring pain in his shoulder that he treated with an over-the-counter ointment. "I used to really push the drums, because I wanted to make money," he explained. "I would move them very fast. But I'm getting old now, and I want an easier job. I don't want to kill up myself." A promotion to a less strenuous job would allow him to extend his employment on the waterfront for several more years. However, the union had not offered him a promotion. Charles felt hurt and disappointed, and he accused other members of trying to "keep him down" by not training him for a less strenuous position. He speculated that he might be more likely to be promoted if he had kin ties to union leaders.

Competition for opportunities to work also created friction among workers and between union members and leaders. Since there were more workers than there were positions in any shift, they had to take turns, and the union kept track of whose turn it was. However, when a ship arrived the union had to assemble a waterfront gang in only a few hours. Most waterfront workers did not have telephones in their homes. Some lived in a village twenty miles from Dangriga. A number cultivated small subsistence farms several miles from town, and others fished. These circumstances made it difficult for union officers to contact workers on such short notice, so workers often missed their turns to work. Since such missed opportunities represented significant financial losses to workers, it was not uncommon for workers to "rail up" at the union office, shouting complaints at union leaders when they felt they had been unfairly denied a chance to work. Missed turns complicated decisions and fueled arguments about whose turn it was each time a ship arrived.

Charles had experienced such problems many times. He had begun fishing as soon as he completed primary school at the age of twelve. He and a partner fished on the offshore cayes several days each week. After he got work on the waterfront at age eighteen, he tried to combine fishing with waterfront work. However, he often returned from fishing to discover that he had missed a turn to work a waterfront shift. Since each missed turn represented a significant financial loss, he finally quit fishing. Instead, to augment the income from his infrequent waterfront shifts, Charles began to buy fish from his neighbors; his wife used the fish to make *panades* (tortillas folded around a fish filling and fried) early each morning. Then Charles sold the panades from his bicycle on the principal streets of Dangriga.

Charles's new strategy allowed him to be available to take each waterfront shift he was offered. He estimated that he earned fifteen to twenty dollars a day with his panade sales, an amount sufficient to cover many daily living expenses; his family utilized his waterfront earnings for larger expenses. Just as Charles had carved out a niche for himself in the local informal economy, other waterfront workers also hustled jobs around town to augment their waterfront earnings. Many offered their services on construction projects that required a large crew for a day or two. However, several blamed immigrants for increasing competition for such jobs: one worker estimated that he managed to get a job doing cement work for no more than a day or two once every two or three months.

As the union's power to assign work shifts produced conflict, so did its ability to make hiring decisions. The union leadership's control over hiring on the waterfront permitted it to maintain a solidly Garifuna workforce, contributing to assertions of brotherhood and ethnic solidarity among waterfront workers. But given the high unemployment in Stann Creek District, competition for waterfront work in Dangriga was intense. As a result, Charles's service on the union's recruiting committee left him feeling frustrated and besieged. "I got a lot of pressure from my friends to include their names or members of their families on the list of recruits," he said. "People got upset if you wouldn't help them." Since the other committee members were under similar pressures, they had great difficulty agreeing on a list of new recruits. Subject to competing pressures and unable to satisfy them, Charles quit the committee. Thus, while the union's control of the waterfront contributed to ethnic solidarity among Garifuna waterfront workers, it simultaneously generated tensions among them, between the rank and file and the leadership, and among Garifuna who competed to fill positions that opened on the waterfront.

Roy Diego

Roy Diego ran the winch that hoisted drums of concentrate from the pier into the hold. At the age of forty-nine, he was one of the oldest workers on the waterfront. He had performed many other kinds of work before getting a job on the waterfront. Born in Dangriga, Roy spent his childhood in Honduras, where his father worked on a banana plantation. The family returned to Dangriga when Roy's father took ill. But his father died soon after their return, leaving Roy's mother with eight children. Though Roy finished primary school, his mother could not afford to send him to high school. Instead, he got a job as a reaper at the Citrus Company's orchards in Middlesex. During the week, he lived in company barracks at Middlesex. On weekends, he traveled the twenty-five miles back to Dangriga to give his mother his earnings. He was promoted to a job keeping records of workers' production, and later he was transferred to the factory at Pomona. During the mauger seasons between harvests, he cultivated a plot of land that had belonged to his father.

Finally, he "decided it's time to take a girl." He had a child with a young woman, but they "couldn't make it." He married another young woman, Delcia, and moved into a house on her family's property, where they began a family. In addition to supporting his wife and baby, Roy continued to give money to his mother, and sometimes he provided support for his "outside" child. "Things became tough, became very tough on me," he said, "because I wanted to please . . . everybody, when it is not a thing that I could have done."

When construction of the new capital, Belmopan, was initiated in the late 1960s, Roy found work in the construction of buildings and roads that provided a good income for nearly three years. But once the construction had been completed, he again found himself out of work and strapped for money. He still farmed his family's plot, but that was not enough to meet his growing family's needs. He managed to find short-term, "catch and kill," work in construction or forestry, earning enough to barely scrape by. But after several months without wagework, Roy decided to try to go to the United States "through the back." He was caught by immigration once and returned to Belize, but he tried again and was successful. He moved in with an aunt, found work in a supermarket, and began to send money back home to his wife and—by now—four children.

When he had saved enough money to build a house in Dangriga, Roy returned to Belize. He had gotten a promotion in the supermarket, "but man I tell you I just wouldn't want to stay in the States another day. I would really want to come home. I wanted to build a house, and then go back into farming." On his return to Dangriga, Roy managed to get hired as a stevedore on the waterfront. When a winchman retired, Roy was given the opportunity to train as his replacement. This enabled him to continue working on the waterfront until the age of forty-nine. At that age, he would no longer have been able to perform the work of a stevedore. But waterfront work was infrequent, so between shipments Roy's family depended on his farming.

Roy bicycled out to the farm almost daily to work. He planted coconuts, plantains, and ground foods—cassava and other root crops—as well as a variety of fruits and vegetables: mango, sugar cane, pumpkins, soursop, okra, cashew, pineapple, papaya. The farm provided much of the family's food, as well as a surplus that the children sold around the neighborhood: "If we don't sell that plantain, we can't buy nothing in the evening," he explained. He had also started a citrus nursery, seeing citrus as his best hope for future income. "Take the men who get severance pay when they retire," he said, "maybe $8,000. They may build a house or something with it, but when the money finish, it's done. Now if they had invested it in citrus, it would be different," he said.

In addition to Roy's income from his waterfront work and the sale of farm produce, Roy occasionally managed to get hired for brief stints as a night watchman. They had also invested in a refrigerator, and now Delcia made and sold ideals (flavoring and water frozen in small plastic bags) for five cents each out of their home. She also raised chickens for the eggs. Roy and Delcia's combination of strategies for generating income—both formal and informal, cash and subsistence oriented—was typical of waterfront workers and their families. Roy's history of migration—between Belize and Honduras, within Belize, and between Belize and the United States—was also not unusual for Garifuna families in Dangriga.

Delcia and Roy assertively identified themselves as Garifuna and displayed a strong sense that they were part of a "people." For example, when Roy once mentioned that he would like to write an autobiography, I asked him what he would write about. He replied: "Well, first of all, I would like to write about the great migration, you know, the migration of the Garinagu from St. Vincent to Honduras and again to their reaching here, to Dangriga and my involvement in it. My involvement, let's say from my birth into it, being born in Dangriga." This conception of his own life as an integral part of Garifuna history, peoplehood, and tradition was shared by his wife. Both Roy and Delcia infused their routine activities with ethnic meanings by referring them to the practices of Garifuna ancestors. They regarded his farming as the performance of a Garifuna tradition. More specifically, they imparted ethnic significance to the foods Roy produced: ground food—root crops such as cassava, coco, yams, or yampi—and plantains were central to Garifuna food traditions. Although people from many ethnic groups eat cassava, the Garifuna process it into a bread (*areba*), a symbolically charged food used in both sacred and everyday contexts (see Gonzalez 1988:107). Delcia used areba consumption to compare neighborhoods of Dangriga to one another in terms of the relative strength of their commitment to Garifuna ethnicity; she praised her own neighborhood as more Garifuna than most, because its residents produced and ate larger quantities of cassava bread. Both Delcia and Roy described their family's consumption of foods their ancestors ate as a means of affirming their own Garifuna identity and instilling that identity in their children.

Roy's class location enabled this particular construction of Garifuna tradition: his intermittent wage labor on the waterfront permitted him to engage in subsistence farming, while people who worked full time were less able to undertake either the farming or the food preparation required to eat traditionally. Another couple, who self-identified just as emphatically as Garifuna, lamented the fact that their office jobs left them without sufficient time to prepare traditional Garifuna foods on a daily basis.

Roy and Delcia also measured other people's Garifuna-ness according to the frequency with which they spoke Garifuna. They always spoke Garifuna to their children and demanded a response in Garifuna. Responses in Creole elicited immediate reprimands, and Delcia criticized parents who did not teach their children to speak the language. Like the waterfront workers on the job, Delcia often used the Garifuna language to draw Garifuna speakers into a circle of commonality and exclude those who did not understand. For Delcia and many others, greetings called to neighbors in Garifuna constituted the streets and alleys of Dangriga as Garifuna space, inverting typical relations of power by marginalizing or excluding monolingual Creole, Spanish, or English speakers.

Dangriga as a community strongly reinforced Delcia and Roy's sense of Garifuna identity. Dangriga is perceived in Belize—and presented by community leaders—as a Garifuna town. Each November the town devotes a week to celebrating Garifuna culture and identity during the days preceding the annual observation of Garifuna Settlement Day, a national holiday that commemorates the arrival of the Garifuna in Belize. Garifuna from Honduras, Guatemala, and the United States converge on Dangriga for the festivities, which encourage and congratulate the mastery of Garifuna expressive traditions. An annual Miss Garifuna Belize Pageant crowns a queen on the basis of her Garifuna-ness, which she demonstrates by speaking the Garifuna language, wearing Garifuna dress, performing Garifuna dances, and answering questions about Garifuna history and culture (Wright 1995). During the weeklong celebration, Roy and Delcia participated in a neighborhood group that performed drumming and dancing at different households in their neighborhood each night. Their group also sponsored a float that portrayed several aspects of Garifuna culture, from dance to traditional food preparation, in the Settlement Day carnival parade, winning first prize for their public performance of Garifuna identity.

However, while Roy explicitly positioned himself as part of a Garifuna people, he was skeptical of some sacred traditions that many Garifuna see as integral to their culture. For example, Roy did not accept the beliefs associated with *dugu* ceremonies, a healing ritual organized by groups of kin and presided over by a Garifuna shaman (*buyai*) to assuage the souls of deceased ancestors (see Foster 1986; Kerns 1983; Wells 1980). "Even when I was a child I didn't believe," he said. "You know, I revolted against most of these stupid ways of talking to us, about these traditions." Thus, Roy initially refused to take part in preparations for a dugu his cousin was organizing for a deceased relative. However, his cousin began to complain to neighbors and friends about his lack of support. When word of the cousin's complaints reached Delcia, she informed her husband of the talk around town. Soon thereafter he contributed to the preparations, and later he participated in the ceremony to avoid censure by the community.

Although he rejected spiritual beliefs and practices that others saw as integral to Garifuna culture, Roy claimed a Garifuna identity and described many of his own activities as Garifuna traditions: farming, eating particular foods, speaking the language, and participating in dancing and other ethnic performances during Settlement Day. This disjuncture indicated a lack of consensus within the community about what constituted Garifuna culture and tradition, though Roy's cousin used the pressure of gossip to push him toward compliance with *her* definition of Garifuna culture. Thus for Roy and Delcia, claiming a Garifuna ethnic identity involved asserting a self-identity, surveilling and evaluating the behavior of others who claimed that identity, and confronting the same techniques of surveillance and critique exercised by others over their own behavior.

These accounts demonstrate how categories of identity were manifested materially as employers, workers, and people outside the industry used them to organize activities and relationships in workplaces, homes, and communities. These workers were acutely aware of how others defined them, and the ways they were positioned by others clearly shaped the identities they claimed for themselves. Though all identified as workers, these accounts also reveal that this designation was fragmented by intersections with other dimensions of their identities and by the variety of different circumstances these workers encountered in their jobs, in terms of pay, hours, supervision, or access to union representation.

A key point of cleavage was the different organization of work between the waterfront and the valley. Over time, confrontations and negotiations between the union and the companies had generated qualitatively different relationships between workers and employers and between workers and the union in the two work locations. On the waterfront the union controlled promotions and work assignments, while in the valley the companies made such decisions. The waterfront foreman was a union member, while the valley's captains and watchimán were clearly aligned with the companies. The inclusion of a paid union representative in waterfront gangs gave waterfront workers greater leverage in negotiating work conditions and pay with management, while valley work crews—which did not include union representatives—were less able to press demands or right perceived wrongs on the job. If they wanted a higher piece rate, or if they had a conflict with a supervisor, they had to wait for a union official to negotiate on their behalf. However, a union intermediary was rarely available. Thus, valley workers often were unable to force the companies to live up to their contract obligations, for fear of being fired.

The citrus companies' hiring of immigrants and workers from other districts of Belize ethnically structured employment opportunities in the industry, as orchard work became associated with Spanish ethnicity. Those workers lumped into the Spanish category by the companies' ethnic typing recognized that they were being lumped together as Spanish (and probable "aliens"), though their number included self-identified Spanish-Belizeans, immigrants from Central America, and some who self-identified as Mopan Maya. The companies' ethnic hiring strategies also circumscribed employment opportunities for Garifuna natives of Stann Creek District, who confronted decreased opportunities for employment by enacting kin and ethnic solidarities in recruitment practices to defend their monopoly over waterfront jobs.

At the same time, differentiation of jobs by work organization, conditions, and wages contributed to further segmentation *among* both valley and waterfront workers. Orchard workers complained that their work was more physically demanding than factory work but paid less. On the waterfront, differences in wage rates and the physical exertion required across positions contributed to competition among longshoremen for promotions into the less strenuous, better-paid jobs.

The companies' hiring of a labor force in the valley that was perceived by many Garifuna and Creole natives of Stann Creek District as largely Spanish and at least partly immigrant contributed to the conflation of "Spanish" and "alien" labels. Many waterfront workers appropriated official discourse that describes agricultural laborers as immigrants, along with Afro-Belizean discourses circulating in the national arena that cast suspicion on the national origins of people classified as Spanish. They expressed suspicion—even certainty—that most groves workers were foreigners. In the context of high unemployment in Stann Creek District and competition for work, official discourses that labeled agricultural workers as "aliens" transformed interethnic competition for work into international competition in the minds of many Afro-Belizean residents of the district.[7]

The companies' hiring strategies also gendered employment opportunities in Stann Creek District, with most citrus jobs being classified as men's work. The strength seen as a requirement for jobs on the waterfront or in the groves and the control over machines involved in factory work or transport affirmed a construct of masculinity as physical mastery; the wages paid for these jobs, equal to three to five times the amount paid for women's work, enabled the people assigned to these jobs to play a breadwinner role that reinforced the "culture of gender" in Belize that casts women as wives and mothers, the economic dependents and property of men (McClaurin 1996).

These accounts reveal that employers positioned workers in ethnic and gender terms in relation to a hierarchical ordering of jobs. However, while employers' strategies shaped workers' collective identities and actions, workers also actively positioned *themselves,* negotiating sameness and difference through exchanges of pronouns and material assistance, labels and epithets. While Hugo and Elena largely accepted the "paisano" label and sought to endow it with positive meanings, many Spanish Belizeans resisted efforts to classify them as paisanos. Waterfront workers used their control over hiring on the waterfront to exercise Garifuna ethnic solidarity, hiring only ethnic "brothers." And, when company management positioned Elena as a woman, undeserving of breadwinner work, she sought to emphasize another dimension of her self-identity by claiming the position of loyal, long-serving worker.

The communities in which workers lived also positioned them. Residents of Dangriga, where most waterfront workers and a few Garifuna and Creole valley workers lived, actively affirmed Garifuna-ness and encouraged—or prodded—one another to speak, eat, and act Garifuna. The company camps positioned workers in a landscape that dramatized class difference and hierarchy. At Alta Vista, administrators' homes sprawled across the hills overlooking the factory and workers' homes below; at Pomona, Stann Creek Valley Road divided administrators and supervisory personnel from common laborers. While workers who lived in Dangriga were directly subject to their bosses only during working hours, workers who lived in the company camps were constantly under the scrutiny of their employers. Thus, living in a company camp made workers continually conscious of class differences, and workers who lived in the camps complained as frequently about the physical manifestations of class in the camps as they did about exploitation in their jobs.

Workers' accounts also demonstrate how different axes of social identity interdetermine and shape one another as they intersect. For example, Charles Nuñez's identity as a waterfront worker and the way in which he performed his job were ethnicized and gendered as Garifuna and masculine. Roy Diego's definition of what constitutes Garifuna tradition, based on the practice of subsistence agriculture, was enabled by his particular class position: his waterfront job afforded him time for agricultural work; more steady forms of employment might not. Hugo Sanchez's status as an orchard worker was integral to the way others classified him as both Spanish and alien. Elena Contreras confronted gender constructs that defined women not as wage laborers at all, but rather as housewives. Though she was the bread-winner for her family, she sometimes had difficulty gaining access to higher-wage work in the citrus industry that was gendered as masculine; at the same time, jobs designated as women's work paid too little to adequately support her family.

As a result of differences in the organization and allocation of work and the ways intersecting axes of identity modified one another, no single kind of solidarity among workers was automatic, and no single identity was accorded supreme importance by all workers across social contexts. If workers' ac-counts demonstrate how class solidarity was interrupted by national, ethnic, and gender affiliations, they reveal that ethnic solidarities were equally prob-lematic. Garifuna brethren competed among themselves for jobs, work shifts, and promotions, perhaps favoring kin over nonkin. They also contested the meaning and content of Garifuna identity. For example, though Roy and Delcia Diego described his farming as the continuation of Garifuna tradition, neither Stan nor Charles engaged in farming. At the same time, Roy rejected aspects of Garifuna ritual practice that others held sacred. And while Roy and Delcia worried about the potential decline of the Garifuna language, Stan Rivers and his wife spoke Creole with their children without concern. Similarly, while Spanish-speaking valley workers were bound together by language and by the stereotypes imposed on them, they routinely drew distinctions among themselves along village, regional, or national lines as they organized their daily interactions.

Workers who owned farms straddled a complex, contradictory set of class positions. They appreciated the security that farming provided to counter the vulnerability of their position as wage laborers in a seasonal industry. Additionally, many viewed their farms as tickets out of wage labor for the future. The use of labor on their farms increased the ambiguity of their class affiliation. Waterfront workers generally had sufficient time to tend to their farms themselves, sometimes asking family members or friends for help. But valley workers had less time available to work on their farms. While some relied on the labor of their children or other relatives, eight of the valley workers sample hired labor to clear land or maintain their citrus groves. Most hired Guatemalans, arguing that Belizean labor was too expensive. Thus, on their farms, they took advantage of the downward pressure on wages exerted by the continual flow of immigrants that hurt them in the workplace.

In these eight cases, each individual was a wage laborer, a farmer, and an employer.

Garifuna waterfront workers as well as Creole and Garifuna workers from the valley drew on African-Belizean discourses that challenged the position of Spanish people in the Belizean nation and official discourses that relegated agricultural workers to "alien" status to claim rights for themselves as more legitimate beneficiaries of Belizean national development. However, some valley workers classified as Spanish rejected official discourse that depicted workers as beneficiaries of, rather than contributors to, national development. For example, Hugo Sanchez asserted that immigrants like himself worked harder than Belizeans, perhaps contributing more to Belizean economic growth than Belizeans themselves. And workers in the company camps continually made reference to the importance of their efforts to the well-being of both the industry and their employers.

5 Brethren and Paisanos
The Mobilization of Collective Agents in Union Politics

Chapter 4 explored how workers fashioned complex, multifaceted identities for themselves through interactions at home, in their communities, and at work. The content of these interactions, ranging from competitive challenges to celebrations of solidarity, invested these identities with meaning and charged them with emotion. Chapter 4 also demonstrated that, on an everyday basis, wage laborers in the Belizean citrus industry did not constitute a homogeneous collective actor: workers. This chapter explores how people strategically deployed particular constellations of categories to mobilize collective agents during a conflict in the United General Workers Union.

Valley Workers Agitate for Improved Representation

As the UGWU's triennial convention approached in the spring of 1986, a few senior valley workers who were dissatisfied with their current representation by UGWU officers—including people from both companies and the Rowan citrus estate—turned to Marcus Cornejo, a worker at CCB, for advice on how to improve their representation. We were aware, explained one of the workers, that Cornejo knew how to organize workers, and we were ready to be organized. A fervent anticommunist, Cornejo had been involved in the formation of the Belize Workers Union in the northern sugar districts in 1982, when the sugar workers broke away from the UGWU under the patronage of a minister from the PUP right wing. Cornejo worked with the BWU in Corozal until the plant closed in 1985. Later, he had found work at Pomona with the Citrus Company of Belize, with the proviso that he not engage in union activities. The valley workers who sought Cornejo's advice also recruited Jorge Villareal, a Spanish Belizean from Cayo District, to help organize workers in the camp at Middlesex.

As we saw in chapter 4, differences in work processes and relations to the union distinguished employment in the valley from work on the waterfront. Waterfront work gangs included a union representative, paid for by the company, to handle on-the-spot negotiations or disagreements, while valley work crews did not. Thus, valley workers relied on union officers to travel up the valley from their office in Dangriga to represent them in conflicts with employers or supervisors or to negotiate increased pay rates for especially difficult work. The disgruntled valley workers who sought assistance from Cornejo and Villareal complained that the UGWU failed to do this. One valley worker asserted, "When you would call on the union officers to solve a problem, it took them about a week, two weeks, and by then it's too late."[1]

Dissatisfaction with the UGWU's representation was compounded by ethnic segmentation between the waterfront and valley, and the fact that all union officers were Garifuna waterfront workers from Dangriga. This combination led many valley workers to characterize the UGWU as an entity that "belonged to" the Garifuna from town in the way that some bars and bus seats did. Further, Spanish-speaking valley workers believed that racial and ethnic considerations led the Garifuna union officers to treat them differently. Elena Contreras's son complained that, when UGWU officers did come up the valley, "they only talked to the Blacks [morenos]. The Black reapers got the best areas, with the most fruit," he charged. The leaders never talked with the Spanish speakers, he added. "That's why we decided we wanted a change: we weren't getting the same attention that the Blacks were getting from the union." Many Spanish-speaking workers felt unable to adequately explain their concerns to non-Spanish speakers. Beyond this, since their Belizeanness was so often publicly called into question on busses and streets, Spanish speakers were well aware that many Garifuna residents of Stann Creek District perceived them as aliens. Thus, many Spanish workers—both immigrants and Spanish Belizeans—suspected that union leaders neglected Spanish-speaking valley workers, because they too assumed those workers were immigrants.

Simultaneous Mobilization of Opposition to Union Leadership

As the UGWU convention approached, another group also began to mobilize workers in opposition to the union's current leadership. The four men spearheading this effort were not employed in the citrus industry, nor were they UGWU members. Cedric Hernandez was a high school teacher in Dangriga, and Peter Ramirez taught primary school in Middlesex. Oscar Samuels worked as a conductor on the local bus line. He and Sylvester Williams, who was unemployed, had worked for the Citrus Company earlier, but they had been dismissed from their jobs. All four men were Garifuna, and all four were seeking election to the union Executive at the upcoming convention. They had recently applied for membership in the UGWU, but the current UGWU Executive had rejected their applications. The general secretary of the UGWU affirmed that the men had applied for membership in the UGWU. However, the union Executive had "directed the two teachers to the union most able to serve them: the teachers union." The other two men, he explained, had been fired from the Citrus Company for their own wrongdoing. "They had no interest in the union while they were working at CCB. Now they do. But since they're not working in the citrus industry, we turned them down."

Hernandez explained that he had become involved with efforts to mobilize citrus workers after "a group of dissatisfied people" had come to him with "certain problems they wanted addressed." "So," he explained, "we all got together to see how we could work out their problems." He had served as an officer in the union during the mid-1970s, under the leadership of Mishek Mawema. But, Hernandez explained, he left for the United States in 1978 to pursue a master's degree. After Mawema left, union leaders had compromised too much, too easily, he charged. Making reference to his university degree, he argued, "I don't think CCB or BFP could manipulate us like they manipulated these guys." Hernandez also complained that union officers' rejection of his application for membership and those of his cohorts was a violation of the Trade Union Ordinance clause that guarantees a worker's right to join a union.[2]

Hernandez further charged the union Executive with corruption in connection with a lawsuit the union had brought against CCB over severance payments. The lawsuit stemmed from a dispute that arose when the Citrus Company of Belize was sold in 1983. The new shareholders claimed that the former shareholders had assured them they would not be liable for severance payments to the company's employees for the years they had worked prior to

1983. The union took the company to court over this stance and won: the court declared that the company was obligated to live up to its severance agreement, regardless of a change in ownership of the company's shares. This victory led many workers to speculate that they would soon receive a lump sum payment for the years they had worked for the company under its previous ownership. Since most workers lived close to the margin, the prospect of obtaining such a sum was very exciting. Many elaborated plans for how they would invest the payment: build a house, begin a farm, emigrate to the United States. However, payments were not forthcoming, for two reasons. First, the union's severance agreement with the company stipulated that severance payments were to be made only when workers retired or were made redundant. Thus, for most workers, the resolution of the lawsuit meant that the years they had worked before the company was sold would be added into the calculations for their severance payment on their retirement. Second, the company claimed that it had insufficient funds to pay workers who had already retired or been made redundant, and it filed suit against the previous shareholders to recover the costs of severance payments for workers' pre-1983 service. Opposition mobilizers played on workers' disappointment that payments for their pre-1983 service had not yet materialized, speculating that union leaders may have stolen the money the court had awarded to workers.

As disgruntled valley workers sought new leadership to improve their representation, these Garifuna men offered themselves as potential leaders. The four Garifuna men began to cooperate with workers in the valley mobilizing for change. Together, they conducted a series of meetings in the work camps in the weeks leading up to the UGWU convention. They criticized the UGWU leadership for "totally neglecting" valley workers, failing to produce the severance payments workers had long awaited, and violating Belizean law in denying these four men membership. Hernandez also criticized the union's ties to Cuba and other Communist countries.

Just a few days before the union's convention, these four Garifuna men distributed an "open letter to labourers" announcing their intention to impeach the governing body of the UGWU in response to "petitions from quite a number of you to act on your behalf." These many currents of tension became obvious as workers assembled for the union convention.

The Union Convention

The convention was held on a Sunday morning in May at a primary school in
Dangriga. When I arrived, a large crowd was waiting outside while the union
officers opened the building. I struck up a conversation in Spanish with a
man who had come from Middlesex for the meeting. As people began to enter
the schoolroom, word passed through the crowd that people whose dues
were not current would not be allowed to enter. The man from Middlesex
appeared concerned: he had not been paying dues for several months, he
explained, because he had been hospitalized with an injury. The announcement about dues payments seemed to provoke several Garifuna men, who
began to complain about the union officers: the officers have the money for
the severance payments, but they don't want to share it with the workers,
one man charged. Another claimed that dues had been deducted from his pay
but not recorded on his membership card. "Where is that money I paid?" he
demanded. Opposition leaders circulated through the crowd, talking to people
as they filed into the schoolroom. As the mood of the crowd—both valley and
waterfront workers—became increasingly antagonistic toward the union leaders, the man from Middlesex standing next to me changed his story: he *had*
been paying dues, but his payments had not been recorded on his dues card.

As workers filed into the meeting hall, waterfront workers—all
Garifuna—sat together on the right side of the hall, while the larger, predominantly Spanish-speaking contingent of workers from the valley assembled
themselves on the left side. Since they outnumbered the chairs that had been
set out, a large group of Spanish remained standing on the left side of the
room, making it obvious that Spanish workers outnumbered the Garifuna.

The Garifuna union officers assembled on the stage and played a record-
ing of the national anthem to open the convention. After the anthem, the
general secretary promised that the majority would rule and urged the members to resolve their differences as brothers. Jorge Villareal, one of the opposition leaders from Middlesex, offered to translate the officers' reports from
English into Spanish for the workers on the left. His translations injected a
negative slant that encouraged heckling from the Spanish-speaking audience. For example, the union president explained that the union's progress
on the CCB case had been slow, because of the legal intricacies of the case
and the large sum of money involved. Villareal summarized in Spanish, "We
didn't accomplish much in these three years," without elaborating. Spanish

workers laughed in agreement. During the general secretary's report, Villareal claimed he was unable to translate a charge that outsiders were attempting to take over the union. He continued to insert criticisms into the portions he was able to translate, eliciting approving responses from the left side of the hall and concern from some who could understand Spanish on the right side.

Following the general secretary's report, a rumbling began among the crowd standing on the left of the hall, and two Garifuna opposition leaders—Peter Ramirez and Sylvester Williams—entered the hall. They marched to the edge of the stage where the Executive was seated and took up positions there.

The officers resumed the meeting with the treasurer's report, which elicited a rising chorus of catcalls and complaints as workers questioned the union's bookkeeping and expenditures of funds. When nominations for officers were opened, one Garifuna union member sought clarification of whether or not nonmembers could be elected to the Executive. Presiding union officials declared that the nomination of nonmembers would violate the union's constitution. Sylvester Williams shouted in response, "We applied for membership!" Jorge Villareal stepped to the stage and declared, "El pueblo manda" ("The people rule"), and Spanish-speaking workers began to shout that they would change the constitution and elect whomever they wanted. Bedlam erupted, as supporters of the union leadership struggled with supporters of the opposition for control of the meeting, the microphone, and the blackboard on which nominations were to be recorded.

Everyone rose and surged forward, many crowding onto the stage. On the floor, workers began to argue with one another in groups of twos and threes, shouting and gesturing emphatically. Behind me, one Garifuna man chided another, "You should know better than to follow a trouble-making group like this. This is the time for Garifuna to unite against the fucking paisanos trying to grab power!"

Unable to restore order, the union leaders announced over the PA system that they were postponing elections. They declared the convention closed, and one union leader placed the names of the current officers on the blackboard next to their respective titles. The opposition erased the names and tried to write in their own. A union officer erased the board again. With the workers still shouting at one another, a union officer wrote "convention postponed" on the board. The opposition erased that declaration and wrote "convention open" in its place. Union officers took down the PA system and shut the windows. The opposition opened the windows. Throughout this struggle, Jorge Villareal controlled the Spanish crowd with his hands, leading their shouts, quieting them with a gesture.

Finally the two Dangriga police officers assigned to the meeting began to close the building, and the union officers left, followed by their supporters. One of the opposition leaders convinced the valley workers to leave, and they filed out slowly, threatening to shut down the union office.

Making Sense of the Convention

On the Monday following the aborted convention, some of the people most alarmed by the rumors about the events of the previous day were processing company administrators and directors. Wesley Spencer, the general manager of the Citrus Company of Belize arrived at his office that Monday morning to confront wild rumors about the union's convention: thousands of dollars were missing from the union's accounts; the keys for the union office had been handed over to the police; the union's books had been confiscated; a "coup" had taken place. Spencer immediately called the district labor inspector to stake out his company's position and seek more information about what had happened. "We just signed a new two-year contract, and it's binding!" he thundered over the phone. "We won't back down!" He and his company's directors feared that the new union leaders might try to show their strength by rejecting the recently negotiated contract with the companies or by calling a strike. Then he demanded, "What's going on?" The labor inspector could tell him little, as she had not attended the convention. But by early afternoon she called him to report that the labor commissioner in Belmopan had assured her that no coup had taken place. The union would have to meet again to complete its elections, but no call for a representational poll had been issued.

A week later, as I talked with Spencer and CCB director Arthur Rowan, they analyzed the man they saw as the leader of the four Garifuna who had emerged as the public spokespersons of the opposition movement. "Hernandez is a radical guy," Spencer asserted. "He's a troublemaker." "Communist?" asked Arthur Rowan, attempting to make sense of the union conflict by placing it in a global cold war context. "Well," responded Spencer, "when CCB was sponsoring the football team from Dangriga, there was a game in Cayo. And Hernandez told the players not to go, unless they got paid!" Whether or not this reflected communist tendencies was left unstated. Ironically, though

Hernandez was railing against union leaders' ties to socialist countries, casting them as dangerous radicals on the wrong side of the cold war, his own demand that Dangriga soccer players insist on payment for playing out of town earned him the label of "radical," which was quickly translated into "communist" in the cold war context of the mid-1980s.

On the Waterfront

If employers were frightened by the conflict that had erupted at the union convention, how did workers make sense of the confrontation, given their multiple positionings and the various possibilities for conflict or alliance presented? During the convention and in the days that followed, citrus workers identified and aligned themselves along a number of axes of difference: as rank-and-file workers opposing union leaders, valley workers challenging the waterfront, Spanish confronting Garifuna, and Belizeans defending their jobs and union against "aliens." Through conversations, posted signs, heated arguments, and public meetings following the aborted convention, waterfront leaders and leaders of the valley workers elaborated competing interpretations that bound together particular identities and urged particular courses of action.

Prior to the convention, some Garifuna waterfront workers had voiced complaints about the union leadership's handling of finances and the lawsuit with CCB. Several railed about missing dues payments and long-awaited severance payments on their way into the meeting hall. However, outnumbered by Spanish workers in the meeting, many Garifuna waterfront workers became concerned that control of the union Executive, and therefore control of the waterfront, might pass into Spanish hands. Thus, when the meeting broke up, they began to urge their Garifuna coworkers to drop their quarrels with the union's leadership and unite along ethnic lines to prevent a Spanish takeover. Such arguments also animated conversations on Dangriga's main street in the days following the convention: for instance, two Garifuna waterfront workers argued in front of the union office, with one expressing support for the opposition and demanding a change in the union's leadership. The other responded, "I want a change too, but not from bad to worse!"

The day after the convention the union office was busy, as workers and union leaders came and went, discussing and arguing about what had happened the day before and offering varying interpretations of the conflict. Some men cast the conflict as a showdown between valley workers and waterfront workers, while others pointed to the way racial/ethnic differences mapped onto the two locales. Ethnic segmentation of the industry's labor force and distinctions in work organization between the valley and the waterfront shaped many Garifuna dockworkers' responses to the challenge posed by valley workers at the convention. Garifuna dockworkers warned each other that, since union officers controlled hiring and work assignments on the waterfront, Garifuna waterfront workers needed to maintain control of the union's leadership or risk losing their jobs. They feared that if the Spanish controlled the union leadership, they might not hire Garifuna. After all, the Garifuna had built and protected their ethnic enclave on the waterfront by recruiting kin and ethnic "brothers"; the Spanish might do likewise. Charles Nuñez, who had his own complaints about union leaders' failure to promote him, was frightened by this possibility: "The Spanish wanted to take over the Executive," he explained. "But the Executive controls the waterfront. So if the Spanish took over the Executive, the Garifuna might lose their jobs; the Spanish could decide who would work. So we had to make a riot at the convention to prevent the Spanish from going through with the takeover." Concerned waterfront workers emphasized this danger to Garifuna dissenters, who had supported the opposition's demands for a change in the union's leadership. Their warning sought to mobilize waterfront workers both as longshoremen and as Garifuna "brothers," to protect their jobs.

While some waterfront workers characterized the union conflict as a confrontation between Black and Spanish workers, or between Stann Creek and Cayo people, others drew on national-level discourses that portrayed Spanish workers as invading aliens to suggest that all of the Spanish workers were immigrants. Such discourses made sense to dockworkers fearful of losing their jobs. One waterfront worker expressed a common sentiment: "There are lots up there [in the valley] from El Salvador, Guatemala. They say they are from Cayo, but cho, that's not true!" If Spanish speakers constituted the majority at the convention, calling them "aliens" or "paisas" questioned the legitimacy of their demands and denied them the rights conferred by Belizean citizenship, the right to aspire to union leadership in Belize or a share of the benefits of Belizean development, for instance.

However, a number of people at the union office defined the valley workers as aliens but suggested that "the poor things" did not really understand the struggle into which they had been recruited. "They're being used," one man asserted. An older man agreed, adding, "There's politics here." He reported hearing rumors of payoffs to opposition supporters by the United Democratic Party. Indeed, UGWU leaders described the opposition movement led by nonunion members as an attempted coup that the UDP had orchestrated to gain control of a union viewed as aligned with the Peoples United Party. The opposition leader Hernandez was head of the liquor licensing committee in Dangriga, a political appointment that indicated he enjoyed good standing in the party in government, the UDP. The fact that the police allowed the opposition leaders to enter the convention was taken as further evidence of the UDP government's involvement. Roy Diego reported that "a teacher" had told him that he was being paid to break up the union. "I told him, 'You will not break up the union; you will break up your *people!*'" he said, appealing for Garifuna solidarity.

UGWU leaders suggested that the UDP had funded and fomented the opposition movement to pursue a dual political agenda. On the one hand, the general secretary suspected that the UDP was responding to CIA pressure: "The CIA's idea is to get rid of communists and that's directed against me." Indeed, the U.S. embassy officer responsible for monitoring labor in Belize had explicitly positioned the UGWU leader as "a communist," which would have been troubling to the UDP, self-described as "unabashedly pro-American."

UGWU leaders also argued that the UDP was unhappy that several of the union's officers were currently active in local politics as PUPs. One UGWU officer (clearly a PUP) charged: "Two executive members are on the Town Board as PUP, and the general secretary has always been viewed as PUP. They want UDP leaders. With UDP leadership the union could be useful to them later on in campaigns, elections." Another officer concurred: "With this regime, their position is that heads of organizations should be UDP."

"Who did the UDP want to install as leaders?" I asked.

"They don't give a goddamn who goes in there so long as those elected will be under their control," he responded. He suggested that the UDP had channeled funds to some of its local loyalists to enable them to buy support. "What is dangerous," he added, "is that . . . if there are certain affairs of Belizeans that should remain with Belizeans, they will automatically be handed into the hands of foreigners. If you noticed there on Sunday, the amount of people that were behind these opposition, there are very few Belizeans among them. . . . That is why I say the opposition do not give a damn who is up there so long as they are within their reach. So gradually Belizean business will automatically fall into the hands of foreigners."

This man believed, along with many others, that the Spanish speakers in the opposition were immigrants, and that the UDP was using them for its own ends. Charges that the UDP was involved in the opposition movement further invalidated that movement's claims in the eyes of many dockworkers, especially those who were PUPs. And it provided the last strand of the argument elaborated by the union's leadership and waterfront workers who supported them: they accused the ruling party of manipulating aliens in order to take over the union. This definition of valley workers as alien pawns of party politics rendered their movement illegitimate and inauthentic, a UDP strategy to expand its own power rather than an attempt by valley workers to obtain more effective union representation. However, if waterfront workers delegitimized the opposition movement with these accusations, it was the fear that a Spanish-dominated union Executive might not give them work that motivated many of them to unite behind the union's Garifuna leadership.

In the Courts

While waterfront workers argued and accused in conversations at the union office, the opposition tried to clarify its own positions and enlarge its following by posting signs on a storefront on Dangriga's main street. One sign listed a set of grievances and demands: "1. We need new man. 2. Where was this union at the sellout? Where is our cutoff pay? 3. Away with Cuba. 4. Down with prejudice. 5. No more bribes. 6. Stop selling our brothers' blood." Point number one called for new leadership. Point two questioned the union's handling of negotiations over severance payments at the time CCB was sold and raised questions about what had happened to workers' severance payments after the court decision in the union's favor. It evoked the accusations heard prior to the meeting, and in opposition lobbying in the valley, that union officers had misappropriated the funds. Point three called for the UGWU to break its relations with socialist trade union federations and Communist countries, in line with the dominant cold war rhetoric of the time. The remaining points accused union leaders of both discrimination and corruption. Cedric Hernandez explained that the sign reflected the complaints and demands valley workers had expressed during meetings in the work camps prior to the convention.

Leaving these signs to speak for them in Dangriga, the Garifuna teachers traveled to the capital to seek advice and support from the Labour Department. Opposition leaders urged the labor commissioner to take an active role in the dispute, but he refused to take action on their behalf. "How would it look?" the commissioner asked me in an interview. "Later people would say the government came down and installed their own officers." Personnel from the Labour Department described the opposition's efforts as politically motivated —backed by the UDP—and expressed doubts that it had the best interests of workers at heart.

The opposition proposed to physically take over the union office, but the labor commissioner advised against it. The action would be illegal, he explained, and the union Executive could bring charges against them. A conviction would jeopardize their goals. He agreed with the UGWU Executive that it was against the union's constitution to allow nonmembers to vote or hold office. Under the union's constitution, he explained, the leadership could stall for up to a year before holding another meeting. Thus, he recommended that the opposition submit to the national UGWU a petition requesting that elections be held at a specific date and time, with 51 percent of the members' signatures. Alternatively, the opposition could request a representational poll. If they won 51 percent of the votes, they could form a second union. But then they would have no access to the UGWU's assets and property. Cedric Hernandez rejected the latter proposal: "They say we can form our own union and have a poll. But then we wouldn't be able to take over the union's books, and we want to see the discrepancies we know are there."

Subsequently, opposition leaders became divided over goals and strategies. Rather than taking the labor commissioner's advice to petition for a new convention, the teachers launched a lawsuit against the union Executive. Meanwhile, Cornejo and Villareal launched a more aggressive organizing campaign in the valley, with an entirely different end in mind: the formation of a new union.

Up the Valley

Ironically, the United Democratic Party's involvement in the opposition may have been more apparent to waterfront workers from Dangriga, who were familiar with local politics and affiliations, than to the majority of valley workers who were from outside the district. Many workers in the valley, including Elena Contreras, were unaware of the Garifuna teachers' role in the emerging opposition movement. Other valley workers were more aware of those figures' involvement in both the valley movement and partisan politics, describing that involvement as "a political thing." "Government was trying to get control of the union," explained one. Another argued that valley workers cooperated with the UDP-linked leaders because "the valley was ready for change, but we didn't know how to go about it ourselves."

Indeed, one worker who had supported the opposition prior to the convention was even more indignant about the UGWU leadership after the convention. I recently had a problem with my employer, he explained. "I went in to the union office to ask them to speak to him. They said they'd be out the next day, but they never went out there at all. Sometimes they would just tell you, 'We don't have time.' Now, I think a union officer should always have time, especially if you're getting paid to be a union officer. And at the convention we found out that we had spent twenty thousand dollars for a pickup. We paid for that pickup, and we expected they would at least use it to come out here and see what was going on!"

Some workers explained that, prior to the union convention, valley workers had supported all of the opposition leaders: the Garifuna teachers and the bus conductor from town, Jorge Villareal from Middlesex, and several men who had helped to initiate the movement in Alta Vista and Pomona, including Marcos Cornejo. But after the convention, the Garifuna men no longer held meetings with workers in the valley.

When a few disgruntled workers from the orchards and transport began to visit Cornejo to discuss how to form a new union, a company spy who lived near Cornejo in the camp at Pomona reported his activities to management, and the company fired him. Out of a job, Cornejo traveled to northern Belize to request support and a loudspeaker from the Belize Workers Union, whose membership had dropped to four hundred with the closure of the Corozal sugar factory (Shoman 1987b:22). With only the Orange Walk branch remaining, the BWU supported Cornejo's plan to reorganize citrus workers into another branch of the BWU. Cornejo returned to the Stann Creek Valley and began working with those individuals from the valley who had spearheaded the opposition, holding meetings several nights a week in the camps. One worker actively involved in these efforts explained, "We had meetings every night—Middlesex, Cow Creek, Salada, Rowan, Pomona—all up and down the valley, telling the workers what they could do to form their own union."

In advocating withdrawal from the UGWU and the formation of a separate union to represent valley workers, they invoked the particular problems valley workers encountered on the basis of their distinct relation to the union and the companies. Unable to press their demands as effectively as waterfront gangs, which include a union representative paid by the company, valley workers depended on the union to send an officer out to represent them in conflicts with employers or supervisors or to negotiate increased pay rates for especially difficult work. Cornejo promised more active representation, with a union office in the valley. Cornejo himself had attended the 1986 UGWU convention and become convinced that valley workers could not elect new officers and take over the UGWU. "We could vote them out of office, but they wouldn't go, because they saw it as *their* union. But those officers never came up here. . . . So after the meeting, I began to tell the workers here that it's the same thing if they vote for these four guys: they're Garifuna from town. I said we can't take over that union. We can only form a new one or a branch of another existing union. But we need officers from the valley." Thus, Cornejo emphasized ethnicity and place in predicting that electing Garifuna men from town would not solve valley workers' problems. His argument tapped into valley workers' perception that the current UGWU leadership—all "Garifuna from town"—had not adequately addressed their concerns and the suspicions of Spanish speakers that there were ethnic motivations behind this lack of attention.

Cornejo, Villareal, and their supporters—whose number included Creoles as well as Spanish—focused their efforts on the Spanish-speaking majority. As chapter 4 demonstrated, valley workers recognized important distinctions among themselves in terms of work situations, pay, and ethnicity; the majority classified as Spanish routinely enacted distinctions among themselves on the basis of narrower village, regional, or national affiliations. However, it appeared to Spanish-speaking valley workers that employers had lumped them together in assigning them work, and many asserted that union officers had conflated Spanish and alien categories to marginalize the concerns of orchard workers, in spite of their numerical dominance in the union. Cornejo's argument in favor of forming a new union made sense to valley workers who had viewed the UGWU as the property of Dangriga's primarily Garifuna inhabitants. Pedro Ruiz explained that valley workers had wanted to elect representatives from the valley to the union Executive at the convention. But "it didn't work, because people from Stann Creek wanted to maintain control of the union." He continued: "Cornejo explained how we could choose a union to look after our interests." (Since Cornejo professed to being a loyal PUP, his campaign against the Garifuna aspirants to UGWU leadership also may have reflected their different party affiliations. At this time, Cornejo's efforts reflected his need for a job as well.)

Jorge Villareal and Marcus Cornejo also used language to target and mobilize Spanish-speaking groves workers. Addressing workers' complaints and needs in Spanish was itself empowering to Spanish-speaking workers who might never have spoken to the Garifuna UGWU leaders because of limited facility in Creole or English. However, at the same time, the Spanish Belizean organizers' ability to speak Creole with workers from other ethnic groups helped to prevent those workers from viewing their movement as exclusively Spanish. Many Creole and Garifuna workers, including Stan Rivers, supported the opposition. "If you have a problem," he complained, UGWU officers "never came up the valley in time to fix it. They would say they're busy." However, one Creole worker from BFP in my random sample adamantly opposed efforts to form a second union. Describing the people who wanted to "change the union" as Spanish orchard workers from the camps at Pomona and Middlesex, he complained, "They're the ones who spoiled it. I never saw any reason to change."

Though Cedric Hernandez claimed that the sign posted on Dangriga's main street following the convention reflected valley workers' concerns, the demand for a break with Cuba and with socialist trade union federations was never mentioned as a concern in any of my conversations with workers, either in the valley or in town. Only Marcus Cornejo and Hernandez himself ever identified the UGWU's socialist connections as a worry. Marcus Cornejo had played the role of anti-communist earlier in the north, when he was involved in ousting the supposed communists from leadership of the cane workers union (when that union was UGWU). The UGWU's socialist affiliations would have been a cause for alarm and embarrassment for the UDP, to which Hernandez belonged, which was preoccupied with casting Belize as a valuable ally of the United States in the circum-Caribbean region. Since the communist bogeyman was the object of daily attacks at that time in the U.S. media, the source of most Belizean television programming, Belizeans were receiving indoctrination in anticommunist ideology in regular doses along with the Chicago weather forecasts. Given this context, it is interesting that none of the workers themselves invoked either communism or anti-communism in explaining the conflict or the positions they took.

Convention, Part Two

Six weeks after the first convention, the UGWU reconvened to complete the election of officers. This time workers from the camps at Pomona and Middlesex did not attend: most had stopped paying dues after the first convention and were no longer members. The Garifuna opposition leaders from Dangriga tried to enter the hall, but the secretary, who was checking union cards at the door, turned them away. They established themselves in the park across the street from the meeting hall, where they chanted, "We want our rights!" and "College graduates not kindergarten graduates!" The first demand referred to the union officers' rejection of their applications for membership, which they claimed violated their right to join a union, as guaranteed by Belizean law. The second demand alluded to Hernandez's higher education in the United States.

Inside the meeting hall, the crowd was rather small. Nevertheless, signs of discord were obvious: several young Garifuna men paced back and forth in the back of the hall, occasionally shouting "Out!" in apparent reference to the union officers. Against this background, the national UGWU president convened the meeting by chiding workers for fighting among themselves. When he opened nominations for the union Executive, the current secretary general announced that he would not run for office again. The young men in the back of the hall continued to rail, but no one offered a nomination. One man grumbled that the people they wanted to elect were not allowed to enter. Then, as if on cue, three Garifuna leaders of the opposition marched in— Peter Ramirez, Oscar Samuels, and Sylvester Williams, accompanied by Jorge Villareal from Middlesex. They made a triumphant entrance to applause, though much of the applause was their own. The UGWU secretary, stationed at the door to check the union dues cards of those who sought to enter, later claimed that the police had allowed the opposition leaders to enter the hall, after they promised not to cause a disruption. However, when the president asked all nonmembers to leave, once again everyone began to shout, to argue, to rail. Unable to restore order, the president again postponed the elections and declared that the current Executive would remain in power until elections were held.

The Resolution

After the second attempted convention, the Garifuna opposition leaders continued their lawsuit against the UGWU's officers, which they ultimately lost. However, even though the Garifuna opposition leaders lost momentum when they moved their attack on the union Executive into the courts, opposition organizers in the valley generated increasing momentum as they campaigned in the company camps. Their appeals mobilized the vast majority of valley workers *as* valley workers and the "Spanish" majority as an ethnic constituency by establishing the legitimacy of their demands and promising to address those demands. By year's end, valley workers petitioned for a representational poll and voted by an overwhelming margin to secede from the UGWU and form a new branch of the Belize Workers Union, the union that represented sugar industry workers in northern Belize.

Solidarity among those who had been classified together as "aliens" emerged as a response to that categorization and its materialization in the differential treatment accorded them by the union. Immigrant workers and Spanish Belizeans' experience of being lumped together as aliens had not convinced them that they were "the same." However, it had convinced them that they shared the consequences of this positioning in union inattention to their concerns and priorities. At the same time, emerging leaders promised timely union representation to resolve disputes with the companies, addressing a problem shared by orchard and factory workers across ethnic and national boundaries. Thus, making their arguments in both Creole and Spanish languages, they mobilized an alliance that incorporated the majority of workers in the valley. After forming a new union, valley workers elected representatives from the different work areas in the valley—factories, groves, transport—to lead the union, producing a union executive whose members' ethnic identities reflected the ethnic segmentation that characterizes the different types of work—comprising Spanish, Creole, and Garifuna—in the hope that these leaders would be more attentive to their specific needs.

The conflict hinged on the strategic use of categories of identity to define workers and their interests. Neither class nor ethnic solidarity could be taken for granted; rather, solidarities had to be actively constructed and continually shored up. Would-be leaders sought to locate potential followers in specific subject positions and attribute to them particular sets of interests.

Leading up to the convention, an alliance of convenience between valley leaders, teachers, and others mobilized a broad swath of the union's rank and file, with varied grievances, in opposition to the union Executive. Dissatisfied workers sought new leadership to address their complaints; would-be leaders sought to attract and mobilize followers by publicly recognizing their grievances—or by recommending issues around which grievances could be generated. (Aspiring leaders with ties to the ruling United Democratic Party thus pursued a dual UDP agenda to expand the party's influence in the region and to please the United States by mobilizing workers to oppose the Communist ties of the current UGWU leadership.)

However, outnumbered by "Spanish" workers in the meeting hall, some waterfront workers began to fear that the election of a Spanish majority to the union Executive would transfer control of work on the waterfront into Spanish hands. As this recognition dawned, many began to cajole their ethnic "brothers" to drop their quarrels with the union's leadership and unite as Garifuna against efforts by Spanish valley workers to attain representation on the Executive. For waterfront workers, their ethnic identities and their fear that Spanish union leaders might not assign them work—since the union's leadership controls such decisions on the waterfront—provided impetus for many of them to pull together to protect their jobs, in spite of their earlier complaints about the union leadership. While those who sought to retain Garifuna control over the waterfront rallied sufficient numbers to prevent valley workers from taking control of the union meeting and electing a valley slate of officers, they never succeeded in uniting all Garifuna waterfront workers behind them. Some persisted in the criticisms of union officials they had voiced as the convention began. Indeed, the elaboration of a discourse to mobilize Garifuna solidarity and delegitimize the demands of valley workers was seen as necessary precisely as a response to Garifuna participation in the opposition movement.

Following the aborted convention, two competing interpretations of the union conflict emerged through conversations, posted signs, heated arguments, and public meetings. Leaders seeking to mobilize support emphasized commonalities among the diverse experiences and interests of those they sought to lead and defined their opponents in terms that powerfully evoked fear or anger among their constituents. Waterfront leaders drew on official discourses that portrayed agricultural workers as immigrants and concerns about political party involvement in the dispute to label the predominantly Spanish/Mestizo valley workers as alien pawns of party politics, diminishing the legitimacy of their demands. At the same time they played on fears of a Spanish takeover of the waterfront to mobilize Garifuna workers to defend their waterfront jobs.

Opposition leaders pursued divergent strategies. While the Garifuna men launched a lawsuit against the union Executive, hoping to ultimately take control of the UGWU, other opposition leaders worked to mobilize valley work-

ers into a new union. Cornejo and Villareal emphasized the insufficient attention union officers had paid to the concerns of valley workers and the ethnic
dimension of this inattention perceived by the Spanish-speaking majority. Among
Spanish-speaking valley workers, unity was not preexisting, since they routinely enacted distinctions among themselves, as chapter 4 demonstrated. However, Spanish workers' perception that UGWU officers had conflated "Spanish" and "alien" categories and discriminated against all of them as aliens
provided impetus for their alliance. Some Maya workers also expressed suspicions that union leaders saw them as Spanish and alien. Although Creole
and Garifuna workers in the valley did not share the same perceptions of
ethnic discrimination, opposition leaders gave voice to problems common to
both groves and factory workers that arose from their distinct relationship to
the union in comparison with waterfront workers: both groves and factory
workers complained about delays in the union's response to disagreements
over wages or conflicts with employers and the lack of a union presence in
the valley. The perception of common problems led both sets of workers to
seek a common solution through alliance, and thus the opposition's promises
also won the support of many—though never all—Afro-Belizean workers in
the valley.

The United Democratic Party, pursuing the traditional path of political
party-union relations in Belize as it attempted to install party loyalists at the
head of the UGWU, had some initial success in defining the issues that mobilized the UGWU's rank and file against its partially PUP-affiliated leadership.
However, the party was unable to maintain a coalition of valley and waterfront workers under its direction. Opposition leaders linked to the UDP were
unable to achieve their own narrow political goal of taking over the UGWU,
because valley workers were more concerned with gaining effective union
representation than with taking control of the UGWU or severing the union's
socialist affiliations. Thus, valley workers responded enthusiastically to the
UDP-inspired leaders' overtures, but they went far beyond those leaders to
create their own union when their demands for representation within the
UGWU were thwarted.[3]

Workers' decisions to organize their struggles around ethnic identities
and interests reflected the ways nonclass identities had manifested themselves materially in their lives, the ways in which their *class* positions had
been shaped by their intersections with ethnic and national positions. They
did not fail to recognize that they shared some interests as wage laborers;

rather, valley workers felt that the union leadership was not addressing their more specific interests. Valley workers acted in this case to redress intraclass inequalities that had become largely ethnicized.

The events that led to the division of the UGWU illustrate the complex interplay between official discourses that attempt to impose particular angles of vision and the discourses workers generate to interpret the circumstances they confront. Garifuna waterfront workers, trying to protect their jobs in a district characterized by high levels of unemployment and high levels of Spanish immigration, drew on discourses that circulated in the national arena to define the predominantly Spanish agricultural workers as aliens and, consequently, to reject their demands for greater representation in the union's leadership. Involvement by the UDP also diverted attention away from the concerns of valley workers. On the other hand, valley workers resisted the definitions imposed on them by official discourses, challenging both official development policies and the arguments elaborated to justify them. Spanish Belizeans rejected attempts to strip them of citizenship and convert them into aliens simply because they worked in agriculture. Further, their perception that both the companies and the union leadership had lumped them together with Spanish immigrants generated a degree of solidarity with those immigrants. Spanish immigrants themselves asserted rights and demands in spite of their lack of Belizean citizenship. Hugo Sanchez cast immigrants as major contributors to Belizean development, since the citrus industry could not function without their hard work. While this assertion echoed the claims of politicians that Belizean agro-industries depended on immigrant labor for their survival, it went far beyond the aims of those politicians in its demand for recognition, rights, and representation for immigrant workers. Significantly, valley workers from other ethnic groups and from the factories supported the claims of the Spanish majority—without regard for their nation of origin—and joined in a coalition with them to demand that the problems of representation they shared as valley workers be addressed. (Though some dissenters rejected the movement and continued to complain about the outcome.)

This conflict was one episode in a continual struggle between employers and workers in the industry, and among workers differentiated by the material manifestations of crosscutting identities. Employers used strategies of hiring immigrant labor and segmenting the workforce by job type and ethnicity to pit workers against one another. However, workers confronted these strategies with struggle, especially those most disadvantaged by them. The companies' fears about the emergence of the new union demonstrate the ongoing, dialectical nature of the engagement between workers and employers. Processing company administrators were surprised and frightened by the aborted convention and its aftermath. If they had counted on the waterfront workers who controlled the UGWU to act as a "labor aristocracy" and to "discipline" orchard workers, the division of the UGWU confronted them with a new reality that would require the development of new strategies of containment.[4]

6 Citrus Growers
Producing Oranges, Producing Identities

Although chapter 4 included some wage laborers who were also citrus farmers, this chapter looks further at the way people who own citrus farms position themselves through their everyday activities and interactions, introducing a number of citrus growers. These farmers' narratives demonstrate how
they interpret the significance of their daily activities and the circumstances
they confront, and what dimensions of sameness and difference they construct among themselves in the process.

Elizabeth Evans

Elizabeth Evans was born in the lower Stann Creek Valley in 1922, toward
the end of a banana boom that had peaked with United Fruit's investment in
1906 and declined after disease struck in 1913. Though her mother had also
been born in the valley, her father had been drawn to Stann Creek from northern Belize by the banana boom, which had also attracted migrants from Central America and Jamaica. The bananas her father cultivated were collected
and transported down to the sea via a railway built to connect United Fruit's
banana plantations at Middlesex to the coast. "At that time, everybody used
to grow only bananas," Miss Liz recalled.

By the time Miss Liz reached adulthood, bananas had "finished," and another small boom had begun in the lower Stann Creek Valley. Empire Starch, a Canadian company, had established a cassava plantation and a factory that processed the cassava into starch for export. Miss Liz's husband was part of their all-male factory labor force. In 1949 she and her husband set up house-keeping on a parcel of land that belonged to Empire Starch and began to produce cassava for sale to the company. "Everybody used to plant cassava right round this area," she recalled. "Nobody didn't worry citrus. Cassava was the one that make the money."

When the starch boom went bust, and Empire Starch pulled out, the government took over the company's land and distributed parcels. The Evans's parcel was surveyed in 1952, and they started to make payments to the gov-ernment for its purchase. "I think this land only cost we 100 and something dollars. . . . Who get land at that time get it very cheap." When the starch factory closed, "then everybody start on the citrus . . . because the citrus was coming up." The Citrus Company was already operating a factory at Pomona, "but it wasn't so big and the fruit wasn't so plenty like now. At that time they were begging for fruit. Most of the people didn't know about citrus, you see."

Miss Liz and her husband both went to work on a citrus estate being established by a well-to-do family nearby: he worked in the field, while she worked in the citrus nursery. She was the only woman working on the estate, until the trees began to produce and the owner hired both men and women to harvest. Miss Liz and her husband drew on this experience to begin planting citrus on their own property, setting out twenty-five trees. At the time, the Citrus Company was offering ninety cents a box for fruit. "It was very very cheap," she recalled. Later, "when they tell us we will get $1.25," she laughed, "we said 'well, we are making money now!'"

When the owners of the citrus estate died, and the place was sold, her husband took a job in the orchards at the Citrus Company. Miss Liz stopped wagework: "At that time we had the citrus here fitting up, you see. So I didn't worry to work." Then, in 1975, her husband "took sick." They traveled to Belize City to seek medical care for him, but he died there. Distraught over how she would return his body to Stann Creek for burial, Miss Liz telephoned Wesley Spencer, general manager at the Citrus Company, to ask for help. He offered to have the company pay the costs of transporting her husband's body back to the Stann Creek Valley and burying him there. She was grateful and relieved: "They let me pay it by deduction, and then they didn't even charge me the hundred dollars for the transport. All I had to do was sign a paper that I would sell all my fruit to CCB. And I had the fruit, so it was no problem."

After her husband's death, Miss Liz did washing and baby-sitting for several years, working for better-off families who lived a few miles up the road to support herself and her nine-year-old son. She also spent more than two years engaged in legal battles to retain the farm. The property had been in her husband's name only, and he had left no will. A shop owner in Dangriga, one Mr. Talbert, took advantage of her ambiguous legal situation to claim that her late husband had sold him the land prior to his death. Mr. Talbert produced a receipt to that effect, with what he insisted was her husband's signature at the bottom. "You see," she explained, "he was basing on the husband dead, and he want to claim the land. He wanted to claims that land, take it away from me, making a false paper and say that my husband sell him the land. He thought he could advantage me. He saw I was small and I didn't say too much and he thought 'Ih fool-fool. [She's foolish.] Ih no got nothing to work with.' They thought it would be easy to get the land from me, but they were surprised how I could fight!"

Claiming to be the new owner of the land, Mr. Talbert obtained a license to deliver fruit from the CGA and then began to reap and sell fruit to CCB. Miss Liz knew that the law prohibits the CGA from issuing licenses to people who are not members. "That's why I go to all the CGA meetings," she explained. "I listen to all what they say about the laws. . . . I go to hear all of that so I could have an understanding of the law, so I know what is right and wrong, what they can do and what they can't do." Miss Liz mustered her courage and went to talk with the chair of the CGA's board of directors, Arthur Rowan, at his estate. She explained the problem and her understanding of the Citrus Ordinance to Mr. Rowan, and the CGA subsequently revoked Mr. Talbert's license and notified the company not to accept any more fruit from him.

In spite of this small success, neighbors were skeptical about her chances for ultimate success in fighting Mr. Talbert, who had retained a lawyer, Mr. Grey. "People tell me, 'You know what? You're going to lose your land, because Mr. Grey is a smart lawyer.' I say 'Yes, Mr. Grey is a smart lawyer. I don't say no. But Mr. Grey must realize that is one smart somebody going in there with him now. I maybe look like I don't smart, but you'll see what I will do with them in that court.' . . . . So we get in court that day, and I never have no lawyer. . . . And when I went in, I take the document [receipt for the land's purchase] and I put it on the table, and I explain that this is the document for the land. . . . And this is the government one: it's stamped." The judge asked Mr. Talbert to show his proof of ownership, but all he could produce was the forged receipt, supposedly signed by Miss Liz's late husband. "And the judge tell him, he said 'Listen, you can't go no further with this case.' Then the judge tell me, he say 'Listen, Mrs. Evans, you go and get a lawyer now and get your land settled.'"

A neighbor put Miss Liz in touch with his cousin, who was a lawyer in Belize City and a prominent member of the opposition party. She retained him to represent her, as the case, now a suit against Mr. Talbert for forgery, was sent to the Supreme Court. "Mr. Talbert never believed I would have taken him to Supreme Court," she laughed. "He believed I would give up, and everything would have been finished, and he would have gotten what he wanted. But when he hear that I was taking him to supreme court, he was shocked. He couldn't believe that I would go so high with it. What, I have to go to get my property! I couldn't let him go like that. I take him for true! He never expected it."

Though she had won the case, Miss Liz would still have to pay death taxes to acquire possession of the property. When the government valuator arrived to appraise the property, he asked her to show him receipts in her name. "I think the only receipt I have was one radio. That's all," she laughed. The valuator allowed her to declare the radio and the bed as her personal property: "He said, 'You could have the bed and the radio, that's all you own. Nothing more.'" When the valuator finished his appraisal, she received a notice that she would have to pay six thousand dollars in "death dues" in order to acquire the property. "I said, 'Oh, what can I do now?' I said 'The best thing, better leave it up and let government take everything and go with it.' And I move out. But you know, good friends talk to me. . . . They say, 'You go and get one lawyer.' 'I no have no money.' 'No,' he say, 'they have a lot of lawyer in Belize who could sympathy with you. They will try for you.' And I said, 'What lawyer?' Well I remember Philip Goldson, he was a good friend of ours. I said, 'Well, I'll go to him.'"

Mrs. Evans traveled to Belize City to put her case to Philip Goldson, a lawyer and the leader of the opposition political party.

I gone to him and I sit down, and I introduce myself, and I tell him, "Mr. Goldson, how much you gonna charge me now for solve this case?" And he said, "I wouldn't charge you one copper." He said "I will fight your case for you without one cent. All what I want you to do for me is to give me all statement correct, so that I don't make no mistake." He said, "Let me tell you something. You're going to have to pay something, but it wouldn't be even quarter the amount what the government want from you." . . . And he took the paper and he gone to court, and they try the case. I don't even know when they try the case, but when I look, one day, I see a letter come for me: eighty-six dollars death dues! And I must immediately pay down, otherwise four months in prison! Well, I had some money in the bank—it wasn't plenty—but when I hear about that I laugh, because I say "Mi gwain a jail fi eighty-six dollar?!" [I'm going to jail for eight-six dollars?!] So I go right down, and I draw the money, and I take the bus and I gone to Belize. . . . And I gone to the office and paid it down. . . . And that was finish. That was finish, but this property give me a hard time.

Determined to acquire the deed for her property, Miss Liz asked Philip Goldson to arrange a meeting for her with Mr. Hyde, the surveyor general. Mr. Goldson explained, "'But Mr. Hyde doesn't see anyone.' 'Well,' I said, 'he's a Belizean just like me.'" Her assertion refused a hierarchical relation between herself and Mr. Hyde, and Mr. Goldson acquiesced. He arranged an appointment for her to meet Mr. Hyde, who listened to her story and subsequently helped her to acquire the deed for the land. "You just have to know how to talk to these people," she explained.

Reflecting on the troubles she had in establishing ownership of the land she and her husband had worked, she felt that Mr. Talbert had tried to take advantage of her precisely because, as a woman alone, she was vulnerable. Since the property was in her husband's name (and Belizean law did not accord her rights to the land as his wife), she was, in fact, vulnerable. But Miss Liz attempted to counter her gender-related vulnerability by invoking a Belizean identity to claim rights (demanding that Mr. Hyde meet with her as a fellow Belizean), and by leveling class differences by visiting Mr. Rowan's estate to demand—as a fellow grower and CGA member—that the association revoke Mr. Talbert's license.

As the years passed, Miss Liz began to feel less and less able to keep up wage labor, and citrus prices were increasing. Thus, she decided to expand her citrus holdings. Since she now held the title to her property, she was able to obtain a four thousand dollar loan for expansion from the CDC-sponsored citrus expansion program managed by the Development Finance Corporation.[1] She thus became a beneficiary of the politicking that had resulted in the loans being directed toward small farmers (see chapter 3). At first she had been reluctant to take up a loan. "I was frightened of losing my land," she explained. Later, the project director from England convinced her that, as long as citrus prices were high, she would have no difficulty repaying the loan. She had expanded her holdings up to five acres of citrus and was paying off the loan through the deduction system: the company deducted a percentage of her payments for fruit deliveries and paid it directly to the DFC. She estimated that she could pay off the loan by the time the trees were fully bearing. After the trouble she encountered in acquiring title to the land, she was anxious to repay the loan and retrieve her deed.

Now the proprietor of a five-acre citrus farm, Miss Liz was confident that she would be able to support herself in her old age. At the age of sixty-eight, she did much of the work on the farm herself: spraying, pruning, reaping. Her son, now grown, helped her with farmwork, and sometimes she hired a neighbor to help circle or reap. Her hands-on involvement with the work of maintaining her orchards was not unusual; at age seventy-eight, Celia Swan was also clearing bush and planting citrus for her "old age." However, her active involvement in farmwork distinguished Miss Liz from women such as Miss Pearl, who declared that she had never done "one lick of work" on her citrus farm. Instead, she hired others to do the work on her twenty-three-acre citrus holding.

Miss Liz lived simply in her small, two-room wooden house on stilts, to which a few patches of paint still clung. She and her son had built a fowl coop under the house, where she kept chickens to supply her kitchen with eggs. Sometimes she had enough eggs to sell as well. In addition, she augmented her citrus income by selling coconuts and breadfruit from trees that grew in her yard. Neighbors passing on bicycle or foot inquired whether she had any ripe breadfruit that day. Since her house lacked running water, she trundled a basket of laundry a half mile down to the river once a week to do her wash.

Miss Liz was somewhat nostalgic about the system of patronage that had previously operated around the Citrus Company of Belize and the Spencer family. She continued to sell most of her fruit to CCB, out of gratitude for the assistance they extended to her at her husband's death, but she asserted that relationships between the company and farmers had changed dramatically with the company's sale. "When the Spencers ran the place, you could get favors from them," she said. "You could go in and tell them you needed to build a house or something like that, and Mr. Spencer would give you the money or send the CCB carpenter down to build it. Then he would give you a job to work off the amount you owed. Now that Mr. Porter is the manager, you can't get anything: Mr. Porter is a hard man."

Miss Liz's relations with economic elites had involved both efforts to level differences, as we have seen, and participation in patronage relations with them. But her relations with elites were also significantly shaped through daily conversations with neighbors, who developed shared perspectives about elites as they passed on information and opinions about them. Miss Liz visited daily with neighbors along a mile-or-so stretch of the Stann Creek Valley Road that ran past her property, as she walked up the road to a small shop, or as they gathered in small groups along the roadside in the evenings. Many of her neighbors were also smallholder citrus farmers, who developed their opinions about current events in the industry through these conversations. Their information about elite activities derived from a combination of rumor and surveillance. Stann Creek Valley Road was the only means for traveling up or down the valley. Thus, from their houses, yards, and orchards, farmers could observe who and what passed on the road and surmise explanations for what they observed. For example, Mr. Bradley, a smallholder with three acres of citrus who was one of Miss Liz's nearest neighbors, regularly bicycled along the road—slowly and not too steadily at the age of seventy-two—stopping to greet each neighbor he encountered. One afternoon, as he joined my conversation with Miss Liz, he complained that the government was giving all of the available land to large growers. He cited three recent examples. Along the Southern Highway, the government made thirty-acre plots available for small citrus producers in Silk Grass Village to expand; but Richard Porter—who was rumored to have contributed significantly to PUP campaign coffers in the last election—used his political connections to snatch all of the land for himself. A small growers' co-op had also requested a parcel of land along the Southern Highway, but the government gave that land to Rolando Hassan. The land at the junction of the Southern Highway and Stann Creek Valley Road shouldn't have been given away at all, he opined, but the government gave it to Oliver Hassan. "I complained to someone in the Lands Department," he said. "I asked him where the small growers must go for land. 'The Cockscomb Basin,' he told me." The Cockscomb, a region of high forest far to the south and far away from roads, epitomized remoteness for Mr. Bradley. "So," he concluded, "the small grower must go way to the back!" Both he and Mrs. Evans laughed at the impossibility of such a solution, since neither of them had means to travel that far "to the back," much less to work lands there.

In addition to sharing information and forming opinions on land dealings, these informal small-grower surveillance networks were also alert to

A small grower's farm climbs the hillside "to the back," behind the roadside orchard of a larger grower.

A small grower calculates his reapers' pay.

the delivery of green fruit to the processing companies. The maturity of the fruit farmers delivered to the factories was a touchy subject in the industry. In order to produce a juice concentrate that is naturally sweet and can demand a high price on the U.S. market, the processing companies establish a ratio of sugar to acid as a measure of a fruit's ripeness. Each load of fruit that private growers haul to the factory is tested for maturity. Having to leave the fruit on the trees until it reaches the required ratio presents a paradox for farmers: in order to receive the best prices for the product on the world market—and hence the best price for their fruit—the concentrate must be high ratio; however, the longer growers wait to begin reaping, the more fruit they lose to birds, insects, or premature fruit drop. The processors have argued that growers make more money selling a smaller amount of high-quality fruit for a higher price than they would if they sold a larger quantity of greener fruit for a lower price. Farmers accepted this argument in principle; however, many smallholders believed that the ratio requirements were not applied equally to all growers. They argued that large growers took advantage of the quantity of fruit they produce to pressure the companies into accepting their fruit, even if it is green.

As small farmers worried about the logistics of having to keep their fruit on the trees longer to meet the companies' maturity requirements, they paid attention to the ripeness of the fruit that passed their farmsteads on the way to the factories. As they monitored passing trailers and trucks full of fruit, word of low-ratio loads being delivered to the companies spread quickly. For example, one afternoon, Miss Liz reported that she had heard that seven trailers of low-ratio fruit from down south—the quantity indicating that it belonged to a large grower—had been delivered to CCB. The company accepted the fruit, according to one of her neighbors, but they paid less for it and set it aside to mix later with higher-ratio fruit. This kind of information, carried neighbor-to-neighbor up and down Stann Creek Valley Road, fueled smallholders' resentment about what they saw as the uneven distribution of the burden of meeting the companies' demands for higher-ratio fruit. Both the process of collective surveillance and the information garnered through such surveillance generated among these neighbors a sense of competition between smaller and larger farmers. Indeed, in spite of efforts to level relations with elites, Miss Liz clearly positioned herself as "small" in terms of her citrus acreage, and through daily conversations Miss Liz and her neighbors confirmed this shared social position and developed shared perspectives.

Miss Liz also consistently saw the world in gendered terms, noting gender differences in employment and other opportunities, recognizing the challenges she had faced because she was a woman, and asserting that others had sought to take advantage of her vulnerable position as a widow. At the same time, the sense of competence Miss Liz had derived from the battles she had fought to retain her land differentiated her from some other older women who owned citrus, such as Miss Pearl, who saw herself as being disadvantaged by her gender, even though she owned twenty-three acres. Miss Pearl had developed her land little by little, complaining, "If I had a husband or a big son, I could go faster, get more land. But I alone can't go." Further, Miss Pearl had never attended a CGA meeting. "I leave that to the big man to take care of it," she commented. Though they perceived the effects of gender on their citrus farming in different ways, all of the single women in the sample of citrus farmers saw gender as a significant factor shaping their involvement in the industry.

Another social identity Miss Liz embraced was that of "UDP." To anyone familiar with Belizean politics, her choice of two lawyers who were leading members of the opposition political party served as a declaration of political affiliation. She also expressed personal affiliations with and loyalty to current UDP politicians, referring to the UDP leader Manuel Esquivel as "*my prime minister.*"

Interestingly, Miss Liz never invoked an ethnic identity for herself, constructing herself simply—and strategically—as Belizean.

Sydney and Violet Cole

Late afternoon visits with Sydney and Violet Cole were always set against the backdrop of broadcasts picked up by Violet's shortwave radio, beginning with religious programs from the United States, followed by the BBC World News. Their small wooden house sat near to the roadside, but a profusion of flowers largely obscured the house from view and prevented all but the most determined breezes from making their way into the still, warm air of their screened porch. The Coles, Violet in her late seventies, Sydney in his middle seventies, had a long history in citrus. Mr. Cole had been born in Mullins River, a village up the coast from Dangriga often described as ethnically Creole. Violet Cole was originally from Belize City, but, as a young woman, she had traveled to Stann Creek District to visit a relative. She found work packing fruit, when the packing shed was located in Dangriga and fruit was transported down the valley to town on the railroad. In the late 1930s, when the Citrus Company moved the packing shed up the valley to Pomona, she moved with it. At Pomona she met Sydney, who also worked for the Citrus Company.

After they married, Violet did domestic work and sold baked goods, while Sydney continued to work for the Citrus Company until 1980, when he retired. During the decades he worked for CCB, he calculated, "I must have done almost all of the jobs available at the company, from orchard to factory work." The Coles lived in the workers' quarters in Pomona for many years, and, as they reminisced, they criticized the company for not providing electricity to its workers, when the other company did so. Since they did not have electricity in their own house on the farm, it was not the lack of electricity that bothered them; rather, it was the fact that the company easily could have provided the service to workers but refused to do so.

During the 1950s, Sydney acquired a twenty-acre parcel of land on lease from the government. They cleared a portion of the land and planted enough plantains and bananas to satisfy their own needs and sell to fellow workers in Pomona. They gradually assembled a wooden house on the property and then moved out of the workers' quarters they had occupied for years at Pomona. Sydney continued to work for the company, and they lived on the farm for about ten years before they began planting citrus. Sydney noted, "It wasn't very encouraging for citrus in those days. The price was very low, down to sixty cents a box." There was only one company then, he explained, and they accepted only a percentage of each farmer's fruit. The one factory was unable to process all of the fruit farmers produced in bumper crop years. Nonetheless, there was a steady market for citrus, so they cleared more of the bush on their property and planted citrus, expanding slowly over the years. When the Coles had planted a total of five acres in citrus, Sydney was able to purchase the whole twenty-acre parcel from the government and secure title to it. The Coles' experience of establishing a citrus farm while working for wages reflects a common pattern for citrus growers. In the random sample drawn from the CGA, 72 percent of the farmers had either worked for wages while they established their farms or were still working for wages as they expanded their citrus holdings.

The Coles had still not developed the other fifteen acres, though Sydney continued to plant a few more trees each year. He had never sought financing, and now, in his seventies, he would not qualify for a loan because of his age. At any rate, the farm was already more work than they could manage by themselves. When he felt well enough, he cleaned under the trees himself with a machete and hired a bushhog to clean between the rows.[2] He usually hired one or two of his neighbors to help with reaping. Violet's heart problems had prevented her from doing farmwork for several years.

Like most farmers, Mr. Cole did not own a vehicle, so he had to hire someone to haul his fruit to the factory. Since it cost the same for them to ship to either company, they usually divided their fruit between the two processors. When BFP was paying more than CCB, he said, I sent most of the fruit there. However, recalling the days when there was only one company that accepted only a portion of each grower's fruit, Violet felt strongly that they needed to sell fruit to both companies in order to keep both operating.

Though they interacted only rarely with citrus elites, both Sydney and Violet spoke with authority and interest about the dealings of larger growers. They acquired information about elite land acquisitions, their alliances and conflicts, and their personal dealings in much the same manner that Miss Liz did, exchanging news with neighbors who passed by on the road and those Sydney encountered in the shop a quarter mile up the road, where he went regularly to sell a few plantains and buy a tin of milk. These neighbors— most of them small farmers like the Coles or wageworkers in the industry— watched the comings and goings of larger growers, questioned their workers about plans for their recent land acquisitions, speculated about the details that remained opaque, and avidly swapped opinions with one another.

However, at the same time that Sydney and Violet Cole—together with their neighbors—constituted small and large growers as oppositional, even antagonistic, categories, they also linked themselves to *some* large growers as Belizean *natives*. Following local custom, as they shared information with neighbors or with me, they referred to elites who were natives of Stann Creek District by their first names: Oliver, Arthur, Wesley. They had known several generations of Hassans, Rowans, and Spencers, and they had known Oliver, Arthur, and Wesley since they were babies. In contrast, the Coles, like other citrus farmers, referred to large growers of Jamaican origin, who had immigrated to Belize after the mid-1970s, by some approximation of their surnames. Small-grower observers almost never got the immigrants' names quite right: Williston became Wilson, Sullivan became Silvan, and Porter became Portapak—after the fruit drink produced by another one of his companies. Sydney and Violet Cole's use of first names to refer to large farmers many years their junior, whom they had known as babies, constructed a more complex relationship with them than the relationships they had with immigrant elites, whose histories, names, and agendas were less known. The use of first names to refer to Oliver, Arthur, and Wesley reflected the intersection of their lives and activities with the Coles' lives and activities in the development of Stann Creek District; their belonging to the same place bound their fates together in easily discernible ways.

Though Violet was from the Creole stronghold of Belize City and Sydney from a Creole village, like Mrs. Evans neither of them ever invoked an ethnic identity.

Alberto Puc

Unlike Elizabeth Evans and Sydney and Violet Cole, who had performed wage labor prior to retiring into dependence on their citrus earnings, Alberto Puc was still working for wages at the Citrus Company, as he planted orange and grapefruit trees with retirement in mind. Thus, in some ways, Puc represents an earlier stage in the life cycle of a majority of citrus farmers. He maintained a foot in each class, as a worker and a citrus farmer.

Alberto Puc was born in the largely Mopan village of San Antonio in Toledo District, to Mopan Maya parents. Though his parents had seven children, only two survived to adulthood. When Alberto was thirteen, his father also died, and Alberto was forced to leave school to work on the family's farm, which he continued until his mother died eight years later. At that time, his older brother was bleeding chicle in Guatemala, and Alberto was alone. He gave up farming and sought wage employment with a merchant in San Antonio. For $2.50 a day, he began learning to do mechanical work and drive the man's truck, hauling cargo between the village and the district town of Punta Gorda. He soon got a driver's license. Though the "bossman" placed a good deal of trust in Alberto, the "bosswoman" (his wife) distrusted him. As a result of conflicts with her, in 1958 Alberto decided to seek work elsewhere. He traveled north to Stann Creek and asked for work at the Citrus Company. "They asked what work I know. I told the man 'Machete, do ax, or farm work.' And I told him I have a driving permit. . . . He was a good man, a white man, bossman, a white Jamaican, so they gave me a chance to drive the tractor." However, Alberto was surprised to discover how little he made driving a tractor with a bushhog. "So I told the boss, I said 'Boss, I am not satisfied for this.' He said 'Why?' I said 'Money too small. I prefer my machete.' He said, "You mean to say you were born and grow with machete, you will die with machete?' I tell him 'Mm hmm.' He say okay. So I start back to chop bush, with my machete."

At the end of the harvest, Alberto returned to San Antonio, where he did chicle work for two years. Then he married a young woman from San Antonio and began to farm again. However, conflicts in the village made him decide to leave again in 1964. This time Alberto traveled to northern Belize to cut sugar cane. His wife accompanied him, but she caught malaria and became very sick, burning with fever and trembling with chills. Alberto decided, "This place is not for us," so they returned to Stann Creek just as the citrus harvest was beginning, and Alberto was rehired at CCB.

After about three months, he was promoted to the position of checker, where he was responsible for keeping records of the amount of work completed by each employee for the purposes of calculating their pay. During the next crop season, he was promoted to field supervisor, and later the company promoted him to the position of foreman, supervising fifty to sixty reapers in the orchards. In this position, he earned $3.27 an hour. The company drew on his ability to speak Mopan to incorporate workers from southern Belize into the harvest labor force. "Sometimes during the heavy crop, and newcomers come in and work, people that don't understand the supervision, then they come and pick me up. When the people come from the south, they speak Mayan with me, because they do not understand so correctly in English, so I have to go interpret or I stay with one group for a week, then I go to another group and I stay one week. Just depends on how many people come to understand, to come to work along with the supervision."

Although some Mopan Maya from southern Belize migrated north for the citrus harvest, Alberto explained, "most of the workers in Middlesex are aliens." He believed these immigrant workers had a depressive effect on wages. "They feel lucky to earn the little bit they get. They feel like it is good money. And they are afraid that if they complain, the boss will fire them. So they say it's better to take what the company gives you and not complain. And the truth is if you make trouble, the company has a system where they give you the worst jobs to try to make you want to leave, so they can get rid of you."

Although Alberto had advanced as far as he could as an orchard worker, he was not satisfied with his income. He saw no prospects that his wages would increase significantly, and he was also getting tired of his job. "When the crop is on, I have to leave my house sometimes five in the morning. Six in the morning, I would be at the orchard, not leaving until all tractors and everything come in, parked. I come in the night. Sometimes I want to stop. I'm getting too old and tired of the job. . . . My health is not like before." Turning the conversation to his farm, he reflected, "I'm very happy that I have this thing for the future."

In 1974 he had gotten a lease on a twenty-acre block just a few miles up the valley from Middlesex. He built a thatched-roof wooden house on the property and moved his family out of the workers' barracks at Middlesex. As the government began to distribute parcels in that area, a number of other Mopan migrants from Toledo District obtained land and established farms. Eventually, they became organized into a village. Ironically, although Alberto was quick to distinguish his community of Mopan Belizeans from immigrant "aliens," as Central American immigrants settled in upper Stann Creek Valley during the 1980s most Stann Creek natives assumed that all of the families settled along the roadside above Middlesex were Salvadoran squatters.

After building a house, Alberto began to clear a section of his land to plant citrus. Because his wage labor left him little time to work on his own farm, it took him more than two years to chop and burn the trees, purchase seedlings, and plant. However, by 1976 he had begun planting about one hundred trees a year, without borrowing money. Initially he invested his wages in citrus seedlings; later, he reinvested his citrus earnings to cover the costs of his slow expansion. He also obtained a second, thirty-acre block a half mile down the valley, which he began to clear and plant. Altogether, by 1989 he estimated that he owned nearly sixteen acres of citrus. He owned neither of his parcels; since he had been planting on both, neither was sufficiently developed to enable him to apply to purchase it. On sections of his twenty-acre block where he had cleared the bush but had not yet planted citrus, he grew coconut and craboo for sale and mango and avocados for home use. He also grew corn and beans for his household, and his wife kept chickens to provide the family with fresh eggs.

Alberto's wages and his citrus income supported a household of six people, including himself and his wife, two daughters aged nine and five, a seventeen-year-old son, and a nineteen-year-old nephew who had just come north from Toledo District to live with them. Alberto calculated that he had earned about three thousand dollars on his previous year's citrus crop and another seven thousand dollars working for CCB. Thus, although much of his citrus was young and not fully bearing, his citrus production significantly boosted his income. However, since both Alberto and his son worked for CCB, they were always short of time to keep up with work on the farm. Alberto sometimes had to hire labor for cleaning or planting, and he often ran out of time to complete all of the work he had planned. In 1989 he had cleared four acres and planted them in corn, planning to plant citrus later in the year. But the time required to keep the bush from overtaking pieces he had already planted in citrus prevented him from preparing the seedlings in his nursery for planting.

Alberto divided his harvest between the two companies, though he shipped the bulk of it to CCB. "We serve the two factories if possible. But I work with CCB, and I get help from them. And they ask for help, for us to deliver our fruit to them. And the first time I reaped they sent a company transport up. Since it was a small amount of fruit, they never charged me for the transport." He was grateful for this favor, and he appreciated the sense that the company was courting him as a citrus farmer, in order to win his fruit. However, he rankled over the way company administrators had treated him and other small farmers at the previous year's "crop over party." Every year, CCB held a big celebration at the conclusion of the harvest. Everyone who had delivered fruit to CCB was invited; indeed, some farmers who delivered most of their fruit to BFP confided that they had delivered a small amount to CCB in order to receive an invitation to the party. This celebration was one of very few social occasions attended by citrus farmers of all sizes. However, Alberto complained, at the party the company had served cheap domestic rum to him and other small growers, while those he referred to as "the big fish"—large

growers and shareholders—drank imported whiskey. Alberto—who could
not afford to purchase imported whiskey but would have dearly loved to sa-
vor a few glasses of it—was deeply offended by this slight. Though Alberto
saw himself as upwardly mobile in status from wage laborer to citrus farmer,
the company's actions diminished his sense of upward mobility by positioning him as *small*. Small and large producers rarely socialized together, and
Alberto's complaint suggests that occasions when they did participate in social activities together only reinforced a sense of distance and hierarchy between them.

Martin and Eva Escobar

Like Alberto Puc, both Eva and Martin Escobar were originally from Toledo
District of far southern Belize. Eva's family was of East Indian descent, while
Martin's father was a Honduran immigrant who married a Belizean. Eva migrated north to Stann Creek District when she was about twenty years old to
work at Pomona for the Citrus Company. Martin had traveled northward from
Toledo to work at a sawmill in southern Stann Creek District. When the
sawmill closed after four years, he moved to the upper Stann Creek Valley to
cut mahogany. After eight months at the mahogany works, he got a job at
Belize Food Products, where he worked for the next twenty-two years.

When Martin and Eva married and began a family, she quit her job to
raise their twelve children. By 1986, when Martin was sixty-one and Eva
fifty-five, only their seventeen-year-old and twenty-five-year-old sons remained
on the farm. Some of their grown children lived just a few miles away in the
Stann Creek Valley, while others had moved to Dangriga or Belize City, and a
few had migrated to the United States and Canada.

Martin acquired his first parcel of land in 1961, when he bought the
piece where his house now stood. "The owner was old and sold it cheap," he
recalled. "He sold me eight acres for one hundred fifty dollars." "One grapefruit tree on the place paid for the whole property!" his wife added. The owner,
a Jamaican, had cultivated bananas. But when the banana boom finished, he
let it grow into bush. After they bought the piece, Martin chopped back the
bush and began to plant citrus, little by little, balancing work on the farm
with his wage labor. Several years later Martin bought another acre a mile
further down the valley, and he obtained three acres on lease beside the first
parcel they had purchased. They cleared the lease parcel and planted citrus;
then they applied to purchase the parcel, made their payments, and obtained

the title. In the mid-1980s they acquired ten more acres next to their earlier lease block, and they had planted six of those. Later, they had managed to get a lease for a fifty-acre block near Middlesex, which they were clearing and planting little by little. They had placed some of the land in his name and some in hers, for income tax purposes. By 1986, they owned forty acres under citrus, but only twenty-four of those acres had mature, fully bearing citrus. All of their holdings had been planted out "piece, piece," in small sections at a time, without financing. Since they had expanded their groves little by little over the years that Martin worked for BFP, he explained, "when I retired, I didn't feel it much [financially]."

Their forty acres of citrus kept all members of the household busy, with a gendered division of labor. Eva did the bookkeeping, while her husband and sons worked in the orchards. In the orchards, the division of labor ran along national lines. Martin and Eva's two sons ran the tractors. Martin explained that his sons were "afraid for machete"; they saw machete work as more appropriate for immigrants than Belizeans. The Escobars owned two tractors, and they hauled fruit and did bushhogging for neighbors as well as in their own groves. While his sons drove the tractors, Martin hired two immigrant men to do machete work or reaping for him on a year-round basis. For clearing land or reaping, he hired as many as three or four casual laborers. Martin noted that every day during harvest season people traveled up and down the Stann Creek Valley looking for work. Most of them are aliens, he explained. "These aliens really work good," he said. "They knows about hard work. People here want to work, but they don't work hard. Then they get vexed when you hire aliens. The first two steady workers I had were Salvadorans. I fixed up their papers and they worked here four or five years. I could really trust them. When I went away to visit my sons in the States, I left them in the house, and when I came back everything was just like I left it."

Martin's reference to "aliens" shifted the conversation to a recent kidnapping in Cayo District, which they suspected was the work of aliens. As they warmed to the topic of violence committed by aliens, they speculated that the recent holdup of a delivery truck on the Hummingbird Highway had been perpetrated by aliens as well. Eva also recalled a murder that had taken place on a large citrus farm nearby, where the checker (who kept records of how much each person worked and how much they were owed) was a Guatemalan who could neither read nor write. A second worker, who was literate, was helping the checker to do his job. But the checker began to worry that the other man, being better qualified, might try to take his job, Eva explained. To foreclose this possibility, the checker shot his assistant, carried his body across the river into some high bush, and chopped off his head. When the body was found two days later, there was insufficient evidence to charge the checker with the murder, but the police did deport him back to Guatemala.

Shuddering at the thought that he was still at large, Eva recalled that when they first hired two Salvadorans to work on the farm, she used to worry that they might kill Martin someday while the three of them were working in the groves with machetes. Luckily, she continued, "they turned out to be good." Nonetheless, the reliability of these particular Salvadorans did not undermine Eva's perceptions of immigrants in general. Like many residents of Stann Creek District, she assumed that Spanish immigrants committed most of the highway holdups and murders reported in the news. Thus, in addition to employing immigrant labor, the Escobars also employed many of the stereotypes about immigrants that prevailed in Belize: they assumed that, while Garifuna from Dangriga "want you to bring the tree to town so that they could reap it," aliens "really know about hard work"; but they also feared those hard workers as a result of the reputation for violence that Belizeans have attached to Spanish-speaking immigrants.

Martin and Eva continued their long association with BFP by delivering most of their fruit there. Martin explained, "It's good to try to support both companies, to keep them both going, but BFP gets the most from me." Just as they divided their land holdings between the two of them, they also delivered fruit in both of their names, splitting the crop and income in a strategy to lower their income taxes.

With forty acres of citrus and two tractors, the Escobars ran a significantly larger operation than Miss Liz or the Coles. In some contexts, people might have classified farmers like the Escobars as "medium" growers—neither large nor small. But the Escobars never situated themselves that way, and they deployed many of the strategies used by farmers with smaller acreages. For example, after clearing land for citrus near Middlesex, they had planted a crop of corn to sell in Dangriga, in order to recover some of the costs of clearing the land. They also grew beans, cassava, plantain, okra, and yams, eating some and selling the excess in Dangriga. They also had fruit trees— guava and mamey apple—planted near their house, and they kept a few chickens. Further, though they were better off than many of their citrus grower neighbors, most of their socializing took place with these neighbors.

Richard and Josephine Fenton

The farmstead of Richard and Josephine Fenton reflected their larger-than-average citrus acreage. Their wooden house sprawled across low stilts, with a screened veranda running the entire length of one side. Though it had clearly not been painted recently, its size would have dwarfed the houses of Mrs. Evans or the Coles. The collection of vehicles rusting in the yard—some of them in running condition—also connoted both a larger investment in citrus and a larger income.

Richard and Josephine Fenton had lived for decades in Stann Creek District, though both were originally from Creole villages in Belize District. From the age of nineteen, Richard had worked in the logging industry, moving from place to place as sawmills were set up in fresh areas and closed down in areas where the timber had been depleted. He established his own farm when he obtained a five-acre block in the Stann Creek Valley on lease from the government. After clearing the land, he built a house on one corner, put the remainder in pasture, and began raising cattle. Later, when citrus prices increased, he decided it would be more profitable to plant citrus on the property. By now that first block of citrus was mature, and he had acquired two other parcels on lease—blocks of eighteen and fifteen acres located a short distance up the road from his house. He had cleared and planted these parcels in citrus, but they were not yet fully bearing. Later, he had bought additional parcels from a neighboring family that owned more land than it could farm. He was in the process of planting fifteen more acres of citrus on these blocks, and he still owned ninety-six acres of land under pasture, where he kept eighty-five head of cattle. With 163 acres of land altogether, he planned to expand up to 105 acres of citrus and leave the remainder in pasture. He had financed all of his citrus investment himself, never seeking loans, because interest rates, he said, were "too damn high."

In their late fifties, Richard and Josephine lived alone on the farm, their children grown and gone. Though he used to do all of the farmwork by himself, Richard explained, he now hired one "Spanish-speaking fellow" to work for him all year long and one or two extra people during the harvest. Listening, his wife Josephine quietly added that she also used to help with all of the different kinds of work related to the farm. Indeed, when we first encountered them, Richard had his head under the hood of an antique pickup in the yard, and Josephine was handing him tools as he called for them.

With thirty-eight acres of citrus, it had become both economically feasible and necessary for Richard Fenton to acquire vehicles for working his farm. In addition to the small pickup he had been repairing, which he used to haul fruit, he owned an older, larger truck he hoped to coax into running condition to haul fruit, once his young groves matured. In addition, he owned two tractors, one of them in running condition, and a bushhogger. He did not do bushhogging for other farmers, because his own place kept him busy enough.

Unlike most of the other growers interviewed, Fenton reported that he rarely attended CGA meetings. "I've only been to one meeting," he said. Farmers with citrus acreages as large as Richard Fenton's tended to be active in CGA affairs, but Fenton explained, "I went to one meeting and saw that it was no use. Small growers might say a lot of things before the meeting, but during the meeting Mr. Rowan or some other large grower stands up and talks and everyone just agrees with him." When I suggested that perhaps he should go to speak his piece, he responded, "No. You stand up and say something. Then, after Mr. Rowan says something against you, everyone agrees with him and leaves you standing alone. So it's no use to go to meetings." Shaking his head, he added, "The large growers are just playing their games—and for nothing. Because they must die, and they can't carry it. Six feet of earth makes us all the same! As long as you have your three meals a day," he asserted, "you don't need to try to get more. The Bible says don't worry about tomorrow. But Arthur [is] greedy," he said, referring to Arthur Rowan in particular, a grower whose orchards abutted one of Fenton's parcels. "He has more than enough, and he still always wants more," he continued. "I sleep at night, and I snore. Arthur has to take pills to sleep, because he has too many worries! But he's going to leave it all behind anyway."

"I won't go to the meeting next Saturday," he continued, "or I will stand up and say something about this thing that they want to raise the ratio." Recalling the issue of fruit maturity ratios that had so interested Miss Liz and her neighbors, Mr. Fenton opined,

> It's the big growers who are mashing up the ratio. I was at the factory twice when Arthur Rowan brought in a load of fruit that was six instead of eight, but they accepted it. If a small grower brings in a load of six, they might reject it, or at least it's only maybe fifty boxes. But he's bringing in maybe fifteen hundred boxes in a load, and maybe five hundred of those are green. I've passed Arthur's groves and seen them picking fruit that is green. Oliver Hassan too. Last year Salada turned away two loads

for Oliver, because they weren't up to ratio. But they didn't turn any away the year before. Now they want to raise the ratio, to make the small grower balance out the problems that the large growers are making, to make sure the ratio of the product is high enough.

Fenton's antagonism toward large growers was fueled in part by a string of personal conflicts between himself and large growers, and in part by a more general sense that the competition between large and small growers over land and services was rigged in favor of large growers. For example, a forty-foot government road—not yet constructed—separated one of Fenton's parcels from an orchard that belonged to Arthur Rowan. One day, he recalled, Rowan's workers were planting citrus seedlings ten feet into the land reserved for the future road. When Fenton complained, he said, Arthur retorted, "I hope the government will know where to put the road when the time comes." Some time later, Rowan's tractor drivers had begun to cut through Fenton's farm. Fenton was furious, certain that his own tractor would one day get stuck in the deep, muddy ruts they were cutting through his property. He was also suspicious that this might be a ploy to undermine his tenure or shift the boundaries of his parcel. When he threatened to prosecute Rowan and his drivers for trespassing, Arthur Rowan directed his workers to stop cutting through his land.

In addition to large growers encroaching on lands that already belonged to smallholders, Richard Fenton complained that they also used their political connections to obtain land that should be allocated to smaller farmers. He cited a recent transaction in which the PUP government had granted large-grower Rolando Hassan a lease for eighteen hundred acres along the Southern Highway, a parcel that a small citrus growers cooperative had already requested. The UDP had criticized the PUP for denying these small farmers the parcel of land that the UDP had already "dereserved" for them, in order to bestow it on PUP and "first family-in-law" Rolando Hassan. Though Fenton was not a member of the co-op, he echoed the UDP's outrage at this government action that favored the interests of a single large grower over the interests of a whole group of smallholders. "The problem," Fenton argued, "is that the big growers are trying to squeeze the little man. They're trying to get all the land close in, along the roads. But the large growers should be the ones who get land to the back. In the next valley behind Pomona there are thousands of acres of land, and they are the ones who have the money to build roads and develop there, not the little man. They should leave the land in close [to roads] for small growers. But that's how it is. The Bible says, 'The big fish eat the little fish.'"

Fenton noted that the Hassans had family connections to the PUP prime minister, since one of the Hassan brothers had married the PUP leader's niece. He believed the Hassans took advantage of their kin connection to obtain land during PUP administrations. For example, he asserted, "Oliver [Hassan] flew over the Melinda Forest Reserve with the minister one day, and the next day he had a title for one thousand acres of it. He had the title, and it hadn't even been dereserved yet!" When Esquivel and the UDP were elected, he continued, they put a stop to that. As Fenton discussed these land acquisitions, he not only positioned himself as a small farmer in competition with large growers, but also as a UDP, through his criticisms of the PUP. Indeed, he did not mention the three hundred acres allocated to Oliver Hassan by the UDP, which had so upset Miss Liz's neighbor.

Large growers also used their political connections to facilitate permits for immigrant workers, Fenton charged. "The laws for work permits are making us all criminals. You have to wait five weeks for a reply from Belmopan. And if that alien works for you without a permit, they can fine you five thousand dollars. You can't wait five weeks to start reaping, when your citrus is ready! Of course, if you are a big grower, like Arthur Rowan, you just call Belmopan and you don't have to go. Or if you belong to the right party, they can give you a permit right away here in Dangriga. But if you belong to the wrong party it takes five weeks, and you have to go to Belmopan personally to check on it." By naming Arthur Rowan specifically, a large grower well known as a PUP, Fenton again criticized both large growers and PUP favoritism, positioning himself again as both a small grower (in opposition to the large growers who sought to take advantage of him and others like him) and a UDP (in opposition to the PUP and its supporters and beneficiaries).

Although both Richard and Josephine Fenton were adamant in their support for the UDP, they did not act on their UDP convictions for personal gain or to benefit small growers more generally. They contrast starkly with Dalton Smith, another small grower with an acreage of similar size and similar views on many issues. Casting himself as a champion of the "small man," Smith regularly attended CGA meetings and spoke out against the schemes and "wangulations" of large growers. He actively deployed both his UDP connections and the "small man" angle of Belizean democracy discourse, seeking advantage for himself or for small growers generally.

The Fentons, like a majority of the citrus farmers in the Stann Creek Valley, are Afro-Belizean Creole speakers. However, unlike Mrs. Evans and the Coles, who did not discuss ethnic identities, the Fentons did position themselves ethnically as *not Garifuna*. Both Richard and Josephine Fenton, from Creole villages in Belize District, saw themselves as quite different from the Garifuna people who predominated in Dangriga. Referring to "these people down here" as "Caribs," a label rejected by Garifuna leaders as pejorative, Richard asserted: "They could learn fast—they're good for school. They can take learning, but they can't take success. If you hire a Carib to work for you and you tell him all what to do, he will do good work. But if you tell him one day 'I'm going to retire and let you run this place,' the next day it will be run down to nothing. They can't take success." The implication was that Garifuna need to be under the direction of non-Garifuna in order to be productive; otherwise success goes to their heads. Area representative Ted Aranda provided an example, they suggested. Aranda became UDP party leader in the early 1980s. But, Mr. Fenton explained, "right away he started giving everybody else in the party orders. They couldn't take that, so they replaced him. But he says they did it because he is a Carib." That is "how Caribs think," they argued.

Oliver Hassan

Oliver Hassan began his adult career as a citrus farmer with thirty-five acres. His father had emigrated from Palestine as a young man, settling briefly in El Salvador and then moving to southern Belize, where he planted a twenty-acre block of citrus in 1955. Over time, he expanded to nearly two hundred acres, "which was considered big at the time," Oliver recalled. One of seven sons, Oliver grew up in Stann Creek Valley and attended high school at the agricultural college in the valley. After high school, Oliver worked with the rest of his brothers on his father's farms.

After his father died in 1971, Oliver bought two farms from his father's estate, totaling thirty-five acres. "Between the years of 1971 and 1975," he explained, "I was really just tagging along with the program, with the system that existed here in the valley. . . . Prior to 1976 we had no price formula, and prices were paid according to the 'generosity,' so to say, of the processors. . . . They came out with a price, and that price was final—whether the growers liked it or not." Hassan described how, before the mid-1970s, the largest independent grower, George Rowan, had controlled the CGA: "George Rowan at that time would meet with the processors, and after the meeting they would come out with a circular to growers stating that the prices for oranges would be X amount of cents or dollars or whatever it was, and for grapefruit the same thing. And they were wishing the growers a very prosperous year and they looked forward to their cooperation." At that time, Hassan complained, there was "no one to champion the part of the growers," no one to mobilize them for collective action. "They would say 'I'm not going to reap.' But eventually they would reap, because some would begin to reap, and it was felt that half a loaf was better than none."

However, as Oliver began to borrow money to expand his citrus holdings, he became determined to push for changes in the industry. "I was very aware of the situation that existed. I had heard my father complain quite a bit about the situation. So I was very adamant, very firm, that I personally would not go through that type of ordeal: just accepting what was paid to the growers by the processors. In 1975, I began to express my feelings among the growers, campaigning. And as a result of this campaign we eventually had a vote of no confidence in George Rowan."

Rowan was replaced as chair of the CGA board of directors by another large grower, who served only briefly before also being removed by association members with a vote of no confidence. At that point, Oliver assumed leadership of the Citrus Growers Association and began to lobby for the imposition of a price formula in the industry. "It took a lot of time. I had to go out and talk with growers, educate them, point out what they stood to lose by not cooperating, by not uniting. And I explained to them exactly what the new management committee had in mind to do. It took quite a bit of time, because most people thought it couldn't be done. It was very frustrating. The processors would have nothing to do with me. . . . They had all sorts of names for me. They said that the price formula was my 'elusive dream,' that we would never see a price formula in this industry. I had to convince government too. That was hard too, because at the time the PS [permanent secretary] for Trade and Industry was very good friends with one of the processors. Very close. And as a result of that . . . he wouldn't even answer my calls. He would tell the minister not to pay attention to the growers, that the growers were disorganized, they had no idea what they wanted, they had no direction, no leadership whatsoever."

Despite opposition, Oliver pursued this cause "tooth and nail": "I didn't spare any effort. Eventually it became a big challenge to me because of all the opposition I was receiving, opposition not only from the processors and from the government but from within the ranks of the growers. Like George Rowan, he was out campaigning too, telling growers, 'Don't associate yourself with that Hassan boy, because he will just break up this whole industry, and he will destroy everything that we have been working for over the years.' . . . I decided at that point I wouldn't back down. I knew that certainly evil could never prevail against good and that eventually what was right had to win!"

Oliver described spending days driving up and down the valley, meeting with groups of growers to explain what a price formula would do for them. Eventually, he won the backing of small farmers: "The small growers is where I got big support. At that time I was a small grower myself too," he reflected. "I just had thirty-five acres. I was a part of them." When fruit began to ripen, Oliver recalled, growers were united in their resolve not to reap until a price formula was implemented. "The fact that the growers were unified to the point that the fruits were dropping off the trees, and they would not go ahead to deliver fruits—that we kept as a block—that was when we got recognition from government," Hassan recalled. Once the government stepped in and forced the enactment of a price formula, the growers saw immediate results, Hassan asserted, as prices for fruit jumped.

Subsequently, Hassan began to focus more of his attention on expanding his citrus holdings, though he served a number of additional terms on the CGA board of directors. By 1986 he had 300 acres of mature citrus trees and 430 acres of young trees. In contrast to farmers who cleared their land with axe and machete, Hassan was running two bulldozers to clear land for further planting. He had also purchased a backhoe to dig drains through and around his orchards, to increase the health and productivity of his groves. To maintain his seven hundred acres and continue his expansion program, he hired a labor force of forty permanent workers, adding sixty more for the harvest season. By 1988, Oliver owned fourteen hundred acres of citrus, though much of it was still young, and he required over one hundred fifty workers for the harvest.

In addition to his citrus holdings, Hassan had diversified his investments in several directions. He owned the bus company that serviced southern Belize, and in the mid-1980s he purchased a banana plantation when the UDP administration privatized the government-owned banana industry as part of the economic restructuring required by USAID and the IMF. The UDP was reluctant to sell to him, Hassan said, because they saw him as PUP. Since the PUP had been in power when he started in business, he explained, he had worked closely with them. However, when the government failed to find an alternative buyer, it did sell to Hassan, who soon demonstrated that he could work closely with a UDP administration as well.

In 1985 Hassan and other large banana growers began working with the Caribbean Development Bank (CDB) on a project to rehabilitate and expand the banana industry, taking advantage of the push by the Belizean government and international development lenders to diversify and expand Belizean export production and increase foreign exchange earnings. Hassan then used the relationship he established with CDB personnel to pitch a citrus project to the bank. The CDB sent a team to study the feasibility of Hassan's proposal, and, subsequently, the bank provided loan funds to finance his citrus expansion. This means of funding expansion clearly set Hassan apart from farmers who financed their own "piece-piece" planting or sought loan funds from the CDC program.

Hassan's increased acreage, together with the expansion of other independent growers, changed the dynamics of price determination in the Belizean industry. With large growers' expansion, the processing companies' relative share of total citrus production had been decreasing. Thus, Oliver and two other large growers devised a new strategy to pit the two processors against one another. Such a strategy became especially important after the sale of CCB, Hassan explained. "When CCB was purchased by growers, it had a fixed share of fruit assured because the shareholders would deliver to their own company. BFP had to do certain things to assure its throughput, like providing loans and services to growers to assure crop commitment. This completely destroyed the competitive spirit between them, because if one gets a certain amount by way of shareholders and the other has an assured quantity in exchange for services, there is no competition. The processors can get together and say, 'Why compete? You have your growers, and I have mine, so let's just set a price.' I recognized that this would be harmful to growers," Hassan explained. "So I got a group of uncommitted growers together who were able to pool a significant amount of fruit, and we got bids for that amount from both processors." "The processors are operating at only about 60 percent capacity, so they want the quantity," he continued. BFP offered the higher price, with the stipulation that all growers who delivered fruit to BFP would receive the same price.

While this strategy led to higher prices for growers for a couple of years, the companies soon developed a counter-strategy of offering to match whichever company's formula price was higher. Thus, by 1986 Hassan had begun to weigh the possibility of establishing a third processing plant. The processing companies' profits are directly related to the quantity of fruit they process. Recent expansion in the industry would have increased the amount of fruit the factories processed, decreasing their operating costs. This, in turn, should have led to better prices for growers, he reasoned. However, the formula that determined the prices growers received for their fruit had a fixed processing cost that had been set in 1982, before citrus expansion began in earnest. Thus, increased throughput had not provided better prices to growers; it had simply increased the companies' profits.[3] After pushing for a new price formula with no success for several years, in 1987 Hassan finally decided to take advantage of the existing formula by going into processing himself.

Hassan offered Nestlé $15 million for its Belize Food Products operation, but Nestlé rejected his offer. Subsequently, he initiated discussions with government officials about opening a third factory. He calculated that the combined production from his orchards and those of Bill Williston, another large citrus grower with whom he had cooperated closely in the banana industry, would soon be enough to support a small factory. In 1988 the UDP government granted him three hundred acres of lease land for the project at the junction of the Southern Highway and Stann Creek Valley Road. Two hundred acres were intended for citrus cultivation, and the remaining one hundred acres were earmarked for a third processing plant. Hassan began clearing and planting citrus on part of the land, while he searched for financing for the proposed factory. However, he complained, all foreign lenders wanted to channel the financing through the Belizean Central Bank, and then through a private bank; "by then," he complained, "the loan is too expensive."

In these examples, Oliver Hassan's biography appears to be more reciprocally intertwined with the development of the citrus industry than the biographies of smaller growers. Rather than simply responding to opportunities, Hassan presents himself as an individual working proactively to shape the industry to accommodate his interests. Hassan worked with great intensity for long hours, meeting with the managers who attended to the day-to-day tasks of operating his farms or the bus company or networking with fellow large growers, politicians, and other Belizean elites to strategize and build alliances in pursuit of particular projects. Thus, although Hassan owned an impressive cement house equipped with its own generator and satellite dish, he spent more time in his offices or in his air-conditioned pickup traveling between farms or meetings. Intensely involved in expanding his businesses, Hassan—in his forties—had never married, though he had fathered children with a number of women. In accord with expectations for a man of his economic means, he supported those children by financing their educations, even sending them abroad for university studies.

Hassan moved in the small circle of social elites in Stann Creek District that comprised the largest citrus farmers, processing company owners and managers, senior bank personnel, and some local merchant families. However, while these elites marked their difference from small farmers and laborers through their consumption patterns—large houses, satellite dishes, air-conditioning, four-wheel-drive vehicles—relations within the circle of elites were often strained by competition. In the mid-1980s some citrus elites waxed nostalgic about earlier times "when we could stand up and argue against one another in a CGA meeting and then joke together over drinks afterward." But by the mid-1980s some elite men had stopped speaking to one another. Hassan's efforts to extract higher prices for citrus fruit had led to serious factionalism among large growers, as those who were not CCB shareholders pitted themselves against the company. Interpersonal rivalries also shaped relations among elites. The Rowans, local elites for several generations, cast themselves as "old money" against Hassan's "new money." And Hassan cited interpersonal rivalry among elites as a motivating factor for his ongoing expansion: when asked why he continued to plant more citrus, he replied, "Do you think I could see Porter put in another hundred acres and sit still?"

But at the same time that Hassan positioned himself as a key member of a somewhat fractious citrus and regional elite, he also drew on his Stann Creek upbringing and former "smallness" to position himself as local, as Belizean, as just one of the growers. Everyone in the district knew him, and all—except for immigrant workers—referred to him as "Oliver." Reciprocally, he sometimes used the nicknames of small growers he had known all his life to diminish the distance created by the varied sizes of their acreages. While elites marked their status by demonstrating their control of Standard English in contexts such as CGA meetings, Hassan often shifted into Creole to persuade or make a point. He skillfully wielded Creole language and proverbs to cast himself as Belizean, local, or simply "a grower." His verbal artistry was unmatched—indeed, unattempted—by rival elites.

The farmers introduced in this chapter made decisions about planting citrus or expanding their holdings within the context of national development priorities and international demand for Belizean citrus products. Locally, farmers perceived citrus as the only option available for those who sought a guaranteed market for their farm produce. Further, the priorities of the Belizean government and foreign development lending agencies to increase citrus production in order to expand and diversify Belizean exports combined in the CDC loan program that encouraged smallholders to expand their citrus holdings, amid assurances that, with citrus prices at record highs, they would have no difficulties repaying the loans.

The overriding construction of sameness and difference that emerges from these growers' narratives is the distinction between "small" and "large" growers. The recurring reproduction of this distinction involves both material differences in the circumstances and possibilities confronted by citrus farmers and their collective efforts to make sense of those differences through discourse. The "small man" rhetoric of Belizean democracy discourse has encouraged and played into the construction of this dimension of difference. As Belizean politicians have wielded democracy discourse, championing the cause of the "small man," smallholder citrus farmers have been "positioned"— taught to recognize themselves—as the "small men" at the center of Belizean democracy. In turn, they have embraced that dimension of democracy discourse, claiming "small man" status for themselves to criticize actions they disapproved and to call for greater consideration or support for small-acreage farmers. In accord with democracy discourse, "small men" in the citrus industry clearly constituted the majority. In the random sample of thirty CGA members drawn in 1989, farmers with fewer than ten acres of citrus accounted for over half the sample but less than 7 percent of its total citrus acreage. Conversely, farmers with more than fifty acres accounted for less than 7 percent of the sample's membership but nearly 70 percent of its total citrus acreage.

Growers' narratives identify a number of differences that distinguish small from large farmers. For example, many of the farmers who describe themselves as "small" had a history of wage labor, and 72 percent of the CGA sample had either worked for wages while establishing their citrus farms or were still working for wages as they planted citrus for their retirement. This contrasts with Hassan's personal history, which never involved wage labor. Smallholders also noted differences among themselves and large growers in terms of the techniques of citrus production and the problems they encountered in the process. While Hassan bought two bulldozers to level the vegetation on his ever-increasing landholdings, small growers cleared trees and brush on their parcels with an axe and machete or paid someone else to do the work by hand. Most of the farmers in this chapter planted their citrus "piece-piece," in small sections, because the costs associated with clearing land, planting, and maintaining the trees until they reached maturity at five to seven years (three thousand to four thousand dollars per acre) prohibited them from planting large blocks all at once. Those who were working for wages were further constrained by time limitations and the need to hire labor to progress in their citrus expansion. Thus, while Alberto Puc was struggling to plant one hundred trees a year, Hassan was planting hundreds of acres a year, with a large hired labor force and financing from an international development bank. Distinctions between small and large growers were also reinforced by the economic activities growers pursued aside from citrus farming: while Hassan had diversified into commercial banana cultivation and transportation, smaller growers' households diversified by working for wages, producing additional foodstuffs for sale or home consumption, or purchasing a tractor to haul fruit or bushhog for neighbors.

Those who considered themselves small farmers also identified aspects of difference between themselves and those growers they saw as "large" that set them in conflict with one another. For example, in struggles over access to land, they saw themselves as constrained by their lack of financial and political clout vis-à-vis large growers. Although both large and small growers applied to lease government-owned land, fertile land close to roads was increasingly scarce. Small growers claimed that large growers used the political clout that resulted from their contributions to election campaigns or their kin connections to government officials to obtain choice parcels. This sense that small growers were pitted against large growers in a competition for land that was rigged against them was revealed in the gossip that accompanied the distribution of land by the government. Distinctions smallholders drew between flat land and hillsides, land near roads and land to the back, and land favorable for citrus in contrast to marginal soils—contrasts in which small growers often got the worse end—contributed to smaller farmers' view of themselves as a class apart from and in many ways opposed to large growers. Those who positioned themselves as small farmers also invoked enforcement of the fruit maturity requirements as another bone of contention that separated them from—and pitted them against—larger producers. These dimensions of difference were identified and elaborated in conversation, as farmers gathered in small groups by the roadside or in the shops in the evenings. In these social contexts, they shared concerns about their own citrus farms; but they also recounted rumors and offered opinions about the activities of larger growers—acquiring more land or delivering green fruit, for example. During their nightly conversations, growers shaped collective opinions and a collective identity that set them in opposition to the large growers, who were almost never present in such contexts.

However, other affiliations sometimes bridged the small farmer–large farmer divide, most notably localness or Belizeanness. The fact that other farmers referred to Oliver, Arthur, and Wesley by their first names generated a greater sense of commonality with them than with the "Jamaican" growers known by their somewhat-mangled surnames. Hassan recognized the utility of this potential and often sought to use it to his advantage.

At the same time, the experiences of those who called themselves "small growers" were not homogeneous. The problems and possibilities confronted by Miss Liz, with five acres of citrus, were different from those confronted by Richard Fenton. Whereas Miss Liz fretted over the difficulties she had in getting the CGA to send a bushhogger to clean her orchards, Fenton operated his own bushhogger. Women also perceived gender as a significant dimension of difference among growers. Although the random sample of citrus growers indicated that citrus acreages were distributed among women roughly in proportion to their distribution among men, with the majority owning fewer than ten acres, all single women farmers I interviewed believed their identity as women had a formative affect on their options and the challenges they encountered as growers. In Miss Liz's narrative, the labor market in the valley was always gender segmented, and the employment opportunities open to her were limited by her gender. Further, she believed that people had tried to take advantage of her because of her gender. She was conscious that others saw and treated her as a woman—with all the connotations that carried—whether she wanted to claim such an identity or not. It is interesting that none of the men interviewed mentioned gender as a significant factor in their lives or work. If gender positioning was so significant as a problem for women, it must have been important for men as well. However, if being positioned as a man meant being able to avoid problems such as limited employment opportunities, lack of rights to a spouse's land, or being seen as easy targets for fraud, the advantages associated with being a man appear to have made gender classification less visible to men.

At the same time, the difference that gender makes was lived in different ways by different women. While Miss Liz did much of the work on her farm, Miss Pearl believed that, as a woman, she was incapable of doing farmwork. Miss Liz was not automatically recognized as the rightful owner of her husband's property after his death, and Miss Josephine was not perceived by her husband as contributing to the work of running the farm, but Eva Escobar managed all of the accounts for the orchards, as she and her husband split both their property and their fruit deliveries across their two names.

Unlike the workers introduced in chapter 4, the growers introduced in this chapter demonstrated a less consistent commitment to ethnic categories and identities. All of the farmers who did not see themselves as Creole, and who would not likely be classified that way by others, placed themselves in an ethnic category: Mopan, East Indian, Spanish. In Alberto Puc's case, he was also singled out by the company that employed him as Mopan (though his community was perceived as a population of aliens by many residents of Stann Creek). However, none of the farmers who would likely be classified as Creole invoked an ethnic identity for themselves at all. This raises questions about whether they understood Creoleness as sufficiently "normal" and normative in Belize to not require naming or elaboration. The Fentons, both from villages in Belize District described as Creole, identified themselves only as *not Garifuna.* As they positioned themselves as different from "these people down here," they posed an unnamed standard against which the behavior and beliefs of Garifuna could be judged; perhaps that standard was a Creole one.

A number of farmers drew distinctions between foreigners and Belizeans. Many of the growers employed immigrant workers, referring to them by a range of terms, from "alien" to the euphemized "Spanish-speaking fellow." The Escobars demonstrated the Belizean assumption that agricultural labor, machete work, was more appropriate for immigrants than for Belizeans. Indeed, the Escobars' sons positioned themselves as Belizean—and thus above the performance of hard, physical labor in the fields—by avoiding machete work in favor of driving tractor, leaving the harder physical work to the immigrants their father hired. In this way, the two Escobar sons upheld and lived out the government's assertions that Belizeans will not do agricultural field labor, even though their father sometimes wielded his machete along with the hired workers.

When they employed these foreign workers, the Escobars also employed stereotypes about Central American immigrants as violent, lawless types who endangered the peace and democracy of Belize. Convinced of the veracity of stereotypes about the violent nature of Central Americans, Eva worried that the workers they hired would murder her husband at the slightest provocation. When these workers turned out to be "good," she perceived this as an aberration. She assumed that every violent crime committed in the rural areas of Belize had been perpetrated by an alien. The implicit subtext of her assumptions, shared by many in Stann Creek, was that Belizeans were too peaceful and reasonable a people to resort so easily to violence. By distancing themselves from aliens, then, the Escobars implicitly asserted moral superiority for themselves as Belizeans.

National identities were also invoked to distinguish among large growers. Through the use of their first names, Hassan, Spencer, and Rowan were all constructed as local, as Belizean, in contrast with Porter, Williston, and Sullivan, who were all cast as foreigners or Jamaicans.

Some of the farmers adamantly claimed for themselves a party identity as well. Miss Liz, the Fentons, and Dalton Smith all claimed a UDP identity, while the small farmer who defended the government's allocation of the land sought by the small farmers co-op to Rolando Hassan could only be PUP. Some of the growers, like Miss Liz and Dalton Smith, put that identity to use in pursuit of personal interests or the concerns of small growers as a group, though the Fentons claimed the identity less as a utilitarian tool and more as a means to position themselves on what they perceived as moral high ground. However, not all growers claimed or hinted at a party identity. At the same time, not claiming a party identity or affiliation did not preclude individuals from being placed in a political category by others. For example, in the mid-1980s Oliver Hassan found himself classified as a PUP by both the Fentons and the UDP government, whether he wanted to claim such an identity or not.

As this last example demonstrates, there were sometimes tensions between the ways individuals positioned themselves—the identities they claimed—and the way they were positioned by others with whom they interacted. For example, Miss Liz explicitly positioned herself as Belizean and as a grower to counter Mr. Talbert's positioning of her as a woman, and hence as vulnerable. In the same vein, Hassan positioned himself as a large grower through virtually all of his activities; but on occasion he verbally positioned himself as just "a grower," without a size modifier to precede the noun. His success in claiming a generic "grower" identity was contextual, as other growers most often positioned him as "large." And Alberto Puc was demoralized by the difference between his self-positioning and his classification by the company. He saw himself as upwardly mobile from the category of wage laborer to that of citrus farmer, and thus he was angered when CCB positioned him as small in comparison to the "big fish" through the differential allocation of liquor at the company's party.

As was the case with wage laborers in the industry, no monolithic, unified collective agent (such as "citrus farmers") emerges from these narratives. Rather, citrus farmers differentiate among themselves along lines of acreages, gender, ethnicity, and nationality. Efforts to construct citrus farmers into collective agents will be examined in the next chapter.

7 The Sale of a Processing Company
Negotiating Class and National Identities

As Oliver Hassan worked to assemble the financing required to open a third processing company, for reasons discussed in chapter 6, he became increasingly convinced that Belize Food Products represented a better investment. Although Nestlé had rejected his initial offer, he later renewed his efforts to acquire BFP, contracting a New York brokerage firm to help him assemble the necessary financing. At the time, Nestlé was interested in selling BFP, which had become "an anachronistic element" in Nestlé's worldwide operations: in other parts of its global operations, the company had extracted itself from agricultural production and shifted its emphasis to processing; thus, the orchards of BFP represented Nestlé's largest remaining agricultural holding ("Belize," *Caribbean Insight*, Aug. 1989, 12). Further, Nestlé had originally purchased Belize Foods to supply its orange juice packaging operation in Trinidad, but the Trinidad operation was experiencing financial difficulties. As Nestlé's interest in divesting itself of BFP became public knowledge, the owners of the Citrus Company of Belize and at least one transnational company also became bidders, competing with Hassan to acquire the company.

During negotiations over the company's sale, competing coalitions of aspiring buyers drew on official discourses on development, democracy, and nation, articulating them in varying combinations in order to channel social collectivity in favor of their own agendas and undermine the arguments of their opponents. Would-be shareholders worked to construct collective agents by defining shared identities and interests principally in terms of class and national belonging. However, these efforts entailed struggles: Are citrus growers a single class with common interests, or do they belong to two—or three— different classes with conflicting interests? What are the requirements for claiming a Belizean identity, and what interests do Belizeans share? Focusing especially on the views of the farmers profiled in chapter 6, this chapter describes the competition involved in negotiations over the sale of Belize Food Products.

More Than a One-Man Show

The New York firm contracted by Oliver Hassan assembled a proposal that called for Oliver Hassan to borrow $23.5 million to buy BFP's processing plant and groves from Nestlé. In turn, he would sell his own groves to BFP for an equivalent amount. Hassan would then sell 40 percent of the company's shares to other growers, retaining 60 percent for himself. Shares would be offered to citrus growers in exchange for their fruit delivery: they could deliver fruit to the company and receive payment in shares. Since the quantity of fruit a company processes directly influences its profitability, Hassan hoped this offer would entice other growers to sell their fruit to BFP; growers who were also shareholders would increase their dividends by supplying fruit to their "own" company. Selling shares only in exchange for fruit deliveries would also keep the company a growers' operation by making it impossible for nongrowers to buy shares. Further, Hassan was gambling that this would prevent the Citrus Company of Belize or its major shareholders from acquiring shares in BFP: they would have to sacrifice CCB's profits—by diverting their fruit to BFP—in order to buy BFP shares. Hassan planned to sell shares to growers for a period of five years. In addition, he planned a two-dollar limit on the value of shares farmers could receive per box of fruit delivered. Preventing large producers from demanding their total payment in shares would force them to deliver their fruit to BFP over the whole five-year period in order to maximize their share ownership.

Hassan presented his plan to the United Democratic Party government to request tax concessions for both the factory and the groves. Prime Minister Manuel Esquivel acceded to a concession for the factory, but he refused to grant a concession for the groves. According to Hassan, Esquivel explained, "This is a one-man show, and we can't give one man all this assistance. With the citrus growers we could give more support." It was an election year, and the prime minister must have seen both a potential public relations problem in providing such assistance to one man and a potential opportunity to widen his party's support among citrus growers if the proposal could incorporate a broader range of growers.

With this incentive, Hassan reconfigured his proposal. He decided to form a holding company that would borrow the money to buy BFP and then sell shares to growers in exchange for fruit deliveries. Rather than setting aside a fixed percentage of the shares for himself, Hassan now proposed to offer all shares for sale to growers in exchange for fruit. However, he had carefully calculated his own fruit production to predict the percentage of shares he would be able to obtain through fruit deliveries. Although he now owned over two thousand acres of citrus, much of it was recently planted and only beginning to produce. Thus, he purchased a mature citrus farm from his brother in order to ensure that he would be able to deliver at least 50 percent of the estimated throughput at the new company—and hence secure controlling shares. This proposal made Hassan's control of the company much less visible, submerging him into the generic category of "growers." Having produced a plan that would provide political mileage for the prime minister and his party in upcoming elections, when Hassan returned to Belmopan with the new plan, he asked the government for more than tax concessions; he asked the government to guarantee the loan that would enable "the growers" to buy the company.

Prime Minister Esquivel was pleased with Hassan's plan to make all of the company's shares available to growers on a delivery basis. Government support for the plan would demonstrate the UDP's concern to help all growers become processing company shareholders. Thus, the prime minister agreed to guarantee the necessary loans and grant tax concessions on both groves and factory. In addition, Esquivel met with a Nestlé representative to inform him that the Belizean government would prefer that Belizean citrus growers be given the first opportunity to purchase Belize Food Products. Nestlé appeared willing to comply with the government's request that growers be given first chance to buy the company, perhaps because both Nestlé and the new owner would require the cooperation of the Belizean government to negotiate tax concessions, licenses, and permits to move money in and out of Belize. If the new owners were foreigners, the government would also have to approve the sale of the company's land. At the same time, the company informed the prime minister that it currently had two other groups of bidders ready to pay cash for the company.

Hassan himself dispatched one of these competitors. Hassan had learned that the British transnational Fyffes had initiated negotiations with Nestlé to purchase Belize Foods. Fyffes was the fruit distributor that purchased all Belizean bananas, so Hassan had dealt with the company in the banana industry. Thus, Hassan contacted Fyffes directly to explain to them that the key to BFP's profitability over the last several years had been the delivery of Hassan's fruit. He recalled, "I contacted Fyffes and made it clear that I would take exception to them coming in at this point. I made it clear to them that, with their big purse, Fyffes could buy BFP, but not the growers and certainly not Oliver Hassan. And so the figures for BFP could change overnight. You know, my pride alone would not let me sell my fruit to the same people who had cut me out, you know? So I would prefer to take my fruit somewhere else." After Hassan "clarified" the significance of his fruit deliveries for BFP's profitability, Fyffes withdrew from negotiations for the company's purchase.

As negotiations continued, rumors about the sale began to circulate around Stann Creek District. One rumor identified the rival Citrus Company of Belize as a bidder for Belize Food Products. The Citrus Growers Association responded to this possibility by sending a delegation to the capital to warn Prime Minister Esquivel against allowing CCB to obtain a monopoly. However, aside from confirmation that Nestlé was negotiating the sale of Belize Foods, the growers were given no further information until August 1989, when Oliver Hassan requested a special meeting of the CGA to unveil his plan.

A "Growers' Company"

At the special meeting Hassan attempted to rally growers' support for his plan by portraying all growers, regardless of their acreages, as members of a single category with common interests. He explained that his proposal provided each grower an *equal* opportunity to acquire shares by delivering fruit to the company. Since growers would not have to put up cash to invest in shares in the company, even farmers without cash on hand could participate. Citrus farmers had always wished for a grower-owned factory, and this plan would make it a reality, he argued.

Prime Minister Esquivel attended the meeting to pledge his government's support for the proposal and to promise a government guarantee for the loan that would allow "the growers" to acquire the company. Like Hassan, he defined the growers as a single category, whose members shared common interests. The prime minister cautioned growers to beware of any attempt by CCB to buy shares in BFP, since a monopoly would not be in the growers' best interests. Thus, he cast CCB shareholders as processors rather than growers, though many of them owned citrus farms themselves. No doubt it was also significant to the UDP that CCB's owners were widely recognized as PUP supporters.

In response, growers passed a resolution to establish a CGA committee to explore the acquisition of Belize Foods and set conditions for participation in the new enterprise. Agreeing with the prime minister that monopoly was not in their interests, citrus growers voted to prohibit anyone with more than a 10 percent share interest in CCB from purchasing shares in BFP. In turn, one of the citrus farmer shareholders of CCB, Arthur Rowan, asked repeatedly whether limits would be placed on the amount of shares in BFP any single individual could acquire. His strategic questioning directed farmers' attention to the probability that Hassan would obtain controlling interest in the company. Hassan replied that growers' purchase of shares would be limited only by the amount of fruit they could deliver to the factory. While most growers favored the idea of a grower-owned factory, many suspected that Oliver Hassan's more than two thousand acres would allow him to gain controlling shares in the new company. Though Hassan's plan would treat all growers the same, smallholders recognized that they were not equal in terms of fruit production; thus they would not be equal in the acquisition of shares. As chapter 6 demonstrated, citrus farmers with small acreages often position themselves as "small growers" in opposition to "large growers," and many smallholders did not believe their interests coincided exactly with Hassan's. They feared that, where their interests diverged, Hassan would pursue his own interests at their expense. These sentiments prompted farmers at the meeting to vote to prohibit any individual from acquiring more than 40 percent of the company's shares.

After the meeting, farmers expressed mixed reactions to the plan for "the growers" to purchase BFP. Richard Fenton—who did not attend but was informed by neighbors about the events that unfolded at the meeting—doubted that purchasing shares would enable him to make a difference in the company's policies: "The problem is that I am so small here that I couldn't get enough shares to have a say in what happens at the factory anyway. I would just have to wait for them to tell me what they decided." The disillusion that had followed growers' initial enthusiasm for the CCB sale in the early 1980s also conditioned their support for the new proposal to purchase BFP. "When CCB was for sale, there was a lot of talk that this was for the growers," Violet Cole remembered. "But they took away some people's shares, and they wouldn't sell more shares to small growers, so I don't think it's true."

Generally, growers supported the idea of a grower-owned factory, but they were afraid that Hassan would control it, whether they bought shares or not. Farmers with small acreages did not believe that Hassan's control of the factory would be in their best interests. Elizabeth Evans explained, "We never wanted Oliver to buy it, because he has too many fruits. He would want to offload his own fruit first. We would have to wait, and our fruit would rot.... [H]e has too much fruit—he wouldn't look upon us." Many smallholders shared Elizabeth Evans's fear that fruit prices would drop if each company was controlled by one or two large growers. When all of their citrus expansion begins to produce, she predicted, the large growers and their factories would have so much fruit that "they won't see us with our little amount of fruit." Those who regarded themselves as small growers were thus disinclined to see all growers as equals who shared the same interests.

Since the prime minister's pledge of support for the growers was made less than two weeks before national elections, Peoples United Party supporters regarded his promise as an "election gimmick" intended to expand support for the UDP. The UDP did carry rural Stann Creek District in the elections, but the PUP emerged as overall winner nationally. The victorious PUP took a dim view of Oliver Hassan's role in orchestrating the special CGA meeting at which the former UDP prime minister had made his promise. Hassan had not openly declared himself a UDP, and, in the past, he had been seen as a PUP, due to his kin affiliations with the PUP leader and the close working relationship he had enjoyed with previous PUP governments. However, in 1989 Hassan was perceived to be supporting the UDP. He was close to the UDP standard-bearer for rural Stann Creek District, and he had been working with the UDP administration on the BFP purchase. Further, advertising for his bus company appeared only in the UDP newspaper. According to Hassan, Richard Porter, the chair of the Citrus Company of Belize, used these facts against him. Porter lobbied new PUP ministers, contrasting his own generous support for the PUP during the recent election campaign with Hassan's "disloyalty," to preclude government support for Hassan's proposal. The result, according to Hassan, was that "ministers [of government] were saying specifically and direct to the point that they were not prepared to buy any factory for Oliver Hassan. . . . Because on a strict deduction basis, I would have had controlling shares."

Rebuffed by both the new government and smallholders in the CGA, Hassan stepped back from his leading role in the acquisition of Belize Foods. He turned negotiations over to the CGA committee created to explore growers' purchase of Belize Foods.

The "Little Man" and the "Belizean Dream": Class Difference, National Sameness

Anxious to learn whether the Peoples United Party government would equal the offer made by its rival prior to the election, the Citrus Growers Association invited PUP prime minister Price to address their annual general meeting in November 1989. The prime minister's speech wove together official discourses on development, nation, and democracy, emphasizing that political independence and a democratic tradition (twin achievements of the PUP) had accorded Belizeans the power to collectively determine the future of Belize Food Products.

> [L]et us go back to the years before 1950. If this happened, our people here would have had no say in what the future would have been. The colonial masters would have decided, and that was it. But now with our government, with the democratic process, our consultation, and our mixed economy, we have a chance to get together and work out a solution. . . . Now what about the future? Well, I think it's a good future. In the first instance, whatever industry—whether it's banana, rice, sugar, fishing— we have stability. Stability and—and I'm being immodest now, and I take credit for the work we have done since 1950. Oh, there were occasions when people say to us "Spill blood! We must start a war!" We never did that. We worked through the ballot; we worked through the democratic process. And we developed a system, even though we may disagree—you belong to one party and I belong to another party, but we can talk. We can reason together. And we reason . . . for the best interest of the people.

The prime minister went on to articulate further links between democracy and development. But whereas the UDP prime minister had addressed the growers as a single category, the new prime minister's speech drew emphatic distinctions between small and large growers. "We needn't hide ourselves from it," he asserted; "this industry is so structured that the few big growers own more acreage than the many small growers. That's the reality." His party was concerned to "make sure that the *little* man is helped." "I was talking to one of your big people here," he continued, "and he said to me what is probably our philosophy: the little man, you have to help him. You have to help him help himself. Sometimes he don't know exactly how to go about helping himself, and I hope the big growers would understand what we are trying to do, to bring them [the little man] in. To bring them in. That's the only way we are going to have stability in our country." The audience applauded in approval. The prime minister went on: "We need to learn from the lessons around us. Why is there civil war in El Salvador? Why is there guerrilla fighting in Guatemala? Why are guerrilla insurgents beginning in Honduras? Because the little man, the majority—the little man is the majority of the people—were neglected."

Directly addressing the question of how the purchase of BFP might be financed, he continued: "We expect the big growers to find the money themselves. They have the access to the markets. And maybe," he added, "something will have to be worked out to help the small growers, some sort of financing." He clarified: "We're not against the big man at all. We're not against the medium man. But a government has the obligation to look after the little man, the little woman—when I say man, I mean man and woman—because that person cannot take care of himself or herself." The prime minister clearly distinguished between large and small growers in his speech and identified small growers as key to efforts to combine development with democracy; "bringing the small man in" to development efforts would maintain Belizean stability. However, the prime minister did not match his predecessor's pledge to guarantee a loan for the company's purchase by growers. Nor did he guarantee financial assistance to the smallholders he promised to look after.

After the prime minister had left the meeting, a grower with several hundred acres of citrus, apparently concerned that the prime minister's speech might foster divisions among citrus growers, cautioned: "A word to my colleagues: certainly we would not like to conduct the affairs of the association in a scenario of big and small farmers, and I certainly hope that when issues of far-reaching importance arrive around our table, it is not . . . the small farmers [against] the large farmers, because that's the beginning of the end. So, my colleagues, let's hope that will not be the trend whereby issues are decided."

Oliver Hassan also spoke against the distinctions Price had drawn among citrus growers, rearticulating nationalist and development discourses to define a "Belizean dream" that combined aspirations for individual and national progress and united all growers as Belizeans.

> At one time, the setting was one that would have embraced all citrus growers as a whole, without exception, which meant that any grower that wanted to participate in Belize Food Products would be able to do so. . . . [A]s long as there will be discrimination within the membership of the Citrus Growers Association, whereby we would be labeled small, medium, and large, I will have nothing to do with that setting. . . . Because I think that . . . it's a Belizean dream. Everybody works, and they work because we want a better way of life for ourselves. And if the rewards that we will get because we have progressed over the years is one of discriminatory rewards, then certainly I am not part and parcel of that.

Hassan's "Belizean dream" echoes the "American dream," in which personal economic progress is encouraged and celebrated as the result of hard work. It would be unfair, he suggests, to discriminate against those who have progressed through hard work. Labeling this dream of progress "Belizean" implies that all Belizeans share in it; indeed, citrus farmers large and small had been clearing and planting for several years in pursuit of personal economic progress and as contributors to their nation's economic development.

Hassan then turned up the pressure on the government to guarantee the whole loan by invoking regional disparities, with their racial-ethnic resonances. He recalled that the government had assisted Spanish cane farmers in the north by actually contributing cash toward the Cane Farmers Association's purchase of shares in the sugar processing plants.[1] "All that we are asking for is a guarantee," he continued. "It will be impossible for the association to raise these monies without the guarantee of the government of Belize." The government's own previous actions—under a prior PUP administration—set a precedent for assisting citrus growers now. Failure to help citrus farmers, Hassan suggested, could be read as government favoritism for the cane growers of the north, which in turn carried implications of racial-ethnic favoritism, since cane farmers are understood to be Mestizo, while the citrus industry is associated with Garifuna and Creoles.

Though the prime minister had been noncommittal about the government's possible role in the sale of BFP, after the meeting smallholders suggested that his recognition and support for them *as* small growers had legitimized their assertions of difference from large growers and their efforts to protect themselves from large growers' power. Indeed, the prime minister had emphatically distinguished between large and small growers, invoking democracy discourse to align his party with the small-grower majority. Though the populist tone of the prime minister's speech convinced many small growers that he wanted the company to belong to the small growers, his failure to make specific promises left them skeptical about their prospects for purchasing Belize Foods. "We were waiting to hear from Mr. Price whether his government would continue the promise of the last government," Elizabeth Evans—herself a UDP—explained, "but we were disappointed. He said he wanted to help the small grower, but he didn't say how. He didn't promise anything." Large growers felt they had been sent dual messages by the prime minister: one apprised them of the costs of political disloyalty; the other reminded them that government support for their plans would be contingent on their winning the backing of the small growers, whom the prime minister had recognized as part of the "small man" majority at the center of Belizean democracy.

The Threat of Monopoly

The CGA committee appointed to explore the purchase of Belize Foods did not meet during the remainder of November or December, as they waited for the government to release the study it had commissioned to explore the feasibility of growers' purchase of BFP.[2] The speeches given by both prime ministers had encouraged growers' expectations that the government would assist them. As chapter 6 demonstrated, small growers were frequently skeptical of politicians' claims of support for the little man—noting land deals that favor the wealthy, for instance. However, since the government had intervened on behalf of smallholder citrus and cane farmers in the past, many citrus farmers expected the government to live up to its rhetoric in this instance. When the consulting firm's study was released, it recommended that the government should guarantee any loan required to purchase the company (BEST 1989); however, it did not provide data about the company's financial position that the government or the growers' committee could use as a basis for action.

Neither the government nor the CGA committee had taken any decisive action by the end of 1989, when renewed rumors of a CCB attempt to buy BFP shook the industry. CCB chair Porter had asked the managing director of BFP, Nathan Clifford, to arrange a meeting for him with Nestlé. Clifford, a Belizean who owned several hundred acres of citrus in addition to having an administrative role at BFP, became alarmed over the prospect of an imminent CCB monopoly in the industry. He informed Oliver Hassan of Porter's request, and Hassan renewed his active involvement in negotiations with Nestlé. Hassan also met with CGA and BWU leaders to urge them to send delegations to the capital: "I began mobilizing all the different interest groups. We held a series of meetings. We made representations to Belmopan, both the growers and the workers, telling Belmopan in no uncertain words that we would not allow a CCB buyout, because obviously it would be creating a monopoly setting, which would be disastrous and destructive."

Rumors about the potential CCB buyout animated conversations throughout the district. Many growers reported hearing that Mr. Porter claimed to have government support for CCB's purchase of Belize Foods. Another rumor suggested that the Belize Foods factory would be shut down. Many growers found the rumors plausible. Some believed the Stann Creek Valley was being punished by the PUP for having elected a UDP representative. Since the largest shareholders at CCB were well known PUPs, some growers speculated that ownership of Belize Foods was to be their reward for supporting the PUP in the last elections. Furthermore, growers reasoned, if PUP loyalists owned both factories, the PUP would be assured complete support from the citrus industry.

CCB's initiative brought to the fore interests smallholders believed they shared with those large growers who did not own shares in the Citrus Company. At this juncture, small and large growers united to oppose the Citrus Company's plans, dispatching a CGA delegation to warn the prime minister that "the growers" would never accept a monopoly. Citrus farmers cast themselves as a single category in this context to emphasize their unity on this issue. However, smallholders believed that a monopoly would have even more negative affects on them than it would on growers with larger acreages. If such a sale ever took place, "the small growers will perish," Elizabeth Evans argued. Then CCB would own all of BFP's groves too, and "they wouldn't look upon us our little fruit." "We remember how it was before BFP opened," smallholder Virginia Small recalled. "A lot of fruit spoiled." Violet Cole, one of many smallholders who believed in selling fruit to both companies to maintain competition in the industry, agreed: "We don't want one company, because we know what it's like. When there was only one factory, the company only accepted about 60 percent of your fruit. They did all of their own fruit first." "And now that there's more fruit," her husband added, "it would be even worse." Martin and Eva Escobar shared this opinion: "Before BFP opened, CCB wouldn't take all of your fruit, and they paid you about seventy-five cents a box. They would tell you, 'You can deliver thirty-five boxes on Monday and forty on Wednesday.' If you couldn't get transport, that was too bad. Now, there is no way one factory could handle all the fruit." Another smallholder, Miss Celia, worried that if Mr. Porter owned both factories, "they could offer us twenty-five cents, and we would have to take it or let our fruit rot."

Although some smallholders tempered their remarks about rumored government involvement with the planned CCB buyout depending on their party affiliation as "PUPs" or "UDPs," most subordinated their political loyalties to the interests they associated with small grower status. In fact, smallholder Carmen Silvers announced that, although she had been a PUP all her life, she was so disgusted with the government's rumored support for Mr. Porter that she was abandoning the PUP. She declared herself "no kind of P" because she did not see PUP and small grower identities as compatible at this time.

Some growers also advanced nationalist reasons for their opposition to the attempted takeover by CCB. A grower with a ten-acre farm explained: "We never want one man to have so much say in the factory, especially since he's not from here. He already has too much say at CCB." CCB chair Porter had immigrated to Belize a decade earlier. He had made a number of investments in Belize, had been living in Belize, and identified himself as a naturalized Belizean. However, legal definitions of nationality aside, many citrus farmers still considered him a Jamaican, someone "not from here." The UDP newspaper expressed a similar point of view, reporting that the cabinet had approved the sale of Belize Foods to "the same foreign interest group that already owns and operates Belize's only other citrus processing plant." This move, the *Pulse* warned, "placed the entire industry in the hands of foreigners" ("Citrus Industry Sold," *Pulse,* 21 Jan. 1990).

CCB refuted the charge that it was foreign owned by initiating its own newsletter, which argued that CCB "is a 50 percent Belizean owned and totally Belizean managed company and has been since 1983, when it was BOUGHT OUT OF FOREIGN OWNERSHIP by a syndicate of Belizeans." To legitimize the Belizeanness of CCB's chair, the newsletter deployed official discourse that celebrates investors as contributors to national economic development. It praised the "Herculean effort" of the "group of enterprising Belizean businessmen/growers," who "expressed their faith in our beloved Jewel in the most tangible way," by investing "their money in buying CCB from its old absentee-owners." "Presently the company has just five shareholders from Trinidad and Tobago and more than forty Belizean shareholders. We find it hypocritical indeed when persons who have been actively encouraged to settle in Belize and who have become Belizeans and who have contributed greatly to Belizean economic growth are still gratuitously labeled 'foreigners' even, in some cases, after being settled in Belize for more than ten years" (CCB 1990). While CCB's argument resonated with official discourses, many growers continued to consider the chair less than fully Belizean. Dalton Smith, a UDP and self-identified spokesman for small growers, argued that Porter had "some kind of special permit to live here," but "he isn't Belizean."

In addition to arguing that the PUP favored "foreigners" over Belizeans, the UDP *Pulse* also painted the PUP as biased in favor of north over south, and hence Mestizos over Afro-Belizeans. Recalling the government's pledge of funds to purchase the sugar factories up north, the *Pulse* declared that "the citrus growers feel that they are being discriminated against" ("Dangriga Rallies behind UDP Condemnation of BFP Sell-Out," *Pulse*, 28 Jan. 1990).

As the possibility of a CCB monopoly became more real, Oliver Hassan assumed a leading role in the CGA committee charged with acquiring BFP on behalf of citrus growers. He was joined by Bill Williston, owner of an eight-hundred-acre citrus farm. Nathan Clifford—managing director of Belize Foods, large-scale citrus farmer, and UDP (manifested in his appointment by the UDP government to serve on national committees)—also took on an active role. The committee held a series of meetings with Nestlé. They also lobbied the PUP representative from the town of Dangriga, Theodore Aranda, to oppose a CCB monopoly. Although CCB shareholders Porter and Rowan were two of the largest PUP supporters in Stann Creek District, animated conversations throughout the district made it clear that the majority of voters opposed a CCB monopoly. Thus, Aranda threw his support behind the CGA committee's bid to purchase BFP and began to pressure both Nestlé and the leaders of his own party to prevent a monopoly in the citrus industry. Hassan and his colleagues soon concluded an agreement for the purchase of Belize Foods. However, it was not clear which faction would win the government backing necessary to conclude the sale, the PUP-affiliated owners of CCB or Hassan's group, which appeared to lean toward the UDP.

Up to this time, workers' main concern with the rumored sale of Belize Foods had focused on severance payments. Both unions wanted the company to make "long service" payments at the time of the sale in order to avoid the problems that had plagued the UGWU after the CCB sale. Suddenly, rumors that the factory would be closed threatened workers' jobs. Encouraged by Hassan, the Belize Workers Union sent a delegation to the prime minister to express their opposition to a factory closure. However, as we saw in chapter 4, workers such as Pedro Ruiz, who had begun investing in citrus, were more concerned about the possibility that citrus prices would fall under a monopoly than they were about losing their jobs.

Grower Unity for a Day: A Message to Belmopan

After a month of rumors about monopolies and plant closings, emotions and fears were running high when a special CGA meeting was convened January 20, 1990. Turnout for the meeting was much larger than it had been for the August meeting. Citrus growers, wage laborers in the industry, and others angered by the rumors filled the schoolroom at Sacred Heart primary school and crowded its doorways. The chair of the CGA committee reported that the committee had signed a memorandum of understanding with Nestlé that committed "the growers" to purchase Belize Foods for $16 million. The growers would also pay $2.5 million in pensions and retirement benefits to BFP's workers, and a block of shares would be reserved for those BFP workers who wanted to invest their long-service pay in company shares.[3] Workers, the committee chair announced, had been "competently represented" in the negotiations by Nathan Clifford.

After the committee chair's announcement, the general manager of CCB, Wesley Spencer, asked to make his own announcement: "Fellow growers," he began, "CCB is interested in buying out BFP."

"No!" "No way!" "No podrian!" ("They can't!") growers shouted in response.

Mr. Spencer attempted to reassure the growers, "We hear that growers are concerned that if CCB bought BFP that there would be a monopoly. But there would have been no monopoly the way that we intended to go about it.

We intended to go about it by offering shares. We also would have . . . asked that no existing shareholder in CCB participate in this new share issue. In other words, the shares would have been put out there . . . for growers to take up, all new growers." Mr. Spencer was attempting to extend the unity of interest that had emerged between large and small growers to define CCB's shareholders as "growers" and to offer once again the opportunity to make CCB a "growers' factory."

"Cho!" a number of growers shouted, using a Creole expression that conveys disbelief and disgust.

Spencer went on: "As throughput increased, because eventually all the fruit would be passing through one company, naturally it would mean that our costs of operation would go down. And we would have been prepared to negotiate with the CGA for a [change in the price formula]. There would be no price fixing, again, because we would be grower owned. Growers would naturally want returns for their fruit."

Mr. Spencer's comment that all of the fruit would pass through a single factory confirmed growers' worst fears about the CCB threat. Growers began to talk among themselves in a crescendo of voices that concluded with more exclamations of "Cho!" Apparently undaunted, Mr. Spencer offered a final sweetener to his proposal, promising that the new CCB would extend electricity all the way up the Stann Creek Valley, from Pomona to Middlesex. "At last," he promised, "the valley would get light!"

The growers, many of whom had worked for CCB and lived in the company camps, hooted, whistled, and jeered. As smallholders loudly rejected Mr. Spencer's offer, their rising chorus of derisive commentary generated a sense of collective identity and interest among small and large citrus farmers allied against CCB.

Taking the microphone, Oliver Hassan built on this sense of shared purpose. He reminded growers of the promises CCB's largest shareholders had made when they purchased the company, calling their enterprise a "growers' factory." He also reminded them of the company's failure to live up to those promises. "We hear of all the generosity, all the sugars that we are getting now. It reminds me of a young man, when he's courting. He promise more, he promise more—. And the day after, we are on the next plane out! The young lady kyaahn find wi [can't find us]!" Loud laughter greeted Hassan's analogy.

His use of Creole pronunciation (*kyaahn*) and Creole grammar in his choice of pronoun (*wi*) heightened the sense of subordinates sharing a joke on elites. Like most formal events in Belize, CGA meetings are typically conducted in

Standard English, characterized as the language of power and prestige in the English-speaking Caribbean, since it implies a certain level of formal education and an ability to deal effectively with foreign elites (Abrahams 1983). In contrast, Creole often serves as a language of egalitarianism and challenges to elites.[4] Belizean smallholders often phrase challenges to elites in Creole (for example, shouting "Cho!" in response to a comment). However, Belizean Creole has additional connotations related to class and national identities: while it is associated with non-elite status, it is also the closest thing Belizeans have to an indigenous national language. Thus, Hassan's code-switching from English into Creole emphasized citrus growers' shared Belizeanness and blurred differences in wealth and power between himself and smallholders to enact class and national commonalities among growers, in contrast to CCB shareholders.

Hassan reminded growers of "all the sufferings we had when we had one plant." His use of the term "we" implied shared suffering and shared interests.

"That's right," several audience members responded with conviction, apparently remembering vividly.

Hassan also reminded them of growers' struggles to create and maintain competition in the past: "Mr. George Rowan, Mr. Arthur's father . . . made every effort to bring about another processing facility here, so that we could have competition in this valley." Applause from the floor interrupted his speech. "Because competition is necessary, competition is a must!" he continued.

"Right!" farmers shouted in response.

Hassan recalled the "gloomy" period in the 1970s, when CCB had gone into receivership and BFP was considering buying out its rival. The CGA management committee, with Hassan as its chair, traveled to Belmopan "every day, requesting government to kindly assist CCB. . . . We made very clear that monopoly would be total destruction." They negotiated an agreement that CCB's shareholders would raise additional funds, and the government of Belize would match those funds. "Those monies were injected in the industry and hence today we still have a competitive citrus industry. Government saw it in their wisdom then that competition . . . was very very vital to this industry, that a monopoly would be damnation!" Hassan concluded.

Several growers shouted, "That's right!"

After establishing agreement about the evils of monopoly, Hassan turned his attention to extracting himself and the association from dangerous UDP–

PUP wrangling: "Our association over the years have gained respect and credibility . . . because we have always been able to keep politics out of the ranks of our association. It was a nonpolitical entity, and we made every effort to keep politics out of the association. And I think this is the way our association has to be run. Otherwise, we will be in serious, serious trouble. . . . So what I'm going to say here. . . . I want you all to understand that it's nonpolitical and has to do with the welfare of this industry. I am not talking politics. I am not talking PUP, UDP, whatever P. I am talking citrus and the only politics I am talking is citrus politics!" Hassan continued, to applause. Hassan thus set the stage for his own announcement by emphasizing the common suffering of *all* citrus growers under the previous monopoly, asserting a nonpartisan basis for "citrus politics," and reminding growers of CCB's empty promises at the time the company was sold.

He then presented the new package the CGA committee had developed, assured that growers would find the plan much more palatable than CCB's. The new plan guaranteed small growers a block of 20 percent of the shares. On Clifford's suggestion, an additional 10 percent of the shares were reserved for BFP's workers. In addition, Hassan reported, the committee had agreed that no individual would be allowed to own more than 30 percent of the shares. He was conciliatory as he explained this limitation: "The fear was that . . . the bigger growers—or to put it very plain, me, the speaker—would have controlling shares. So that has been dispelled." In spite of the emphasis in this meeting on the interests all growers share as growers, Hassan apparently no longer hoped to use these commonalities to persuade smallholders that his control of the company would be in their best interests. Indeed, the new plan recognized smallholders' assertions of difference and addressed concerns that smallholders had raised earlier: the plan limited Hassan's acquisition of shares and explicitly differentiated small growers from large growers by establishing a separate block of shares for small growers.

Hassan reported that the committee's request for a loan guarantee from the government for the blocks of shares to be held for small growers and workers had been denied. "What!?" a chorus of growers and workers shouted, surprised that the prime minister had responded negatively to the request after emphasizing the government's "obligation" to "look after the little man" in an address to the CGA only two months earlier.

However, Hassan assured them that the committee itself would locate the finances for growers' and workers' purchase of BFP. But, he cautioned, again using Creole terms to position himself and his audience in shared class and national categories, "Even though we are very optimistic . . . that we will be able to do this, we have just heard Mr. Spencer saying that "If unu [Creole plural "you"] fall down, if unu drop through, we are right there. . . . They are just waiting for us to slide, and they will step in. So then . . . I am saying that if . . . we are not able to bring this deal to reality, . . . growers must not sit here idle and must not entertain a CCB buyout of Belize Food Products."

"No, no way," the audience assured him loudly, applauding.

If we can't do it, Hassan suggested, then it would be better to have Mr. Gorbachev buy BFP rather than letting CCB buy it. The growers burst into applause and laughter, as an older woman shouted, "I'll give you a kiss for that, bwai [boy]!" The irreverent tone of her response and the fact that she addressed Hassan as "bwai" demonstrated his success in blurring differences among growers and mobilizing them as a collective agent in opposition to the proposed monopoly.

To absolutely preclude the rumored possibility of the government supporting CCB's bid, Hassan continued with exaggerated emphasis that provoked more laughter, "I understand that the big boys from [CCB] are going around—now I'm *sure* that this is not so. I am *sure* that this is not so. I *hope* it is not so! They are going around telling everybody that they have the blessing of the prime minister and the cabinet. I don't believe that. But if it is so, it is something very very serious. And if it is so, we have to send a very clear signal to Belmopan."

"Yes," the audience agreed, applauding, "That's correct!"

"Belmopan has to realize that the people are power," he said.

"Correct!" they responded again. "We put them there!"

"And if the wishes of the people will not be adhered to, then we don't have a good government," he added.

"That's right!" "Yes!" they shouted, amid applause. Growers had spoken in a united voice, and their message had been sent, loud and clear, to Belmopan. At the previous CGA meeting, the prime minister had invoked democracy discourse and positioned small growers at its center. Now, Hassan had appropriated the themes of democracy discourse, reframing the "small man" majority as "the people," a potentially broader term that might include even those who were not "small," though it certainly excluded the "big boys" of CCB. In doing so, Hassan and his fellow growers were able to turn democracy discourse back on the government and demand that it respect their wishes.

The New Coalition: "Oliver and the Growers"

If the delegations of union leaders and citrus growers that had visited
Belmopan had left any doubt, the overwhelming expression of collective will
at the January CGA meeting made growers' opposition to CCB's overture
manifestly clear. After the meeting, ministers of government categorically
denied that they had ever supported Porter's bid to buy BFP. Such sugges-
tions were "vicious rumors," the prime minister stressed. Indeed, the government sought to capitalize on the impending sale of Belize Foods, headlining
its report in the PUP *Belize Times* "Belizeans First: Citrus Growers and Workers Buy BFP." The article credited the government with being "fully involved
in monitoring the discussions," in order "to ensure the best possible outcome
and stability of the industry." Now, rather than "discriminating" among citrus
farmers, the newspaper announced that "Government placed particular emphasis to ensure the participation of Belizean citrus growers as a whole to
become shareholders in the new enterprise" (*Belize Times*, 4 Feb. 1990).

Those who identified themselves as small growers were elated that a
CCB buyout of BFP had been averted. Alberto Puc explained, "We don't want
one man to boss two factories." Miss Celia elaborated: "Mr. Portapak wanted
to buy the factory. But we said we don't want either CCB or Mr. Portapak to
buy BFP . . . and Oliver Hassan is our spokesman." However, most farmers
were also relieved that Oliver Hassan would not wield controlling shares in
the new company. Though they had collaborated with Hassan at the January
meeting, afterward nearly everyone—from Richard Fenton to Elizabeth
Evans—phrased their approval in terms that signaled a coalition between
two distinct kinds of people, "Oliver and the growers." Some included workers at BFP in the coalition. Many suggested that democracy, as the rule of the
majority, had been well served by the January CGA meeting. As Dalton Smith
explained, "Politically, the politicians would look at the benefit they can derive from a hundred men against what they can derive from one."

Though some small growers began to consider purchasing shares in BFP,
most growers remained skeptical. They had been far more concerned with
preventing a CCB monopoly than with purchasing shares in the company
themselves. Many doubted that they would have control over the funds they
invested in the company or a say in running the company. Elizabeth Evans
said she would not buy shares, because, based on past experience with the
companies, "I don't trust. Last year we thought we would get back pay, and
at the end of the crop they said no back pay. So I don't trust to leave my

money with them that they will give me something back later. I prefer to have the money in my hand. Then I could be sure of it." Similarly, another small-holder reasoned, "The fifteen hundred dollars that I might invest in shares I could also invest in expanding my citrus acreage. But if I expand my farm, I would have more control over my investment."

For other growers, buying shares was out of the question, because their families made too many demands on the household income already. Still others were wary of committing themselves to one company, preferring to remain neutral, able to sell to the highest bidder. All considered the agreement for BFP's purchase a victory, however, because it protected them from a CCB monopoly or from a company dominated by a single large grower.

Wage laborers were taken by surprise by the plan unveiled at the January meeting, which offered shares to workers for the first time. They were even more surprised to hear the chair of the CGA committee announce that the workers had been "competently represented" in negotiations with Nestlé by Mr. Clifford, BFP's managing director. "How could management represent the workers?" waterfront worker Roy Diego wondered. They also questioned whether workers' shares were intended for workers or staff. The UGWU leadership met with Mr. Clifford to discuss these questions and request that workers be represented in the negotiations by union officers rather than by their employer. Though the union did not win a place at the negotiating table with Nestlé, union members were happy to learn from Mr. Clifford that severance payments would be made at the time of the sale, and that all workers would have the option of investing the amount owed them in shares or receiving the payment in cash. Most workers were eager to receive their long-service payments but not very interested in buying shares; they had more pressing plans for the money: building a house, expanding a farm, migrating to the United States.

Following the January meeting, the CGA's committee appointed a sub-committee to negotiate the financial arrangements to implement the memorandum it had signed with Nestlé in January. The subcommittee on finance consisted of three elites: Oliver Hassan, Bill Williston, and BFP managing director Nathan Clifford. When the Belize Bank offered to support the venture, the bank's chair, Michael Ashcroft, also became involved in the negotiations. Ashcroft, a British financier, had been granted Belizean citizenship by the former UDP administration in return for his investments in Belize. He was subsequently made ambassador to the European Community by the PUP administration.[5] Working with Ashcroft, the finance subcommittee substantially revised the financial plans for the company's purchase. After the sub-committee had signed a sales agreement with Nestlé in May, the CGA scheduled a meeting for July to present the package to the CGA membership.

The "First 100 Percent Belizean Citrus Company"

Turnout for the July meeting was much smaller than it had been for the January meeting. Since growers no longer felt their futures were threatened by the sale of Belize Foods, many had lost interest. Hassan announced triumphantly that the finance subcommittee had signed a sales agreement with Nestlé that would "eventually bring the ownership of Belize Food into the hands of Belizeans, 100 percent Belizeans!" The declaration of "100 percent Belizean" status for the new company was intended to contrast favorably with CCB's "foreign" ownership, since Trinidadians owned controlling shares in CCB and Richard Porter's Belizeanness had already been questioned. Framing the sale of Belize Foods in this way suggested that buying shares in the company was a means for Belizeans to take control of their economic destiny. Although Hassan's own faction included both a naturalized immigrant from Jamaica, Bill Williston, and the British financier Michael Ashcroft, who had become Belizean through the government's economic citizenship program, Hassan cast them both unproblematically as Belizean in his claim that the new owners of Belize Foods would be "100 percent Belizeans." Hassan's aims were twofold: he needed to convince growers to deliver their fruit to the new company, and he sought to use citrus growers' support to press the government to facilitate the sale and grant the company concessions.

The audience clapped in approval, and Hassan went on to summarize the negotiations and their results. Michael Ashcroft's "ingenious" negotiating tactics had saved growers $5 million: they would now pay $13 million for the company, plus the costs of severance payments. Thirty percent of the company's shares would be reserved for growers who produced more than ten thousand boxes of fruit per year, and 18 percent would be reserved for growers who produced fewer than ten thousand boxes. These shares could be purchased either in exchange for fruit delivery or by paying cash before the sale. The second option provided an avenue for raising cash toward the purchase price, but participation was limited to citrus growers only. Growers could purchase shares according to a formula that multiplied their annual production by the number of years (one to five) for which they were willing to commit their fruit to Belize Foods. Those who failed to deliver their fruit to

BFP after buying shares would have their shares revoked. A third block of 16 percent of the shares would be reserved for the staff and workers of Belize Foods, and the remaining shares would be allocated "according to how the finances will be made available by the various different parties." The ambiguous "various different parties" included Hassan, Mr. Williston, Mr. Clifford, and a company called Belize Holdings Limited. Together, these parties would put up the money to buy BFP and then hold the shares in the growers' and workers' blocks for their future investment.

Hassan encouraged all farmers to participate for their own good and the good of their nation. To enable smallholders to participate and feel a sense of ownership in BFP, it was necessary to establish a means for them to acquire shares without having to put up cash. Hassan explained that his group had worked very hard to assemble financing that would allow a block of shares to be held for small growers to purchase through fruit deliveries rather than cash. "This is in keeping with our commitment to the small farmers, because . . . we want to encourage small farmers to participate in buying shares. . . . We want to know that, after all the shares have been issued out, that all farmers will be able to say that they had an opportunity, an opportunity to own shares in what will be our first truly one hundred percent Belizean-owned citrus industry." Having conceded to small growers' insistence that they were distinct from large growers, Oliver Hassan now addressed them as small growers. He cast himself in the role of protector in terms that resonated with the PUP prime minister's earlier speech about "helping" the "little man."

Farmers in the audience raised several concerns. One complained that small growers, "the majority of this industry," were allocated too few shares. Hassan disagreed, taking pains to quantify the extreme consideration that the large-grower negotiators had exercised toward small growers: "If you have your figures correct you will note that growers under ten thousand boxes deliver 12 percent of the total crop, okay? Thirty-four growers with production of over ten thousand boxes, including the two companies, produce the rest. So when we look at the amount that the small grower is getting in comparison with what the big grower is getting, the small grower is far much more protected and considered in this setting."

Following his line of questioning, the same grower asked, "Has the government of Belize approved this percentage distribution of shares?"

"The government of Belize has nothing to do with this setting," Hassan replied. "The government . . . no di put in [is not putting in] one cent! So the government of Belize have nothing to do with this." As growers began to protest to one another, Hassan quickly added, "However, they are abreast of what's happening. They are in tune with our recommendation, and they have given this whole setting one hundred percent support." Hassan attempted to use the government's professed support to rally small growers behind the plan, so that he could use small growers' support to press the government for concessions.

Another grower challenged Hassan: "Who is or who are the main shareholders in Belize Holdings Company? Is it a public company? Are they nationals?" This grower was clearly aware of allegations published in the UDP *Pulse* that BFP was being sold to Michael Ashcroft, a "foreigner." Although the UDP had granted Ashcroft Belizean citizenship in recognition of his investments in Belize, during the PUP administration the *Pulse* had run articles critical of Ashcroft's business and political dealings in Belize. Indeed, after the July CGA meeting, it ran an article about Ashcroft titled "Billionaire Buys Belize." The article was accompanied by a cartoon showing kneeling members of the PUP government proffering gifts—exemptions from taxes and government controls—to an octopus labeled "Ashcroft," seated on the throne of Belize Holdings Limited. The octopus grasped in its tentacles the citrus processing company, his ambassadorship, shares in the Belizean telecommunications company, and bags of money (*Pulse,* 5 Aug. 1990). In the cartoon, one of the government ministers says, "Oh great foreign one, we give you these special privileges that you may dominate all business in Belize for all times."

Hassan, also mindful of the UDP's charges, explained that Belize Holdings "is a public company registered in Belize which owns . . . one hundred percent shares of Belize Bank." Identifying Belize Holdings as a public company, Hassan sought to dispel rumors that Ashcroft as an individual would control the company. So, he assured the growers, "the rumors that have been circulating that it's Mr. Michael Ashcroft that's buying shares into this company, that's falsely and mischievously spread by people who want to create mischief." Hassan then introduced "His Excellency," Ambassador Michael Ashcroft, to provide further clarification. Ashcroft explained that he presently held controlling shares in Belize Holdings, a fact that undermined Hassan's assurances. However, during his brief presentation, Ashcroft cast himself as a Belizean nationalist, explaining that he had taken the lead in assembling a group of investors in Belize Holdings to purchase the Royal Bank of Canada branch in Belize. This effort had "brought back to Belize one of its banking institutions," making the Belize Bank the first *Belizean* bank. His involvement in the current negotiations for BFP aimed to accomplish for the citrus industry what he had already done for the banking industry, making BFP a *Belizean* company. Growers politely applauded his presentation.

Small growers also raised a number of practical concerns during the meeting. Many small growers sold fruit to both companies, out of concern to maintain competition in the industry and to foster good personal relations with both companies. The idea of committing their fruit to one company appeared risky: if BFP had mechanical problems and could not accept fruit they had already reaped, would CCB accept it? Or would they have to watch it rot? And if everyone began to sell to BFP, what might happen to the competition that in January they had emphatically agreed was necessary to the industry? Further, small growers pointed out, CCB had always sent transport to pick up their fruit. Would BFP offer the same service? Hassan assured growers that the directors would discuss that issue at their next meeting. Small growers also worried that if large numbers of growers began supplying fruit to BFP exclusively, the factory would not be able to handle all of the fruit. If not, small growers were sure that the company would accept large growers' fruit first and might not "look upon" those with smaller amounts of fruit. In response, Mr. Clifford outlined BFP's plans to double its facilities for fruit delivery and storage and assured growers that the factory was operating at only 60 percent of its capacity. Thus, smallholders continued to position themselves as "small growers" and to pursue concerns and problems specific to that social location. In doing so, they forced those planning the sale to continue courting them *as* small growers.[6]

After the meeting, small growers expressed surprise and disappointment that the government had provided no financial support or loan guarantee for them. Growers spoke favorably about two parts of the final agreement. First, the five-year period for the purchase of shares would allow them plenty of time to consider the advantages and potential pitfalls of participation. Second, some hoped that increased Belizean ownership of the processing side of the industry might keep more of the industry's profits in Belize to create jobs during the off-season.

However, many complained that Hassan had not given them sufficient information about how the sale would work. One skeptical smallholder wondered if this was done intentionally to dissuade them from buying shares: "The growers are not educated, and they don't understand. But they need to be educated if they are going to participate. If they don't want to take the time to educate small growers about their plans, is it because they really don't want them to participate?" While some farmers expressed enthusiasm about buying shares, others predicted that BFP would become another CCB. One farmer with twenty-seven acres of citrus complained: "They made lots of noise about the small growers buying shares at CCB, but in the end only a few large growers own the company. The same thing will happen at Belize Foods: they have 30 percent for some group, 16 percent for another group, and 18 percent for someone else. And the rest of the shares? They must be for Oliver, Williston, Clifford, and the bank manager. . . . [T]hat's what it has to be: those are the only people who know what's going on. It's all a secret, and the small growers only hear shush-shush here and shush-shush there, only whispers. No one tells them anything." He suggested Hassan was just trying to use the small growers. "Oliver could talk and talk, and say a lot of pretty things to make everyone agree with him. . . . But he only tells you what he wants you to know. He didn't tell us a lot of things on Saturday."

Struggle over the purchase of Belize Foods involved competing efforts to define and mobilize collective agents around class or national identities. Oliver Hassan initially attempted to mobilize citrus farmers behind his proposal in broad class terms. Both his rhetoric and his code-switching from English into Creole asserted common class—and national—identities and interests for all Belizean citrus growers. The UDP prime minister's promise to guarantee the entire loan that would enable "the growers" to purchase BFP echoed Hassan's arguments, embracing all growers as equal members of a single category. In contrast, his warning to growers to guard against a CCB monopoly positioned CCB's PUP-affiliated shareholders as *processors* rather than growers and ascribed to them interests contrary to those shared by growers.

However, farmers with relatively small citrus acreages rejected these attempts to define all citrus growers as members of one big class with common interests. Drawing on understandings they had generated on the basis of the practical activities involved in citrus production, which often place them in competition with estate owners, they defined themselves more narrowly as small growers, who share certain interests in opposition to large growers. Envisioning themselves as a class separate from large growers and vulnerable to large growers' self-interested actions, they amended Oliver Hassan's package to prevent him from obtaining controlling shares in the company. By pointing out and emphasizing Hassan's probable control of the company, CCB shareholders contributed to small growers' resolve to limit Hassan's participation.

The distinction perceived by small growers was reinforced after the 1989 elections, when PUP Prime Minister Price emphatically distinguished between small and large citrus farmers. His positioning of "small growers" as part of the collective "small man" of official democracy discourse reinforced the legitimacy of smallholders' previous appropriations of "small man" rhetoric and their assertions of difference from large growers. The prime minister's assertions and small growers' embrace—once again—of the position of "small man," whose interests Belizean democracy is pledged to serve, forced competing economic and political elites to seek alliances with smallholders to further their own agendas.

However, just a few months later the threat of monopoly provoked by CCB's bid to buy Belize Foods prompted all citrus growers who did not own shares in CCB to unite in opposition to CCB's efforts. Self-identified small growers believed that they *did* share *some* interests with *some* large growers, and they allied themselves with Hassan's large-grower faction when they saw those interests threatened by monopoly. At the January CGA meeting, growers' opposition to monopoly was nearly unanimous; CCB's grower-stockholders were the exception. When Mr. Spencer from CCB sought to appropriate the grower unity generated at the meeting by asserting "grower" status for CCB's shareholders and reviving the "grower-owned factory" promise of 1983, jeers from the floor indicated that smallholders were not willing to extend grower unity that far. In response to rumors of government support for CCB's bid, small and large growers together drew on the positioning of small growers as the "small men" at the center of Belizean democracy to pressure the government not to act against what they defined as their best interests.

However, despite the striking unity among citrus farmers at the January meeting, Oliver Hassan no longer attempted to persuade smallholders that his control of the company would be in their best interests. Instead, he abandoned his argument that all citrus growers belonged to a single class and shared common interests, conceding to smallholders' concerns by limiting his own participation to 30 percent and setting aside a separate block of shares for small growers. Thus, by insisting on defining themselves as "small growers," whose interests overlapped but did not coincide with the interests of "large growers," smallholders had forced Hassan to court them *as* small growers, recognizing their identity claim and addressing their issues.[7]

As negotiations with Nestlé drew to a close, Hassan increasingly deployed discourses that articulated nationalism with development. He solicited support from both growers and the government by promoting the new Belize Foods as the first "100 percent Belizean owned" citrus company. This argument, as well as earlier debate over the national status of CCB director Richard Porter, injected contests over the definition and allocation of national identities into efforts to mobilize collective agents for the purchase of BFP. To claim Belizean identities for themselves, both Porter and Michael Ashcroft invoked official discourse that defines investment as a contribution to national development worthy of membership in the nation.

However, though smallholders accepted the argument that investment was a contribution to Belizean national development, they were unconvinced by assertions that investment provided a sufficient claim to Belizean identity. At the same time, though most citrus growers were skeptical of Hassan's claims to "100 percent Belizean" status for the new company, they did not mobilize in opposition. Hassan's rhetoric appeared to work more effectively on those who had disseminated it in the first place: the government agreed to grant the company a fifteen-year tax concession, which exceeded the concession bestowed on CCB when it was sold in 1983 (BFHL 1990:15).

In the struggle for control of Belize Foods, competing groups of economic and political elites sought to mobilize collective agents behind their own agendas. They invoked official discourses on development, nation, and democracy to construct often-conflicting versions of class, regional, and national identities and interests. Large grower-processors, large growers who hoped to become processors, and political elites all attempted to create alliances with smallholders by imposing their own definitions of the relationships between smallholders and themselves. Smallholders responded to elite overtures with efforts to minimize their vulnerability to elites and protect their investments in citrus. During negotiations for the sale of BFP, smallholders insistently asserted a collective identity *as* "small growers," constructing this collective identity in CGA meetings through their questions and responses and outside of the meetings through discussions with family and neighbors.

Throughout the negotiations over the sale of Belize Foods, small growers strategized to pursue both the interests they believed they held in opposition to citrus estate owners and the interests they believed they shared with estate owners, with some success. They were primarily concerned to avert a CCB monopoly or the ownership of controlling shares by Oliver Hassan. Both scenarios, they argued, presented the danger that small growers would not be "looked upon" and their fruit would be disregarded. They achieved their goals by taking advantage of factionalism among large growers, between those who owned shares in CCB and those who did not, a distinction compounded by differences in political party affiliations. They allied themselves first with CCB shareholders to oppose Oliver Hassan's control of BFP and then with Hassan and other elites to oppose CCB's control of BFP. While both factions at some point sought to portray themselves and small growers as a unified class of growers, the faction that was ultimately successful was able to construct the sought-after alliance with small growers only by dropping this claim and addressing the issues raised by those who classified themselves as small growers.

However, small growers did not define owning shares in Belize Food Products as one of their major interests. Most believed they would have no say at the company and no control over the money they invested. They also recognized potential practical problems arising from transportation difficulties or the vindictiveness of CCB, which might refuse their fruit if Belize Foods were unable to accept it. Further, they valued continued competition between the two companies, so many were reluctant to commit all of their fruit to a single company. Thus, most smallholders did not buy shares in BFP, and large-grower shareholders dominated the new company.[8]

In their competing efforts to define and mobilize collective agents around class or national identities, politicians, farmers, and processing company shareholders advanced different versions of class collectivity. CCB owners sought to include as "citrus growers" all who owned citrus farms; Hassan and Esquivel excluded CCB shareholders from the citrus-grower category; and self-identified "small growers" found support from the PUP prime minister for their efforts to mobilize in narrower class terms. The insertion of the share offer to "workers" in January raised additional issues of class identity. While the use of the term "workers" played well on the national stage, in fact most of the block of shares reserved for workers was purchased by BFP's managing director, Nathan Clifford. Most self-identified "workers" did not count Clifford as a member of their class, and they rejected the notion that he could represent them in negotiations with Nestlé. Beyond this, workers who owned citrus themselves identified more readily as "citrus growers" during struggles against a potential CCB monopoly: some were more concerned about the potential impact of a monopoly on citrus prices than on their jobs.

It is interesting to note that although many citrus farmers used racial-ethnic and gender categories to organize daily activities and interactions, they did not mobilize around them in this struggle. The invocation of regional identities and loyalties by both Hassan and the UDP newspaper, comparing the government's assistance to the north with its support for the south, raised the potential for racialization of the contests surrounding the sale of BFP. Small growers' identification of "large growers" and "foreigners" also carried such potential; however, in neither case was this possibility pursued.

8 Conclusion

Collective Agency and the Direction of Development

The goal of this study has been to understand how collective identities and interests are formed, how collective agents are mobilized, and how the resulting social alliances shape development trajectories. This has involved, first, examining the everyday processes through which participants in the Belizean citrus industry construct—and are constructed into—collective identities and interests. Chapters 4 and 6 revealed the complexity and contingency of the personal identities assigned to or embraced by workers and farmers, as well as overlaps and contradictions among them. The multiplicity of each individual's social positionings provided an array of identities and interests as raw materials for coalition building and rendered collective agency a contingent, continually emergent phenomenon. Indeed, an individual's perception that a particular dimension of identity held special salience for him or her provided no guarantee that that individual would mobilize around that identity. The examples of women workers and farmers, who saw their gender positioning as a significant liability, is instructive in this regard.

Second, I have explored the ways workers, citrus growers, and political elites have strategically deployed the resulting politically charged identities to define both their interests and the issues that confront them, in order to mobilize collective agents behind specific agendas. The mobilization of such collective agents has played a significant role in shaping the development process in Belize. For workers and smallholder citrus farmers who control few material resources, such mobilizations have provided their primary means of exercising power. But even for political and economic elites, their control over material resources was insufficient to attain their goals without marshaling collective agents to lend their support. For example, while Citrus Company of Belize shareholders claimed to have the finances in place to purchase Belize Food Products, they were unable to do so, since they were unable to persuade their "fellow growers" that a CCB monopoly owned by "growers" would be in the best interests of all citrus farmers. Similarly, Oliver Hassan could not have prevented a CCB buyout of BFP by himself; it was the alliance of small and large growers in vociferous opposition to monopoly at the January Citrus Growers Association meeting that sent a message to Belmopan powerful enough to prevent a monopoly.

As they constructed shared identities and mobilized around them, farmers, workers, and processing company executives drew on discourses with diverse, yet interrelated, origins in transnational, national, and local arenas. For example, official discourses on nation, development, and democracy reflected the priorities of foreign governments and multilateral agencies as well as those of Belizeans. Indeed, over time, the former have informed the latter in important ways: the Belizean government has been extremely susceptible to the priorities of more powerful nation-states, as a result of Guatemala's long-standing threat to its sovereignty. Moreover, during the first decade of Belizean independence, the United States was determined to play a leading role in shaping agendas and priorities throughout the Caribbean and Central America.

The official discourses that mediated foreign and local interests generated interrelated objects (development, democracy, the Belizean nation) and a range of subject positions with different implications for individuals' exercise of power in shaping the trajectory of national development. For example, official discourses on nation and development cast both small and large investors as contributors to development, while workers were cast as development beneficiaries. Thus, although chapters 4 and 6 reveal that to a large extent citrus farmers and wage laborers in the industry are *the same people*, some dimensions of their identities—as citrus farmers—provided them with both options and legitimacy not accorded to other social positions they occupied. Official discourses on development and nation also privileged Belizeans over non-Belizeans as appropriate development beneficiaries. The government's designation of agricultural laborers—overwhelmingly classified as "Spanish"—

as "foreigners" contributed to the conflation of racial-ethnic and national identities, while Afro-Belizean discourse and practice completed that conflation, privileging Belizeans of African descent as more legitimately Belizean than those classified as Spanish. Official democracy discourse opened up possibilities for interventions in state policymaking by those recognized as "small men" (citrus farmers) and "true" Belizeans (not Spanish-speaking agricultural workers).

Workers and farmers appropriated—or were recruited into—some of these national-level discourses, which they deployed to interpret and respond to the circumstances they confronted daily, to define what was at stake in the two struggles explored above, and to mobilize collective agents behind particular agendas. For example, both Richard Porter of CCB and Michael Ashcroft of Belize Holdings Limited drew on official discourse that proclaimed investment a contribution to the Belizean nation worthy of citizenship to claim Belizean identities and tout their contributions to Belizean development. Smallholders repeatedly positioned themselves as the "small man" celebrated in democracy discourse, wielding this designation to shape policies, win access to land and credit, and judge the propriety of actions taken by political and economic elites.

Like citrus farmers and processing company shareholders, workers also selectively deployed official discourses. Garifuna workers echoed government pronouncements about the use of immigrant labor in agriculture when they defined Spanish agricultural workers as aliens while positioning themselves as core members of the Belizean nation and thus appropriate beneficiaries of national development. United General Workers Union leaders also drew on the government's designation of agricultural workers as foreign to delegitimize valley workers' demands and justify their exclusion from union leadership. At the same time, leaders of the opposition to the UGWU Executive invoked anticommunist discourse to discredit the union's current leadership, though they were unsuccessful in recruiting workers into this perspective.

Throughout the previous chapters, government officials, would-be shareholders, and aspiring union leaders have been shown working to "subject" potential followers to particular identities, to locate them in certain subject positions from which they could be exhorted to recognize and pursue specific sets of interests. However, the selective engagement and refusal of their efforts by their intended subjects reveals the agency that accompanies subjection to official or elite discourses. Those who were subjected to official discourses to such an extent that they embraced them in the construction of collective self-identities were often able to use those discourses to advantage; they sometimes deployed them *against* the government, using the government's own terms and arguments to exert pressure on the government to comply with their demands.

However, others who were subjected to official discourses—in the sense of having those discourses imposed on them by both government officials and people they interacted with on a daily basis—rejected the subject positions offered by those discourses and elaborated alternatives. In fact, those who stood to lose the most within the terms of official discourses—agricultural workers classified as aliens and hence excluded from the Belizean nation, Belizean democracy, and Belizean development—appear to have been least persuaded by them. Spanish and Mayan Belizeans who worked in the Stann Creek Valley rejected efforts by the government and by Garifuna natives of Stann Creek District to define them as foreigners and deny them rights to representation. Immigrant workers in the valley, such as Hugo Sanchez, elaborated counter-discourses that emphasized the contribution their hard work made to Belizean agricultural development. Aspiring leaders such as Marcus Cornejo mobilized both self-identified Spanish Belizeans and immigrants who recognized that they had been lumped into the Spanish category in response to UGWU leaders' perceived positioning of them as a unitary entity—Spanish "aliens"—not worthy of representation. If individuals are "always in the position of simultaneously undergoing and exercising" power (Foucault 1980:98), participants in the Belizean citrus industry are always simultaneously attempting to shape (more cynically to manipulate) the understandings and actions of others and undergoing others' efforts to shape or manipulate their own understandings and actions. In the cases explored in this study, manipulation was most often mutual.

The examples presented above also demonstrate that people's perceptions of their interests depended on how their identities were defined—and with whom they were being lumped—in specific contexts. Along these lines, this study contributes to research on social movements by offering a detailed analysis of how collective agents were constituted in particular contexts, despite the multiple, crosscutting nature of participants' identity commitments in general, and by exploring how and why particular definitions of shared interests were embraced by these collective agents. In doing so, this study provides a model for engaging the recent concern with identities in social movements research, without assuming the a priori existence of collective actors (with a requisite set of interests) and without detaching discursive struggles over identities and interests from their material contexts and stakes.

Collective Agency and the (Re)Production of Social Alliances

Negotiations over the sale of Belize Food Products ultimately renewed a loose alliance of large- and small-scale export commodity producers in support of a development strategy based on agricultural production for export. Such a strategy is also favored by the government's foreign creditors as well as the transnational—or Belizean?—companies involved in the processing of agricultural exports, both of whom support and benefit from this development direction. In this alliance, large producers and processors account for most of the growth in export production and reap most of the benefits of state efforts to promote this growth. Small producers contribute a small share to economic growth; more importantly, their integration into this development strategy through the provision of land and credit underwrites the legitimacy of Belizean democracy discourse and bridges the potential disconnect between what Belizeans want and what development experts prescribe as good for the nation's economic development. Such an alliance has a long—but discontinuous—history in Belize, since large producers and smallholders have mobilized against each other as frequently as they have mobilized together.

Since achieving self-government, Belizean political leaders have sought to balance development with democracy, growth with equity, and economic efficiency with political expediency, by supporting both smallholder participation and large-scale investment in sugar and later citrus production. First in sugar and later in citrus the PUP supported the demands of smallholders and wage laborers for land at the same time that it facilitated the acquisition of land by transnational companies and wealthy individuals. In turn, smallholders appropriated the rhetoric of Belizean political leaders, claiming "small man" status to make demands on both the state and agricultural elites. Their demands introduced deviations from what foreign and local experts deemed the most economically efficient avenues for pursuing an agricultural export-led development strategy, but they were accommodated without threatening the overall strategy.

Small growers' success in casting themselves as the "small man," officially defined as the key to wedding democracy and development, provided them a degree of leverage with the government, processors, and citrus estate owners that exceeded the leverage wielded by wageworkers. While

small growers' demands have decreased the efficiency of the government's
development strategy, workers' demands threaten a strategy that depends
on holding down wages. Thus, while the government recognized small growers as the "small men" at the heart of Belizean democracy, it defined agricultural workers—the largest employment sector in Belize—as "aliens." While
this characterization of predominantly Spanish agricultural workers as aliens
has contributed to division and conflict among workers that might depress
wages, it has also exacerbated racial-ethnic tensions that threaten the
multiethnic character of the officially imagined nation. Government policy
and rhetoric, together with the hiring practices of the citrus processing companies, divided orchard workers from other workers along lines that enabled
the conflation of racial-ethnic distinctions with national ones, such that the
largely Spanish-classified labor force came to be perceived as "foreign." Thus,
when conflict emerged in the UGWU, union leaders drew on official discourse
to define their predominantly Spanish-speaking challengers as aliens, excluding these agricultural workers from the nation, its democratic practices,
and a share in its economic development.

However, if efforts to segment the workforce diminished cooperation
across waterfront and valley workers, the strategy also led to new solidarities and collective agency among those most disadvantaged by it. Opposition
leaders who tapped into Spanish-speaking valley workers' perceptions of
discrimination by employers and the UGWU leadership forged an alliance
between immigrant and Belizean workers that alarmed both their employers
and waterfront workers. Leaders of the opposition movement did not convince Spanish-speaking workers that they were all the same, but they did
convince them that they experienced a shared injustice associated with others' efforts to position them as foreign. Thus, in spite of the forces arrayed
against them, agricultural workers in the citrus industry united to demand
greater union attention to their concerns.

The broad outlines of alliance that emerge from this study bind large-
and small-scale agricultural export producers together with the transnationally
owned processing companies in support of the agricultural export-led development strategy prescribed by foreign experts. This reflects the type of alliance predicted by neo-marxist models based on a structuralist logic (deJanvry
1981). However, this exploration of some of the episodes involved in generating or sustaining such an alliance in Belize demonstrates that the process is
much more complex and contingent than structuralist approaches are able to
account for. This study began with the premise that collective identities and

shared interests are both more contingent and less continuous than structuralist models would allow. It has thus examined the mobilization of collective
agents as the outcome of *struggles* rather than structure. Consequently, this
research has also approached the formation of social alliances as a contingent and discontinuous process, examining *how* alliances are forged and how
they may be fractured or sustained across time.

Challenges to Continuity

Indeed, the loose alliance between small and large export producers renewed
through mobilizations during the sale of BFP has never been a stable alliance
that, once constituted, could perpetuate itself indefinitely. Although it has
been continually renewed over decades through conscious efforts and com-
promises, the alliance has been—and continues to be—vulnerable to pressures generated inside and outside of Belize. Internally, this alliance has
often been sundered by competition between political parties, between
smallholders and large growers, between factions of large growers, and between the processing companies. It is also vulnerable to mobilizations among
those excluded from the benefits of the development direction supported by
the alliance, such as wage laborers in agriculture. Their efforts to improve their
representation and to claim rights challenged the perceived requirements for
successful agricultural export-led development.

The alliance has been continually regenerated through political struggles
in which wage laborers and smallholders have won access to resources that
enable them to participate as agricultural export producers. Government provision of land to smallholders and wage laborers, who are often the same
people, has permitted the cultivation of citrus (or sugar in decades past) to
provide a ticket out of wage labor. But this avenue for upward mobility remains an option only so long as resources such as land and credit continue to
be allocated to workers, and only if "inefficiency" in export production continues to be both tolerated and profitable.

This latter condition points to ways that this loose alliance is vulnerable
to pressures generated outside of Belize, where priorities and agendas shifted
over the 1990s. In the cold war context of the 1980s, as insurgent movements described by the U.S. government as instances of Soviet aggression
gained ground in several countries of the Caribbean Basin, U.S. policy and
discourse prescribed—and linked—capitalist economic growth with democracy, the latter defined in terms of "free and fair" elections. To encourage

capitalist economic growth, development lenders pushed the small economies of the Caribbean to expand their export production, and both the United
States and Britain facilitated this expansion by extending privileged access
to their protected markets for some Caribbean products. Access to these
protected markets neither required nor encouraged efficiency in Caribbean
production. However, by the end of the 1980s, the Soviet Union had dissolved,
with most of its former constituent states embracing capitalism and some
form of multiparty electoral politics; democracy, according to the U.S.
government's definition, also spread across Latin America during the 1980s,
as military rulers were replaced by civilian leaders elected in multiparty political contests deemed "free and fair" by international observers. Declaring
capitalism and democracy victorious, the U.S. government shifted its rhetoric and policies to aggressively pursue increased opportunities for investment and trade for U.S. business through the promotion of free trade. Markets were hailed as more efficient allocators of resources than states; their
now global extension would contribute to a more efficient division of labor on
a global scale. The neoliberal discourse and policies that contributed to the
increased momentum of globalization over the 1990s foregrounded the cou-
pling of economic development with efficiency and "free and fair" trade, while
the earlier emphasis on links between capitalist economic development and
democracy in the form of "free and fair" elections receded into the background.

These shifts in the international political-economic context confronted
the Caribbean with what Dominguez (1995) has called the "threat of peace."
The key political motivation for the industrial West to accord trade privileges
to the Caribbean disappeared with the end of the cold war; no longer strategically important, the Caribbean's trade privileges began to be eliminated as
free trade expanded. The majority of Caribbean countries produce a rather
narrow range of commodities at relatively small scales and depend heavily
on more developed countries both as suppliers of imports and markets for
their exports. Belize is no exception, as it depends on preferential market
access for its three major agro-exports: sugar, citrus, and bananas. However,
Caribbean agriculture has been diagnosed with "structural problems" that
arise from "low productivity per man and per acre" combined with "relatively
high wages," which "leads to high production costs in relation to world market prices" (CDB 1993:37). Again, Belize is no exception. Even after expansion, the Belizean citrus industry is minuscule in comparison with industry
giants like Brazil. Further, most Belizean citrus growers are smallholders,

who attain yields below world averages. As free trade initiatives increasingly pit small-scale Caribbean producers head-to-head against large-scale producers in other countries, what consequences will Caribbean economies and peoples confront? Prognosticators envision two potential scenarios: (1) the collapse of many key Caribbean export industries and the marginalization of the Caribbean as a relatively high-cost, small-scale producer in a world of expanding free trade; or (2) the reorganization of production in Caribbean export industries to become more efficient and more competitive with larger-volume producers. Scholars, political leaders, and international lenders addressing the challenges the Caribbean faces at this juncture present a near consensus: the Caribbean must aggressively pursue efficiency in order to avoid marginalization (Bryan 1995a; CDB 1993; Watson 1994a).[1]

The Belizean citrus boom of the late 1980s and early 1990s was spurred by trade advantages extended to the Caribbean under the U.S. Caribbean Basin Initiative, but free trade initiatives now emanating from the United States threaten the Belizean industry's viability. The shift in U.S. priorities and policy from the 1980s to the 1990s and the new emphasis on efficiency pose a dilemma for Belize. Although Belizean development experts have deemed smallholder production inefficient, smallholder citrus planting has raised income levels for many in the citrus belt of underdeveloped southern Belize and provided an avenue for upward mobility to wage laborers desirous of higher incomes. The government has traditionally sacrificed a measure of economic efficiency in order to maximize the political support of small growers, legitimize Belizean democracy discourse, and forge a broad social alliance between small and large growers that has underwritten its agricultural export-led economic development strategy. But the U.S. promotion of free trade has the effect of making economic efficiency a higher priority in an increasingly competitive global marketplace.

Belizean citrus growers responded to the shift in U.S. policy by pressing their government to lobby U.S. officials to extend the Caribbean's trade privileges and by forging new strategic alliances. The CGA allied itself with Florida citrus growers during negotiations over the North American Free Trade Agreement (NAFTA) to lobby the U.S. government against the inclusion of citrus, though their efforts were unsuccessful. Belizean citrus farmers also allied themselves with the processing companies to lobby the U.S. ambassador to Belize. Resuscitating CBI rhetoric linking development with democracy, they argued that the Belizean citrus industry provided a shining example of how capitalist economic growth and peaceful democracy are mutually reinforcing. Free trade agreements would threaten that exemplary linkage, they cautioned. The chair of the CGA warned U.S. and Belizean officials, "Very few of us could make the infrastructural changes necessary to compete with [the economies of] First World countries" ("Jenkins Shoots Straight!" *Amandala*, 19 April 1991), suggesting that free trade would drive many Belizean citrus producers—especially smallholders—out of business. Processing company administrators and shareholders echoed these concerns, arguing against free trade, which would force Belize to compete head-to-head with countries such as Mexico and Brazil, and advocating instead "fair trade" that would allow "special and useful provisions for small underdeveloped citrus industries like Belize's" (quoted in "Jenkins Shoots Straight!"). In this context, farmers and processing company executives highlighted interests they perceived themselves to share.

However, the U.S. ambassador's response suggested that, in a post–cold war world, the United States did not believe it needed Belize to serve as a model of the happy combination of capitalist development with democracy. Reinterpreting the CBI's goals from a more neoliberal vantage point characteristic of the 1990s, the ambassador explained that the initiative had been designed to afford small countries in the Caribbean Basin an opportunity to "capitalize on their economic strengths and time to address their weaknesses." "However," he asserted, "the CBI's long term objective has always been to help industries in these countries to become more efficient and competitive in the world market" ("Letter from U.S. Ambassador Scassa to Norris Hall," *Amandala*, 26 April 1991). Further, he emphasized, "free trade is the fairest form of trade."

A "more efficient and competitive" future does not bode well for Belizean agro-exports. The vulnerability of the Belizean citrus industry was demonstrated repeatedly over the 1990s, even though Belize still enjoyed protected trade status in U.S., European, and Caribbean markets vis-à-vis industry giant Brazil. World prices for citrus fell drastically because of increases in Brazilian production in the early 1990s (FAO 1994:142–44). As a result, the prices Belizean growers earned were halved: while citrus prices had increased from $6.85 to $10.75 per box with the implementation of the CBI, in 1992/93 prices fell to $4.22 per box. As prices continued low over the decade, many farmers negotiated to reschedule payments on the loans that had financed their expansion, and a small number sold their farms or lost them to foreclosure. International funding agencies stopped funding the expansion of citrus (and other export crops) in Belize. The prices Belizean growers receive would

drop further under hemisphere-wide free trade: not only would Belizean citrus producers be forced to compete directly with Brazilian producers, but
U.S. market prices for citrus would also fall, if legislation enacted to protect
U.S. domestic producers were repealed. Some Belizean citrus farmers argue
that further steep declines in fruit prices would lead to the consolidation of
citrus holdings in the hands of the largest estate owners, who could increase
their efficiency more easily than smallholders. Others fear that increased
competition and declining prices could lead to the collapse of the industry.

Unfortunately for Belize, similar concerns confront its other two principal agro-export industries. The profitability of both banana and sugar industries in Belize has depended on access to protected markets in Europe and
the United States. That access is increasingly in question. Trade preferences
extended by the European Union (EU) for bananas from African, Caribbean,
and Pacific (ACP) countries had helped to revitalize Belizean banana production. However, at the behest of banana giant Chiquita, the United States lodged
a complaint with the World Trade Organization (WTO) charging that the EU
policy was unfair to Latin American banana producers. The WTO ruled in
support of the U.S. position, declaring that the trade preferences enjoyed by
ACP bananas in Europe were unfair barriers to free trade. Though negotiations in these "banana wars" are ongoing, Belizean banana growers have
lamented the impending curtailment of preferential access to European markets for Caribbean bananas as a "death sentence" for their industry ("7 Banana Farms to Close: 450 Workers Jobless," *Amandala*, 18 May 1997). Though
the banana industry in Belize incorporates relatively few smallholders compared to citrus, a process of consolidation has begun in that industry, with
some plantation owners buying out smaller producers in order to increase
efficiencies of scale. Jobs have also been eliminated, and remaining workers
have been pushed to become more productive ("7 Banana Farms to Close").
Thus both citrus and banana industries that were expanded during the 1980s
to diversify the Belizean economy and make it less vulnerable to market
shocks in sugar are threatened by free trade. They must become more efficient
or risk collapse.[2]

The sugar industry itself, still the largest of the three main agro-export
industries, may be equally vulnerable. Sugar's profitability has depended
heavily on U.S. measures enacted to protect domestic sugar producers. These
measures boost prices for sugar on the U.S. market above prices available in
global markets. By issuing quotas for the sale of sugar in the U.S. market to
Caribbean countries that have cooperated with U.S. agendas, the United States

has sustained the profitability of Belizean sugar production. If free trade initiatives undermine U.S. protective legislation for sugar, however, the Belizean industry's viability would be thrown into question. Thus, Belize's whole agricultural export development strategy, prescribed by foreign development experts and pursued avidly by the Belizean government, is increasingly vulnerable to shifting global political-economic currents.

Rearticulations

In response to neoliberal discourse and policies, Belizean citrus farmers and processing company shareholders have embraced initiatives that mightily contradict the arguments that mobilized collective agents in the struggle over the sale of Belize Food Products. In the late 1990s, the former British government development agency, the Commonwealth Development Corporation, offered to purchase majority shares in both processing companies. The offer itself reflects the ways neoliberal policies have reconfigured development practice. The Commonwealth Development Corporation (formerly the Colonial Development Corporation) was established by the British government in 1948 to provide low-interest loans and some venture capital to businesses in developing countries or colonies. In the late 1990s the British government directed the CDC to curtail its practice of providing loans for development (as it had done in Belize in the citrus expansion/rehabilitation program of the 1980s) in favor of providing equity investment in developing countries. This shift prompted the CDC, which already owned citrus operations in Costa Rica, to make an offer to purchase a majority stake in the two citrus processing companies in Belize. Against the global political-economic context of citrus production in the late 1990s, most shareholders were willing—even eager—to sell, notwithstanding the struggles in which they had engaged to purchase those shares in the first place.[3]

Given the difficulties faced by Belize and its citrus industry at the time, citrus growers appeared to have significantly reconfigured their interests. Thus, growers voiced few complaints about the purchase of the companies by foreigners or the imposition of a monopoly. Rather than defining this move toward monopoly as a threat, the CGA described the CDC's investment as an opportunity to make the industry viable. CGA officials hoped that the CDC's experience in managing citrus operations in Costa Rica and selling its products in global markets would enable it to operate the new consolidated company with greater efficiency, perhaps combining its Costa Rican and Belizean citrus production in a single marketing strategy. They hoped that increases in efficiency would in turn lead to higher prices. The rearticulation of "growers' interests" in this case reveals the malleability of perceptions of collective interests across shifting contexts, as well as citrus growers' own adoption of neoliberal discourses of efficiency, as applied to the factories at any rate.

However, the CDC's purchase and consolidation of the processing companies yielded mixed results. The CDC did win new loan funds from the European Investment Bank (EIB) in 2001 to rehabilitate old orchards and update the processing plants, both of which continued to operate (EIS 2000).[4] Some of these funds were invested in a system to recover citrus pulp, so that the company could sell what it had previously dumped as waste. However, world market prices for citrus products continued very low, and so did the prices Belizean farmers—by now numbering over a thousand—received for their fruit. Some citrus farmers complained that the lack of experience in Belize on the part of the foreign management staff put in place by the CDC prevented the company from realizing its goals of increased efficiency.

Subsequently, the expanding neoliberal agenda in Britain again reconfigured the CDC's priorities and engagement in the Belizean citrus industry. As part of the drive toward privatizing state functions, the British government privatized the CDC, offering 60 percent of its shares to the public while retaining a minority stake for itself. The new CDC, now renamed CDC Capital Partners, has a mandate to continue to invest 70 percent of its funds in developing countries. But as a joint public-private company, it faces increased pressure to generate profits in order to attract and hold investment. This represents a new model for development efforts; if successful, the privatization of the CDC could have a major impact in restructuring the whole development industry. However, it is not clear that it can follow its mandate for investment in developing countries and provide the kind of returns investors seek. Faced with a new imperative to generate profits, the CDC decided to shift its investments away from agribusiness operations, such as its factories and orchards in Belize, to focus on sectors deemed to have higher earnings potential: power, infrastructure, financial services, telephones, and technology.

As a result of this shift, the CDC engaged the CGA in negotiations for the sale of the newly consolidated processing company. The CGA established the Belize Citrus Growers Association Investment Company Limited to acquire the processing company on its behalf, and in late 2002, after two years of negotiations, the CGA signed an agreement to acquire 99 percent of the company's shares for the price of $2. At the same time, however, the CGA assumed the company's U.S.$18.9 million debt ("Growers Buy Del Oro by Assuming Company's Debt," Channel 5 News, 21 Oct. 2002). Signing the purchase agreement on behalf of citrus growers were Nathan Clifford, chair of the Belize Citrus Growers Association Investment Company Limited, and Arthur Rowan, chair of the CGA ("Belize Citrus Growers Buy Processing Plants," BIS press release, 9 Oct. 2002), both of whom had ceased being processors and become "citrus growers" when the CDC bought out the two companies and installed its own staff. The CGA announced that it would retain at least 51 percent of the company's shares under its collective control, but it planned to offer the rest of the shares for sale to CGA members ("Growers Buy Del Oro"). The CGA subsequently announced plans to initiate payments to growers on the basis of the quality of the fruit they delivered, rather than just the quantity. This strategy aims to capitalize on high product quality to seek a competitive edge in global citrus markets over the quantity offered by large-scale producers such as Brazil.

The CGA also initiated plans to increase efficiency in processing operations. In December 2002 the CGA announced that it would terminate all workers at both factories, with severance payments, and then restructure the workforce. While former workers could reapply for jobs, the company argued that restructuring was necessary to improve efficiency and lower production costs, as the enterprise confronted low citrus prices on the world market and its large debt ("Citrus Industry Merger Could Leave Hundreds Jobless before Christmas," *Amandala*, 15 Dec. 2002). Thus, in the case of its newly acquired labor force, the CGA adopted the efficiency discourse of neoliberalism, whose application to citrus growers it had earlier rejected. For its part, the union countered with efforts to make the restructuring process the subject of negotiations rather than company fiat.

The eventual outcome of the expanding neoliberal agendas that are reconfiguring citrus production in Belize and around the world will depend on the outcome of mobilizations both for and against these changes in numerous national and local arenas. In addition to struggles over the costs and benefits of increasing efficiency among participants in the Belizean citrus industry, the future of the industry hinges on the outcome of struggles waged by U.S. citrus producers against efforts to eliminate the legislation that protects them and struggles waged across the Americas in favor of and in opposition to efforts to establish a hemisphere-wide free trade agreement.

Even if efforts to increase the efficiency of citrus production and processing in Belize are successful enough to prevent the industry's collapse in a free-trade-dominated future, those efforts may unravel the alliance between small and large export producers and processors that has for decades underwritten the implementation of a development strategy based on agricultural production for export. The government has had success in establishing economic growth through the expansion of exports as an overriding "national interest," due in part to its incorporation of smallholders into the expansion process: through the provision of land and credit, the government offered a stake in agro-export development to some of the people who considered themselves members of the "small man" majority. If small-scale agro-export production becomes uneconomic, the current stake held by the "small man" in the agro-export-led development strategy would disappear, and democracy as the rule of the majority would become less compatible with the definition of development as agricultural export expansion.[5] If small citrus growers were transformed into wage laborers (or unemployed), and wage laborers no longer saw citrus production as a ladder out of the working class into higher standards of living, the articulations of identities and interests that have loosely bound together a significant block of the Belizean population behind agro-export expansion would be unlikely to hold. New articulations will be offered and contested, appropriated and rejected.

This study has used the Belizean citrus industry and the Belizean state as sites where local and global forces are mediated, in order to explore how actors in local arenas shape the structures imposed on them by global capitalism—and vice versa. In the Belizean citrus industry, farmers, wage laborers, processing companies, and government officials maneuver both within and against international flows of capital, labor, concepts, and priorities, as they compete to define and pursue collective interests. The construction of collective identities and interests and the mobilization of collective agents has proven to be central to such mediations in the past. Indeed, the efforts of participants in the citrus industry to mobilize collective agents and to negotiate or renew social alliances have pushed the industry's development in directions that conform in many ways, but diverge in others, from the trajectories laid out by transnational development experts. For example, smallholders repeatedly mobilized to pressure the government to provide them with the land and credit that enabled them to incorporate themselves into citrus production for export, despite the warnings of foreign and national experts that their incorporation into the industry represented an economically inefficient use of investment funds and land. While Belizean citrus farmers have not reconfigured the external forces that condition and discipline Belizean citrus production for export, they have played a key role in organizing the industry in Belize, even in the face of transnational ownership of the processing companies. However, if this study has shown collective agents and social alliances to be contingent, negotiated, and unstable entities, it has also demonstrated that the successes attained through social mobilizations are themselves contingent and unstable. Losers often contest the victories of their opponents, and continually changing external circumstances can also erode successes. Thus, there is no ultimate success, only ongoing strategizing and struggle. Any victory may be undermined, eroded, or turned into a liability by subsequent events and struggles.

Recent victories of citrus growers demonstrate this assertion. In a recent book titled *Peasants against Globalization,* Edelman (1999) examines the mobilization of peasant movements in Costa Rica in reaction to neoliberal reforms that smallholder agriculturalists understood as threats to their survival. Though the present book shares many concerns with Edelman's work, recent mobilizations among citrus farmers in Belize have aimed to *integrate* Belizean farmers more deeply *into* processes of globalization, rather than to oppose globalization. Fearful of witnessing yet another agricultural bust in the Stann Creek Valley (recalling earlier busts in banana and starch production for export), Belizean citrus farmers struggle against the threat of being completely marginalized by globalization. Their efforts to integrate themselves more deeply into global markets increasingly subject them to the discipline of the global political-economic processes in which those markets are enmeshed. Thus, their successes have simultaneously increased their peril; over the last couple of decades, citrus growers increased their investments and at times their incomes, but they also increased their vulnerability to global political-economic forces. Currently, both farmers and wage laborers grapple with the implications of increased global competition and consequent efforts to increase efficiency for the Belizean citrus industry as a whole and for different categories of people within it. The future direction of the industry—how participation will be structured, whether it will survive or collapse—will depend on the outcome of interrelated struggles over neoliberal policy and practice both within Belize and beyond its borders.

In studying such struggles and their impact on the direction of development, this ethnography demonstrates the importance of examining the construction of collective identities and interests and the mobilization of collective agents as processes integral to the ongoing production and re-production of the social alliances that shape economic development trajectories. Such an approach enables us to better understand both the "how" and the "why" of struggles over the course of development across intersecting local, national, and global arenas.

Notes

Chapter 1. Introduction

1. Workers employed by other large citrus estates and small growers were not unionized.

2. The analysis of discourse may permit us to avoid reifying the categories we study, since it pushes us to problematize and investigate the conditions that have made it possible for people inside or outside of the academy to think those categories. The potential for the reification of discourse itself remains. While in many cases such a reification would be an error, in other contexts such a move might legitimately represent repetition and standardization of an argument. The official discourses disseminated by the Belizean government, which I delineate more fully in chapter 2, are examples of constructions that have been formalized and standardized in five-year plans and campaign manifestos, reiterated in speeches and press releases.

3. It is common for studies of identity formation to apply this approach to examine how gender and racial differences and inequalities are produced or how ethnic and national collectivities are constituted. The production of collective class identities has received less attention, and scholars have not problematized the social construction of class identities and interests in the same way. Although "orthodox" marxism has never been monolithic, this failure to deconstruct class can be traced to key assumptions shared across its multiple strands and even beyond marxism. Although Marx himself took a more complex approach in some of his work, orthodox marxism has traditionally distinguished a material "base" from an ideological "superstructure," prioritizing the material over the ideational. This perspective reflects a "realist" approach to knowledge that assumes that

"the real world indelibly imprints its meanings and interests directly into our consciousness" (Hall 1988:44). In this perspective, ideas merely *reflect* material relations, and the positions people occupy in the process of capitalist production automatically impart to them particular class identities, particular sets of interests, and particular forms of class consciousness. At the same time, orthodox models allow that dominant classes may use ideology to subvert the class consciousness of subordinates by inculcating in them a "false consciousness" that diverts them from the pursuit of their shared class interests. Within the orthodox marxist opposition of the material to the ideological, class directly corresponds to material relations by definition, while other axes of identity do not; hence, class is seen as more *real* than other dimensions of identity, which are deemed ideological (Bourgois 1989; Moberg 1990). As a result of these assumptions, while identities defined in terms of race, ethnicity, nation, or gender are seen to depend for their existence on people's consciousness of their meanings, classes are seen to exist even if their members have the "wrong" (i.e., false) consciousness. Within this perspective, the existence of class does not have to be explained; only people's failure to comport themselves in accord with the interests prescribed to them by marxist analysis requires explanation.

This dichotomous distinction between the material and the ideological fails to account for either the mechanisms by which material conditions might directly produce the "proper" class consciousness, or the mechanisms through which that consciousness could be subverted (Hall 1988:44). From within marxism, Gramsci (1971) began to address such questions by attributing to ideology more powerful and autonomous effects in relation to material conditions. He focused on the role of ideology in constituting "social blocs," political alliances that united people across class boundaries by defining interests shared across those boundaries. Gramsci recognized that neither class solidarity nor broader social alliances are the automatic consequences of particular material conditions. Rather, such solidarities are forged through struggle, and ideas are central to those struggles; indeed, Gramsci's notion of "war of position" posits the renegotiation of social meanings and identities as a necessary step toward the forging of new social blocs and the transformation of material relations. The role ideology plays in such struggles is to provide individuals and groups with "conceptions of the world" that shape their actions (Gramsci 1971:377).

Working at the borders of marxism and poststructuralism, Hall (1988) refined Gramsci's approach, by arguing that ideology works or is elaborated through discourse; discourse thus provides the mechanism required to explain the production of consciousness or subjectivity that orthodox marxist perspectives lack. Rather than casting ideas as *reflections* of material relations, poststructuralist approaches undermine the dichotomous opposition of the material to the ideological by defining discourse and material conditions as *mutually constitutive* (Laclau and Mouffe 1985). From a poststructuralist perspective, material conditions are not autonomous, and discourse does not simply comment on material reality; rather, discourse both interprets the material world and shapes the way we act to reproduce or reconfigure the material conditions we apprehend.

If the material and the conceptual are mutually constitutive in the formation of classes and class interests, then material conditions "structure the range of possibilities" for class formation, "but precise outcomes emerge directly from struggles" (Przeworski 1977, quoted in Gilroy 1987:30). The construction of class identities and agents in concrete historical contexts is contingent, and class collectivity must be understood as perpetually emergent—always in the process of becoming, but never guaranteed (Gilroy 1987:30; Hall 1986:14; Medina 1997b).

4. Within new social movements research, resource mobilization approaches share many of the assumptions of orthodox marxism, positing the existence of shared goals and grievances based on the researchers' own readings of social structures and their logics. These approaches also assume the existence of calculating rational actors whose ledger of the costs and benefits of participation in collective action matches the researchers' (Buechler 1995; Cohen 1985). In contrast, identity-oriented approaches to new social movements have begun to explore how shared goals and grievances—and shared identities themselves—are constructed through the very process of collective mobilization.

5. This involves a Gramscian approach that focuses on the use of ideas and arguments to mobilize social blocs, rather than defining hegemony simply in terms of dominance or domination. Hall asserts that the question of whether such arguments are true or false is misguided: there must be *something* that "makes good sense" about any argument that moves people to action (1988:46).

6. See also Johnson (1998).

Chapter 2. The Articulate State

1. I refer to this territory as Belize, though it was called British Honduras during much of the colonial period.

2. This rendering of Belizean history must be schematic. For more complete accounts, see Bolland (1977, 1988), Grant (1976), Shoman (1994), and Stone (1994).

3. The primary form of wealth in the settlement was enslaved human labor, since during this period settlers were not allowed to own land. What they parceled out among themselves were use rights to particular tracts of land.

4. Belize was the only West Indian colony that allowed free colored people to participate in its legislative system (Dobson 1973:113).

5. It has often been argued that the first Africans reached St. Vincent in 1635, when two slave ships were wrecked nearby; however, Gonzalez (1988) presents evidence that Caribs had raided European colonies and carried away slaves prior to that time. "Black" Carib (now called by the term *Garifuna*) histories usually use this data to explain their origins, though recently some Garifuna invoke the work of Van Sertima (1976) to suggest that Africans were incorporated into Carib society prior to the European discovery of the Americas. The manner in which Africans were incorporated into Carib society has been a matter of speculation, with some suggesting that they were enslaved by the Caribs, others that they were incorporated as full members into the society, and others suggesting that they came to dominate the society.

6. Most of the Chinese either died under the harsh working and living conditions or escaped into the forest and became incorporated into Mayan communities. The contemporary Chinese population is the result of later immigration (Ropp 1996).

7. The designation "East Indian" is used in the Caribbean to distinguish people born

in India from two other categories of people named as a result of Columbus's misperception that he had discovered a western route to the Indies: Afro-Caribbean people of the Caribbean have been called "West Indians," while indigenous peoples of the Caribbean have been termed "Amerindians."

8. For insight into the politics behind the shifting numbers of appointed and elected members, see Ashdown (1979) and Shoman (1994).

9. Though Price sought to integrate Belize into Central American political and economic networks, Belizean overtures to Central America were unsuccessful, and the PUP was ultimately forced to seek economic and political alliances in the Caribbean.

10. The U.S. commitment to economic development in the post–World War II period reflected a number of U.S. priorities. The United States was concerned to maintain the high levels of production and employment it had attained during World War II, which would require expanded markets for U.S. goods and capital and continued access to raw materials. This goal shaped plans for the United States to rebuild Europe and then to develop the colonies and former colonies of Latin America, Asia, and Africa (Escobar 1995; Esteva 1992; Meier 1984; Rostow 1984). As the cold war set in, nationalism and anticolonialism in Latin America, Asia, and Africa provided openings for Soviet interventions that threatened to remove emerging countries—both their markets and their resources—from Western spheres of influence and commerce. To avert this, development assistance from the United States and other Western countries offered poor countries incentives to remain in the Western fold.

11. Although the idea of development was associated with both economic growth and the alleviation of poverty, its measurement in terms of GNP per capita links development more closely to the former than the latter. However, development discourse posited that economic growth would lead to the alleviation of poverty through the downward trickle of income.

12. While the analysis of development as a discourse has facilitated critical exploration of the processes through which development has been defined and implemented, Escobar (1995) has been criticized for his portrayal of development discourse as a monolithic, hegemonic, global force. Grillo and Stirrat (1997) argue that, although in some ways development discourse may function hegemonically, it is less monolithic and more multivocal than Escobar suggests. Though I agree with Grillo and Stirrat, I focus here on some of the relatively hegemonic assumptions about development that became articles of faith among national and international policymakers: the priority of economic growth and the need for investment to fuel such growth.

13. The causes of UBAD's demise were complex. They include tensions between middle-class and working-class goals and perspectives, between those who saw themselves as "brown" and those who claimed a Black identity, between Garifuna and Creoles (Macklin 1986:147), and between political-economic and cultural agendas.

14. On the tenth anniversary of Belize's independence in 1991, the president of Guatemala recognized Belize. Subsequently, British troops handed over responsibility for defense to the Belize Defense Force and began to withdraw from Belize. However, after the Guatemalan president staged a "self-coup" and was subsequently forced into exile, Guatemala renewed its claim in 1994.

15. The expansion of tourism and light manufacturing enterprises was also prioritized.

16. Monetary sums are given in Belizean dollars unless otherwise specified. One Belizean dollar equals U.S.$0.50.

17. Elsewhere (Medina 1997a), I have elaborated another strand of official nationalist discourse, a synthesizing nationalism that plays down ethnic difference and the potential conflicts it may engender through construction of a synthetic national culture shared by all.

18. These categories are in flux. For instance, the term "white" is a construct that has traditionally conflated light skin color, putative European ancestry, and economic power and privilege; however, Judd suggests that recently "the economic success of mestizo and non-European immigrants has obliged local whites to open their ranks—at least to Lebanese and Palestinians, if not Indians and Chinese" (1992:117). Mennonites, who immigrated to Belize in the 1950s and maintain a large degree of social separation between their communities and the rest of Belizean society, were formerly classed as Whites but are now classed separately. Over recent years, as the Chinese category has incorporated rising numbers of immigrants, it has been increasingly defined as outside the Belizean nation.

19. The dominant ethnic group in Guatemala categorizes itself as Ladino, but its members are defined as Spanish or Mestizo in Belize.

20. This racializing process does not completely deny multiethnic constructions of the Belizean nation: Creoles and Garifuna often recognize Spanish Belizeans who were born and raised in their local area as legitimately Belizean. However, the large number of Spanish Belizeans who migrate from their home districts to other regions of Belize in search of employment are likely to be classified as aliens.

21. The policies and rhetoric that characterized the CBI were accompanied by military action, including the U.S. invasion of Grenada, U.S. funding of the Contras to fight the Sandinista government in Nicaragua, and assistance to Salvadoran and Guatemalan militaries. Indeed, the CBI was viewed in some quarters as a fig leaf for U.S. military intervention.

22. Bolland (2001) describes Belize as an "authoritarian democracy" where a small elite controlled political parties and political processes, including the trade unions.

23. The Belizean education system, which devalues manual work and encourages students to prepare for higher-status office jobs, is partly responsible for negative attitudes toward agricultural work. The prestige associated with urban consumer lifestyles through trade, travel, and television contacts with the United States also lessens the attraction of agricultural labor for young Belizeans (Bolland 1986:95). However, wages, working and living conditions, and employer hiring preferences also shape Belizeans' involvement—or lack of involvement—in agricultural labor. Nonetheless, many Belizeans are involved in agricultural labor; they are rhetorically converted into "aliens" rather than recognized as Belizeans.

24. The government does not collect such data, so policy is based on popular assumptions and perceptions. A study of communities known as "refugee," or immigrant, communities revealed these assumptions to be inaccurate, since a large percentage of the

residents were actually Belizeans who had migrated there from other parts of the country (Stone 1990). Further, though immigrants can apply for refugee or permanent resident status and eventually become naturalized citizens, they will not necessarily be accepted as true Belizeans.

25. There are subtleties in these labels that should be noted. When the minister uses the terms "foreign workers" and "refugees" interchangeably, he is following standard Belizean usage of the terms that departs from official international designations. In Belize, "refugee" is understood as the most polite term to use in referring to someone perceived as foreign, rather than as a technical term for someone who has sought and received political asylum. Its perceived politeness makes it the appropriate term for a government minister to use in a radio interview. The less polite term "alien" is more commonly used to refer to the same population in everyday speech. The least polite term is "paisa."

Chapter 3. Citrus History

1. Some growers explained the Citrus Company's imposition of quotas as a response to reduced market share in Europe as citrus production from Israel and Spain increased.

2. Abrahams (1983) suggests that, in the Caribbean, Creole functions as an anti-elite language, in contrast to the prestige language of Standard English. In many parts of the Caribbean it also functions as a local/national language that distinguishes its speakers from non-natives.

3. Several large growers sought alternative sources of funding for their expansion. However, the DFC later dropped some limitations on large-grower access to CDC funds. The DFC needed to disburse the funds more quickly than small growers were able to absorb them, so that it could begin receiving interest payments with which to make its own payments to the CDC.

4. The government owns over 50 percent of the land in Belize, a quarter of it in forest reserves (Barry 1992:132). The government has made land available for citrus expansion to both small and large growers on a lease basis. Once the land has been developed, the farmer can apply to purchase the parcel for below-market rates.

5. The Coca-Cola/Minute Maid purchase was part of a larger deal involving 686,186 acres. Coke purchased 50,000 acres, 50,000 acres were acquired by Houston business partners Walter Mischer and Paul Howell, and 50,000 acres were retained by the former owner Barry Bowen. The remaining land in the parcel was owned jointly by the parties on a 30:30:40 basis (Petch 1986:1014).

6. Although the Belizean government projected the growth of an independent sector of citrus producers in northern Belize, Coke mentioned no such plans and made no promises to purchase citrus from independent producers (Petch 1986:1015). In fact, Coke was concerned to avoid being forced to purchase fruit from independent growers.

7. One citrus grower also reported having been interviewed by a British spy who was investigating Mawema's activities.

8. The Orange Walk leadership of the UGWU had actively campaigned against the PUP representative from Orange Walk during the 1979 elections.

9. The energy workers' departure from the UGWU had roots in disagreements within

the UGWU over how to respond to the Heads of Agreement, the document negotiated with Guatemala as a step toward settling the ongoing Belize-Guatemala land dispute and moving toward Belizean independence. While angry protests against the agreement erupted in the streets of Belize City, the UGWU remained neutral. The PUP Right took advantage of some electricity workers' dissatisfaction with this stance, in combination with their discontent over the progress of contract negotiations, to win them away from the UGWU (Shoman 1987a:21).

Chapter 4. Citrus Workers

1. However, Aurelio's uncertainty contrasts with the certainty—and greater specificity—of Mayan identity claims made by workers from southern Toledo District. For example, four migrant workers from Toledo District asserted identities as Maya Mopan and identified Maya Mopan as their first language.

2. The Citrus Company began recruiting workers from Cayo and Toledo in the 1960s (White 1968:59). Although there are no figures available to document the extent of this migration, one scholar who conducted research in Bullet Tree Falls asserted, "I met no young adult who had not spent at least one season (and generally they had spent many more) cutting sugar cane or picking oranges. In the appropriate seasons Bullet Tree appears bereft of men" (Sullivan 1978:7).

3. While town-dwellers who could afford to pay a monthly cable bill of twenty-five dollars could receive any of the major networks from the United States, those who lived outside of Dangriga or who could not afford cable could receive only the signal from Pomona.

4. Even some work that was not gender typed paid women less than men. For instance, women who worked in the factory selecting fruit earned $2.45 an hour, while the men working beside them received $2.90 for the same work. The union's contract with the companies also restricted women's work hours to 8 A.M. through 6 P.M., since the Belizean Labour Ordinance prohibits the employment of women and males under the age of eighteen at night. Male workers sometimes began work as early as 5 A.M. and worked as late as 10 P.M., making significant amounts of overtime. But Belizean law distinguished women and minors from men and equated women with minors. Although Belizean law did not mandate distinct wages for women, neither did it prohibit wage discrimination. In fact, the government itself set a precedent for wage differentials between men and women in 1968, when a government wages council for the citrus industry set the minimum wage at $2.50 a day for men and $1.60 a day for women (Labour Department 1968).

5. On the other hand, some immigrant workers began to Belizeanize their Spanish over time, adopting the pronoun *tu* more commonly used among Spanish-speaking Belizeans as a means to blend in or assert Belizeanness.

6. Many families that identify as Garifuna possess Spanish surnames that reflect Honduran or Guatemalan origins. Others bear traditional Garifuna names, and still others carry names that derive from encounters with British colonial systems or intermarriage with Belizean Creoles.

7. In the random sample of valley workers, foreign-born workers' length of resi-

dence in Belize ranged from two to twenty-three years, with an average of ten and a half years. Five of the immigrant workers had obtained Belizean residency or citizenship. Belizean-born workers were from five of the six districts of Belize, with Stann Creek (25 percent), Cayo (21 percent), and Toledo (13 percent) most heavily represented. Immigrant workers and migrants from Cayo District accounted for most of the workers classified as Spanish in the valley.

Chapter 5. Brethren and Paisanos

1. In their defense, local union leaders suggested that workers would view the situation differently if they themselves experienced the demands of leadership.

2. This clause of the Trade Union Ordinance was directed at employers, not at unions.

3. From this vantage point, the strategies of workers themselves, invisible in the top-down analysis of political competition for control of unions presented by official reports, secondary sources, and union leaders that informed chapter 3, appear to be much more significant than that chapter could document.

4. Moberg also notes the companies' strategic segmentation of their labor force along ethnic lines to divide workers and render them more malleable. However, in suggesting that "when wage differentials and hiring practices are employed to exacerbate ethic antagonism within the work force, hegemony becomes a *fait accompli*," he fails to account for the ways that this strategy helped to generate militance and mobilization among relatively disadvantaged orchard workers (Moberg 1990:205; 1993).

Chapter 6. Citrus Growers

1. Unlike Miss Liz, one-third of the CGA sample held only leases for their land.

2. A bushhog is a farm implement akin to a lawn mower, but it is larger and pulled behind a tractor. It is used to cut the grass/bush between the trees in the citrus groves.

3. The price formula allocated to the companies an additional percentage of the revenues when prices for citrus concentrate were high, as they were during the late 1980s. The formula dictated a 75 percent/25 percent split between growers and processors of the amount of net revenue in excess of $10.60 per box of fruit. The net revenue per box equals the company's gross revenue minus shipping and selling expenses, divided by the number of boxes of fruit the company processed. The price determination works as follows: in 1990 CCB's early estimated price predicted a net revenue per box of $19.86. This figure exceeded $10.60 by $9.26, and CCB retained 25 percent of the $9.26 for itself ($2.32). Then CCB subtracted the set processing fee of $4.32, leaving $13.22 as the estimated price to be paid to growers for each box of fruit.

Chapter 7. The Sale of a Processing Company

1. As world market prices for sugar declined in the early 1980s, Belize Sugar Industries, under pressure from North American banks, threatened to close the two plants in

Belize unless the Cane Farmers Association agreed to buy majority shares in them. The government of Belize agreed to pay a half million dollars to Belize Sugar Industries (which was paid) and "made a commitment on behalf of cane farmers to buy shares." However, when the UDP won the 1984 elections, Esquivel reneged on the agreement, and BSI closed the factory in Corozal District (Henderson 1990:73).

2. Hassan expressed doubt that the special committee would be able to conclude an agreement with Nestlé and finance it. But he refrained from stepping back into the negotiations to renew his own offer to Nestlé in order to avoid alienating small growers, whose support he would need if he renewed his offer at a later date.

3. The inclusion of workers was suggested by Nathan Clifford, who intended to use his own severance payments to invest in shares.

4. Kernan, Sodergren, and French (1977:43) suggest that Abrahams errs in according greater prestige to Standard English than to Creole. They argue that rather than simply valuing Standard English over Creole, Belizeans value a speaker's ability to use the proper code at the proper time.

5. Later, Michael Ashcroft became treasurer for the Tories in Britain, as well as a major party contributor. In turn, the Tories nominated him repeatedly for knighthood. After much debate, which included Ashcroft's efforts to take the title "Baron of Belize," he was finally knighted.

6. In October the company changed hands. The prospectus for the sale of Belize Foods, released in September, presented the final arrangements, which followed closely the numbers presented in the July CGA meeting. Thirty percent of the shares would be reserved for large growers, paid for either by fruit delivery or cash up front with a fruit commitment; 17 percent was reserved for small growers producing fewer than 10,000 boxes of fruit on the same basis; 16 percent was reserved for employees; and 37 percent was reserved for Oliver Hassan, Bill Williston, and Belize Holdings, who funded Belize Food Holdings Limited, a holding company that put up part of the purchase price (BFHL 1990:14). Any shares that remained after the completion of grower and employee offers would be divided among Hassan, Williston, Clifford, and Belize Holdings (BFHL 1990:14).

The prospectus also addressed some of the problems growers had raised in meetings. It declared that "the offer is only open to Growers. All Growers are entitled to apply under the Offer except any Grower who, in the opinion of the Directors of BFHL, has a significant interest in any business which is competitive with any business carried on by BFHL" (BFHL 1990:8). Further, it provided that fruit commitment would not be binding in case of "factory equipment breakdown, natural disaster, crop failure, strike action, riot and transportation difficulties" (BFHL 1990:10). It advised that the growers scheme would run three seasons and that the directors would then decide whether or not to extend it two more years (BFHL 1990:12). It also named the new company's directors: Hassan, Williston, Clifford, and a representative of the Belize Bank. Belize Holdings retained 20 percent of the shares ("Belize," *Caribbean Insight,* Nov. 1990, 7).

7. In fact, the actual process of negotiations with Nestlé reinforced distinctions between small and large growers. Hassan initiated the process and put together the first packages. Once responsibility for negotiating was handed to the special CGA committee,

the process stalled, largely due to their lack of information with which to proceed. When the threat of monopoly produced a crisis, the committee stepped aside and appointed Hassan, Bill Williston, and BFP's managing director to assemble the finances. The package they assembled was never put to a vote in the CGA, and some smallholders complained that information was being withheld from them.

8. However, after its first year of operations, the company had 120 shareholders (compared to fewer than 50 at CCB).

Chapter 8. Conclusion

1. Recommendations to increase Caribbean competitiveness include deepening and expanding CARICOM to increase the size of the regional market and enable more rational use of resources (Bryan 1995b; Harker 1995) and using technology to increase productivity (CDB 1993; Watson 1994b). Some scholars argue for greater investments in human capital to increase productivity (Dupuy 1994), though wage suppression to decrease costs has been a more widely used strategy in the past.

2. Across the Caribbean, industries that flourished under CBI provisions, principally garment assembly and fruit and vegetable production, are now threatened by free trade expansion; some have already lost ground. Citrus producers in Jamaica and Trinidad face the same pressures as their Belizean counterparts, while garment manufacture, the industry that expanded most under the CBI, lost investment to Mexico with the implementation of NAFTA (Watson 1994b:83). The erosion of trade privileges in the EU by WTO rulings on bananas also has implications for Caribbean nations other than Belize. Many Caribbean banana industries comprise smallholder producers who own between 0.5 and 40 hectares (Harker 1995). While Caribbean producers are less efficient than the high-volume corporate plantations of the Latin American mainland, their bananas account for over 50 percent of total export earnings in places such as the Windward Islands (Harker 1995). Caribbean banana farmers seeking international support for continuing their EU trade privileges have echoed Belizean citrus farmers' defense of their own trade privileges: "We have avoided the strife and turmoil that has plagued Latin America precisely because we don't have a plantation economy and our distribution of income is better," the chairman of the St. Lucia Banana Growers Association asserted (Rohter 1997). His assertion suggests that the mutual causality between democracy and capitalist development posed by CBI discourse resonated widely in the Caribbean region. However, throughout the region, this logic and the social configurations it helped to shape are confronted by the competing logic of efficiency and its aim to reconfigure Caribbean societies.

3. As a result, though the CDC had originally intended to acquire only 51 percent of CCB's stocks, it ultimately purchased more than this amount.

4. This agreement prompted Florida Citrus Mutual, Belizean growers' sometime ally/sometime adversary, to complain to the U.S. government that Belizean citrus was being subsidized, an argument CGA executives worked to counter.

5. The other major threat to the continuation of the alliance that backs the agricultural export-led development strategy is the growing pressure to discontinue the practice

of allocating government lands under tropical forests for conversion to agriculture. This pressure derives from activism by environmentalists in Belize and beyond, as well as the adoption by the government and much of the tourism private sector of an ecotourism strategy for tourism development.

References

Abrahams, Roger. 1983. *The Man-of-Words in the West Indies.* Baltimore: Johns Hopkins University Press.

Abu-Lughod, Lila. 1991. "Writing Against Culture." In *Recapturing Anthropology,* edited by Richard Fox, 137–50. Santa Fe, N.Mex.: School of American Research Press.

Anderson, Benedict. 1991. *Imagined Communities.* New York: Verso.

Appadurai, Arjun. 1996. *Modernity at Large.* Minneapolis: University of Minnesota Press.

Ashdown, Peter. 1979. "Race, Class and the Unofficial Majority in British Honduras 1890–1949." Ph.D. diss., University of London.

———. 1985. "The Growth of Black Consciousness in Belize 1914–1919." *Belcast Journal of Belizean Affairs* 2(2):1–5.

———. 1986. "Race Riot, Class Warfare and Coup d'etat." *Belcast Journal of Belizean Affairs* 3(1–2):8–13.

Barham, Bradford. 1992. "Foreign Direct Investment in a Strategically Competitive Environment." *World Development* 20(6):841–57.

Barry, Tom. 1992. *Inside Belize.* Albuquerque, N.Mex.: Inter-Hemispheric Education Resource Center.

Belize Enterprise for Sustainable Technology (BEST). 1989. *The Current Status of the Citrus Industry.* Report presented to the Ministry of Industry and Natural Resources, November 1989.

Belize Food Holdings Limited (BFHL). 1990. Prospectus.

Birdwell-Pheasant, Donna. 1985. "Language Change and Ethnic Identity in Eastern Corozal." *Belizean Studies* 13(5–6):1–12.

Bolland, O. Nigel. 1977. *The Formation of a Colonial Society.* Baltimore: Johns Hopkins University Press.

———. 1986. *Belize: New Nation in Central America.* Boulder, Colo.: Westview Press.

———. 1987. "Race, Ethnicity, and National Integration in Belize." Paper presented at the First Annual Studies on Belize Conference, Belize City, May 25–26.

———. 1988. *Colonialism and Resistance in Belize: Essays in Historical Sociology.* Benque Viejo del Carmen, Belize: Cubola Productions.

———. 1991. "Society and Politics in Belize." In *Society and Politics in the Caribbean,* edited by Colin Clarke, 78–109. New York: St. Martin's Press.

———. 2001. *The Politics of Labour in the British Caribbean.* Princeton, N.J.: Markus Wiener.

Bolland, O. Nigel, and Assad Shoman. 1977. *Land in Belize: 1765–1871.* Mona, Jamaica: Institute for Social and Economic Research, University of the West Indies.

Bourgois, Philippe. 1989. *Ethnicity at Work.* Baltimore: Johns Hopkins University Press.

Bowman, W.A.J. 1955. *Citrus Culture in British Honduras.* Stann Creek, British Honduras: n.p.

Brockmann, Thomas C. 1977. "Ethnic and Racial Relations in Northern Belize." *Ethnicity* 4:246–62.

———. 1985. "Ethnic Participation in Orange Walk Economic Development." *Ethnic Groups* 6:187–208.

Brown, M. 1987. *World Orange Juice Trends.* Gainesville, Fla.: Department of Citrus.

Bryan, Anthony, ed. 1995a. *New Dynamics in Trade and Political Economy.* Miami: North-South Center, University of Miami.

———. 1995b. "Coping with the New Dynamics." In *New Dynamics in Trade and Political Economy,* edited by Anthony Bryan, 239–52. Miami: North-South Center, University of Miami.

Buechler, Steven. 1995. "New Social Movement Theories." *Sociological Quarterly* 36(3):441–64.

Burdon, John. 1931, 1934, 1935. *The Archives of British Honduras.* Vols. 1–3. London: Sifton Praed and Co.

Cal, Angel. 1991. "Rural Society and Economic Development: British Mercantile Capital in Nineteenth-Century Belize." Ph.D. diss., University of Arizona.

Cardoso, Fernando Henrique, and Enzo Faletto. 1979. *Dependency and Development in Latin America.* Berkeley and Los Angeles: University of California Press.

Caribbean Development Bank (CDB). 1993. "The Adjustment Problems of the CARICOM States." In *Caribbean Economic Development: The First Generation,* edited by Stanley Lalta and Marie Freckleton, 35–46. Kingston, Jamaica: Ian Randle.

Central Bank of Belize. 1990. *Quarterly Review* 13(1–4).

———. 1991. *Quarterly Review* 14(4).

Central Statistical Office (CSO). 1984. *Belize Labour Force Survey, 1983–84.* Preliminary Report. Belmopan.

———. 1992. *1991 Population Census Major Findings.*

———. 1994. *Abstract of Statistics 1993.*

Chatterjee, Partha. 1993. *The Nation and Its Fragments.* Princeton, N.J.: Princeton University Press.

Citrus Company of Belize (CCB). 1990. *Citrus News.* Pomona.

Citrus Growers Association (CGA). 1981. *Annual Report, 1979–80 Crop Year.* Dangriga.

———. 1985. *CGA Membership Survey.* Dangriga.

———. 1990. *Annual Report, 1989–90 Crop Year.* Dangriga.

———. 1991. *Annual Report, 1990–91 Crop Year.* Dangriga.

Cohen, Jean. 1985. "Strategy or Identity." *Social Research* 52(4):663–716.

Deere, Carmen Diana, Peggy Antrobus, Lynn Bolles, Edwin Melendez, Peter Phillips, Marcia Rivera, and Helen Safa. 1990. *In the Shadows of the Sun.* Boulder, Colo.: Westview Press.

deJanvry, Alain. 1981. *The Agrarian Question and Reformism in Latin America.* Baltimore: Johns Hopkins University Press.

Development Finance Corporation (DFC). 1989. *Report on the CDC Citrus Rehabilitation Programme for Period 1/6/89 to 30/9/89.* Belmopan.

Dobson, Narda. 1973. *A History of Belize.* London: Longman Caribbean.

Dominguez, Jorge. 1995. "The Caribbean in a New International Context." In *New Dynamics in Trade and Political Economy,* edited by Anthony Bryan, 1–23. Miami: North-South Center, University of Miami.

Dreyfus, Hubert, and Paul Rabinow. 1982. *Michel Foucault: Beyond Structuralism and Hermeneutics.* Chicago: University of Chicago Press.

Dupuy, Alex. 1994. "Free Trade and Underdevelopment in Haiti." In *The Caribbean in the Global Political Economy,* edited by Hilbourne Watson, 91–107. Boulder, Colo.: Lynne Rienner.

Edelman, Marc. 1999. *Peasants against Globalization.* Palo Alto, Calif.: Stanford University Press.

Escobar, Arturo. 1992. "Culture, Economics, and Politics in Latin American Social Movements Theory and Research." In *The Making of Social Movements in Latin America,* edited by Arturo Escobar and Sonia Alvarez, 62–85. Boulder, Colo.: Westview Press.

———. 1995. *Encountering Development.* Princeton, N.J.: Princeton University Press.

Esteva, Gustavo. 1992. "Development." In *The Development Dictionary,* edited Wolfgang Sachs, 6–25. London: ZED Books.

European Information Service (EIS). 2000. European Report, 2 December 2000, sec. 2549. Headline: "EIB Lends Belize Euro 13.2 Million to Revitalize the Citrus Industry."

Ferguson, James. 1990. *The Anti-Politics Machine.* Cambridge: Cambridge University Press.

Fernandez, Julio A. 1989. *Belize: Case Study for Democracy in Central America.* Brookfield, Vt.: Avebury.

Food and Agriculture Organization (FAO). 1991. *Commodity Review and Outlook 1990–91.* Rome: FAO.

———. 1994. *Commodity Review and Outlook 1993–94.* Rome: FAO.

Foster, Byron. 1986. *Heart Drum.* Benque Viejo del Carmen, Belize: Cubola Press.

Foucault, Michel. 1973. *The Order of Things.* New York: Vintage Books.

———. 1979. *Discipline and Punish.* New York: Vintage Books.

———. 1980 [1972]. *Power/Knowledge.* New York: Pantheon.

Frank, Andre Gunder. 1966. "The Development of Underdevelopment." *Monthly Review* 18(4):99–105.

Gilroy, Paul. 1987. *There Ain't No Black in the Union Jack.* Chicago: University of Chicago Press.

Gonzalez, Nancie Solien. 1988. *Sojourners of the Caribbean: Ethnogenesis and Ethnohistory of the Garifuna.* Chicago: University of Illinois Press.

Gramsci, Antonio. 1971. *Selections from the Prison Notebooks.* New York: International Publishers.

Grant, Cedric. 1976. *The Making of Modern Belize.* Cambridge: Cambridge University Press.

Gregory, James. 1984. *The Mopan: Culture and Ethnicity in a Changing Belizean Community.* University of Missouri Monographs in Anthropology, no. 7. Columbia: Department of Anthropology, University of Missouri.

Grillo, R. D., and R. L. Stirrat. 1997. Preface to *Discourses of Development,* edited by R. D. Grillo and R. L. Stirrat, vi–viii. New York: Berg.

Hall, Stuart. 1983. "Ideology in the Modern World." Transcript of an address and discussion held at La Trobe University, April 14, 1983, jointly organized by Media Centre, Department of Sociology and Department of Legal Studies.

———. 1986. "Gramsci's Relevance for the Study of Race and Ethnicity." *Journal of Communication Inquiry* 10:5–27.

———. 1988. "The Toad in the Garden." In *Marxism and the Interpretation of Culture,* edited by Cary Nelson and Lawrence Grossberg, 35–73. Urbana: University of Illinois Press.

Hall, Stuart, Bob Lumley, and Gregor McLennan. 1977. "Politics and Ideology: Gramsci." In *On Ideology.* Center for Contemporary Cultural Studies, 45–75. London: Hutchinson.

Haraway, Donna. 1988. "Situated Knowledges." *Feminist Studies* 14:575–99.

Harker, Trevor. 1995. "Caribbean Economic Performance in the 1990s." In *The Caribbean in the Global Political Economy,* edited by Hilbourne Watson, 9–27. Boulder, Colo.: Lynne Rienner.

Henderson, Peta. 1990. "Development and Dependency in a Belizean Village." *SPEAReports 4,* 71–91. Belize City: Society for the Promotion of Education and Research.

Johnson, Melissa. 1998. "Nature and Progress in Rural Creole Belize." Ph.D. diss., University of Michigan.

Jones, Grant D. 1971. *The Politics of Agricultural Development in Northern British Honduras.* Developing Nations Monograph Series, no. 4. Winston-Salem, N.C.: Overseas Research Center, Wake Forest University.

Judd, Karen. 1989. "Cultural Synthesis or Ethnic Struggle? Creolization in Belize." *Cimarron* 2(1):103–18.

———. 1992. "Elite Reproduction and Ethnic Identity in Belize." Ph.D. diss., City University of New York.

Kaufman, Georgia. 1997. "Watching the Developers: A Partial Ethnography." In *Discourses of Development,* edited by R. D. Grillo and R. L. Stirrat, 107–31. New York: Berg.

Kernan, Keith T., John Sodergren, and Robert French. 1977. "Speech and Social Prestige in the Belizean Speech Community." In *Sociocultural Dimensions of Language Change,* edited by Ben Blount and Mary Sanchez, 35–50. New York: Academic Press.

Kerns, Virginia. 1983. *Women and the Ancestors: Black Carib Kinship and Ritual.* Chicago: University of Illinois Press.

Labour Department. 1956–57. *Annual Report.* Belmopan.

————. 1958. *Annual Report.* Belmopan.

————. 1960. *Annual Report.* Belmopan.

————. 1965. *Annual Report.* Belmopan.

————. 1968. *Annual Report.* Belmopan.

Laclau, Ernesto. 1977. *Politics and Ideology in Marxist Theory.* London: New Left Books.

Laclau, Ernesto, and Chantal Mouffe. 1985. *Hegemony and Socialist Strategy.* New York: Verso.

Levine, Daniel. 1993. "Constructing Culture and Power." In *Constructing Culture and Power in Latin America,* edited by Daniel Levine, 1–39. Ann Arbor: University of Michigan Press.

Macklin, Catherine. 1986. "Crucibles of Identity: Ritual and Symbolic Dimensions of Garifuna Identity." Ph.D. diss., University of California, Berkeley.

McClaurin, Irma. 1996. *Women of Belize.* New Brunswick, N.J.: Rutgers University Press.

Medina, Laurie Kroshus. 1990. "'For the Good of the Small Man': The Source of Small Growers' Power." *SPEAReports 6,* 44–51. Belize City: Society for the Promotion of Education and Research.

————. 1997a. "Defining Difference, Forging Unity: The Co-construction of Race, Ethnicity, and Nation in Belize." *Ethnic and Racial Studies* 20(4):757–80.

————. 1997b. "Development Policies and Identity Politics: Class and Collectivity in Belize." *American Ethnologist* 24(1):148–69.

————. 1998. "The Impact of Free Trade Initiatives on the Caribbean Basin: From 'Democracy' to 'Efficiency' in Belize." *Latin American Perspectives* 25(5):27–49.

Meier, Gerald. 1984. "The Formative Period." In *Pioneers in Development,* edited by Gerald Meier and Dudley Seers. Oxford: Oxford University Press.

Melucci, Alberto. 1988. "Social Movements and the Democratization of Everyday Life." In *Civil Society and the State,* edited by John Keane, 245–60. New York: Verso.

Ministry of Foreign Affairs and Economic Development. 1985. *Five Year Macro-Economic Plan for Belize 1985–1989.* Belmopan.

Moberg, Mark. 1990. "Class Resistance and Class Hegemony: From Conflict to Co-optation in the Citrus Industry of Belize." *Ethnology* 29(3):189–207.

————. 1992. "Structural Adjustment and Rural Development: Inferences from a Belizean Village." *Journal of Developing Areas* 27:1–20.

————. 1993. *Citrus, Class, and Strategy.* Iowa City: University of Iowa Press.

————. 1997. *Myths of Ethnicity and Nation.* Knoxville: University of Tennessee Press.

National Bipartisan Commission on Central America (NBCCA). 1984. *The Report of the President's National Bipartisan Commission on Central America.* New York: Macmillan.

Omi, Michael, and Howard Winant. [1986] 1994. *Racial Formation in the United States.* New York: Routledge and Kegan Paul.

Ong, Aihwa. 1987. *Spirits of Resistance and Capitalist Discipline.* Albany: SUNY Press.

Peoples United Party (PUP). 1989. *Belizean First, PUP Manifesto 1989–1994.* Belize City.

Petch, T. 1986. "Dependency, Land and Oranges in Belize." *Third World Quarterly* 8(3):1002–19.

Pollard, Nicholas. 1986. "Secrets of a New Nation." *The Voice* 6(12):4–5.

Rattansi, Ali. 1995. "Just Framing: Ethnicities and Racisms in a 'Postmodern' Framework." In *Social Postmodernism,* edited by Linda Nicholson and Steven Seidman, 250–86. Cambridge: Cambridge University Press.

Rohter, Larry. 1997. "Trade Storm Imperils Caribbean Banana Crops." *New York Times,* 9 May.

Ropp, Steven Masami. 1996. "Chinese in Belize: An Examination of Nationalism, Development, and Social Conflict." Master's thesis, University of California, Los Angeles.

Roseberry, William. 1993. "Beyond the Agrarian Question in Latin America." In *Confronting Historical Paradigms,* by Frederick Cooper, Allen Isaacman, Florencia Mallon, William Roseberry, and Steve Stern, 318–70. Madison: University of Wisconsin Press.

Rostow, Walt. 1960. *The Stages of Economic Growth: A Non-Communist Manifesto.* New York: Cambridge University Press.

———. 1984. "Development: The Political Economy of the Marshallian Long Period." In *Pioneers in Development,* edited by Gerald Meier and Dudley Seers, 229–61. Oxford: Oxford University Press.

Rutheiser, Charles. 1990. "Culture, Schooling, and Neocolonialism in Belize." Ph.D. diss., Johns Hopkins University.

Scott, James. 1985. *Weapons of the Weak.* New Haven, Conn.: Yale University Press.

Shaw, Kathryn. 1988. "Capitalizing on Success." *Grassroots Development* 12(3):20–27.

Shoman, Assad. 1979. *The Birth of the Nationalist Movement in Belize 1950–1954.* BISRA Occasional Publications, no. 7. [Belize City: Belize Institute of Social Research and Action].

———. 1987a. "Double Jeopardy: Trade Union Relations with Party and State—The Case of the UGWU." Paper presented at the First Annual Studies on Belize Conference, Belize City.

———. 1987b. *Party Politics in Belize, 1950–1986.* Benque Viejo del Carmen, Belize: Cubola Productions.

———. 1992. "The Making of Belize's Foreign Policy." *SPEAReports 8,* 13–31. Belize City: Society for the Promotion of Education and Research.

———. 1994. *Thirteen Chapters in a History of Belize.* Belize City: Angelus Press.

Smith, Carol. 1993. "Local History in Global Context: Social and Economic Transitions in Western Guatemala." In *Constructing Culture and Power in Latin America,* edited by Daniel Levine, 75–117. Ann Arbor: University of Michigan Press.

Society for the Promotion of Education And Research (SPEAR). 1990. "Profile of Belize." *SPEAReports 3.* Belize City: Society for the Promotion of Education and Research.

Stone, Michael. 1990. "Backabush: Settlement on the Belmopan Periphery and the Challenge to Rural Development." *SPEAReports 6,* 82–134. Belize City: Society for the Promotion of Education and Research.

———. 1994. "Caribbean Nation, Central American State: Ethnicity, Race, and National Formation in Belize, 1798–1990." Ph.D. diss., University of Texas at Austin.

Sullivan, Paul. 1978. "Bullet Tree Falls." *Belizean Studies* 6(6):1–22.

Thompson, J. Eric S. 1988. *The Maya of Belize.* Benque Viejo del Carmen, Belize: Cubola Productions.

Tout, G. M., A. G. Anderson, D. A. Estall, T. A. Freeman, and J. Ryan. 1979. *Belize Citrus Industry.* Commonwealth Development Corporation. London.

Tylor, Stephen. 1986. "Post-Modern Ethnography." In *Writing Culture,* edited by James Clifford and George Marcus, 122–40. Berkeley and Los Angeles: University of California Press.

Van Sertima, Ivan. 1976. *They Came before Columbus.* New York: Random House.

Vernon, Dylan. 1990. "Belize Exodus to the United States." *SPEAReports 4,* 6–28. Belize City: Society for the Promotion of Education and Research.

Visweswaran, Kamala. 1994. *Fictions of Feminist Ethnography.* Minneapolis: University of Minnesota Press.

Watson, Hilbourne, ed. 1994a. *The Caribbean in the Global Political Economy.* Boulder, Colo.: Lynne Rienner.

———. 1994b. "Global Restructuring and the Prospects for Caribbean Competitiveness." In *The Caribbean in the Global Political Economy,* edited by Hilbourne Watson, 67–90. Boulder, Colo.: Lynne Rienner.

Wells, Marilyn. 1980. "Circling with the Ancestors." *Belizean Studies* 8(6):1–9.

Wetherell, Margaret, and Jonathan Potter. 1992. *Mapping the Language of Racism.* New York: Columbia University Press.

White, Michael. 1968. "The Citrus Industry of the Stann Creek Valley, British Honduras." Master's thesis, Michigan State University.

Wilk, Richard. 1986. "Mayan Ethnicity in Belize." *Cultural Survival Quarterly* 10(2):73–77.

World Bank. 1984. *Belize Economic Report.* Washington, D.C.: World Bank.

———. 1988. *Staff Appraisal Report. Belize Agricultural Credit and Export Development Project.* Report No. 7011–BEL. Washington, D.C.: World Bank.

Wright, Pamela. 1995. "The Timely Significance of Supernatural Mothers or Exemplary Daughters." In *Articulating Hidden Histories,* edited by Jane Schneider and Rayna Rapp, 243–61. Berkeley and Los Angeles: University of California Press.

Index

About the Author

Laurie Kroshus Medina is an associate professor of anthropology at Michigan State University. She teaches courses on economic development, political ecology, collective identities, and social movements in the Anthropology Department's program in Culture, Resources, and Power. She earned her Ph.D. in anthropology at UCLA. After doing research since the mid-1980s on agricultural development in Belize, her current research explores an alternative development strategy Belize embraced in the early 1990s: ecotourism. Her work focuses on efforts to implement ecotourism in Mayan villages in southern Belize, where villagers negotiate with Belizean and transnational conservation NGOs, government departments, upscale ecotourism entrepreneurs, and tourists themselves over how to combine development aspirations with conservation priorities.